Preparing the U.S. Army for

HOMELAND SECURITY

Concepts, Issues, and Options

Prepared for the United States Army

Approved for public release; distribution unlimited

WITHDRAWAL

Eric V. Larson, John E. Peters

Arroyo Center

RAND

The research described in this report was sponsored by the United States Army under Contract No. DASW01-96-C-0004.

Library of Congress Cataloging-in-Publication Data

Larson, Eric V. (Eric Victor), 1957–
    Preparing the U.S. Army for homeland security : concepts, issues, and options /
Eric V. Larson, John E. Peters.
        p. cm.
    Includes bibliographical references.
    MR-1251-A
    ISBN 0-8330-2919-3
    1. United States. Army. 2. United States—Defenses. I. Peters, John E., 1947–
II. Title.

UA25 .L27 2000
355' 033273—dc21

00-045819

RAND is a nonprofit institution that helps improve policy and decisionmaking through research and analysis. RAND® is a registered trademark. RAND's publications do not necessarily reflect the opinions or policies of its research sponsors.

Published 2001 by RAND
1700 Main Street, P.O. Box 2138, Santa Monica, CA 90407-2138
1200 South Hayes Street, Arlington, VA 22202-5050
RAND URL: http://www.rand.org/
To order RAND documents or to obtain additional information, contact Distribution Services: Telephone: (310) 451-7002; Fax: (310) 451-6915; Internet: order@rand.org

This report addresses the many conceptual, programmatic, and practical issues associated with an emergent mission area for the U.S. Army and Department of Defense (DoD) called "homeland security" (until recently the mission was known as "homeland defense").

At the most basic level, the report seeks to provide Army and other DoD audiences with an introduction to, and overview of, four of the five homeland security task areas,[1] and the various organizations at the federal, state, and local level that the Army and DoD may need to interface with under different circumstances. More ambitiously, it seeks to define homeland security in a concrete way and to provide the necessary background and conceptual and analytic constructs for wrestling with the key issues and choices the Army will face as the mission area matures.

The research reported here was initiated as homeland security was emerging as an issue of policy concern and was conducted during Fiscal Year 1999, a year in which the Army and Department of Defense considered but had not yet resolved many key homeland security–related issues. These include a definition of homeland security, the key task areas that constitute homeland security, and the programs and capabilities needed to respond to these various threats. In a similar vein, the broader federal government enacted or

---

[1]Because it already is the focus of substantial analytic attention, national missile defense is not addressed in this report.

refined numerous programs to combat terrorism and weapons of mass destruction and to mitigate the threat to critical infrastructure.

While we have made every effort to stay apprised of these developments, the complexity and dynamism of the broader policy environment led to a conscious choice to focus on broad issues, principles, and options in this report, rather than specific organizational solutions. Indeed, at the time the report was being completed, a new Unified Command Plan (UCP) was announced, specifying responsibilities for some homeland security activities. We have, nevertheless, provided observations regarding organizational issues where we felt it useful and appropriate.

The research was sponsored by the Office of the Deputy Chief of Staff, Operations and Plans, Headquarters, Department of the Army, and was conducted in the Arroyo Center's Strategy, Doctrine, and Resources Program, and was concluded in September 1999. The Arroyo Center is a federally funded research and development center sponsored by the U.S. Army.

For more information on the RAND Arroyo Center, contact the Director of Operations, (310) 393-0411, extension 6500, or visit the Arroyo Center's Web site at http://www.rand.org/organization/ard/

CONTENTS

FIGURES

TABLES

The overall objective of the research reported here is to help the Army understand a new mission area called homeland security. To achieve this, the research had the following principal, more instrumental, objectives. They were to (1) characterize the range of threats that need to be considered; (2) provide a methodology for homeland security; (3) delineate Army responsibilities; (4) describe additional force protection requirements that might be necessary; (5) evaluate capabilities, provide options, and highlight risks; and (6) help the Army explain its role in homeland security. A summary of our principal findings with regard to each of these six objectives follows.

CHARACTERIZING THE RANGE OF HOMELAND SECURITY THREATS

A Taxonomy of Threats

Chapters Four through Seven characterize the range of threats facing the nation in the four homeland security task areas and describe the most relevant policy considerations for dealing with these threats. Although most of these threats seem relatively remote now, the Army and DoD should continue its planning and preparations for the following:

- The threat of weapons of mass destruction (WMD), including high explosives, either against the population; critical national infrastructure; elected and appointed leaders at the local, state, or federal level; or U.S. military forces.

- The threat of specialty weapons, such as mortars, rocket-propelled grenades (RPGs), and man-portable air defense missiles, against the same targets.

- The threat of cyber attacks on mission-critical systems aimed at disrupting the continuity of military operations.

- The threat of WMD smuggling into the United States.

- The threat of large-scale refugee flows that can create threats to national security.

- The threat of the use of ballistic or cruise missiles against the nation.[2]

Our analysis suggests that most of these threats are relatively modest but possibly growing, as is the risk of surprise. With cyber attacks, it is particularly difficult to establish the degree of threat because of poor data and the somewhat alarmist nature of the debate.[3] These "low but possibly growing" threats clearly justify planning and selective enhancement of local, state, federal, and military capabilities, but the Army needs to ensure that it is neither overrating the likelihood or consequence of future attacks nor beguiled by the most advanced threats at the expense of preparing for the most likely ones.

During the course of the study, the study team was asked to address the issue of threat campaigns directed at the continental United States (CONUS). Although such threat campaigns appear to be unlikely at present, they could pose important challenges if mounted by a committed future adversary. In particular, civilian and military leaders could face a dilemma if simultaneous attacks were made against military and civilian targets in the United States. Attacks on the military could disrupt mobilization for a major theater war (MTW), while simultaneous attacks on civilian targets could further tax mobilization capabilities, sapping those "dual-missioned" to warfighting and homeland security. Consequently, planning and capability development should consider the possibility of a sustained

---

[2]Because it already is the focus of substantial effort, national missile defense is not addressed in the present report.

[3]We generally agree with Betts's (1998) argument that "the probability that some smaller number of WMD will be used is growing."

campaign that includes multiple attacks separated in space and time, and assigning missions to forces in ways that minimize potential tension between warfighting and homeland security activities. In particular, the Army should perform analysis, planning, and training to field multiple simultaneous Response Task Forces (RTFs).

A Definition of Homeland Security

Because at present no agreed-on definition for homeland security exists, we now provide our working definition:

> Homeland [security] consists of all military activities aimed at preparing for, protecting against, or managing the consequences of attacks on American soil, including the CONUS and U.S. territories and possessions. It includes all actions to safeguard the populace and its property, critical infrastructure, the government, and the military, its installations, and deploying forces.[4]

While other definitions are certainly possible, the merit of the definition just presented is that it is clear about homeland security's focus on military activities (as distinct from the activities of civilian organizations), its geographic specificity, and the potential targets it seeks to protect.

The taxonomy of threats and definition of homeland security suggest five key military task areas:

- WMD domestic preparedness and civil support;

- continuity of government, i.e., operations to ensure or restore civil authority;

- border and coastal defense, including the prevention of WMD smuggling into the United States and management of large-scale refugee flows that can create threats to national security;

---

[4]We recognize that other departments and agencies have important roles to play in many areas related to homeland security. For example, and most notably, the FBI and FEMA play the key roles in crisis and consequence management. However, we reserve the phrase "homeland security" for the tasks performed by the armed services and the Department of Defense.

- continuity of military operations, including force protection—primarily for deploying units—protection of mission-critical facilities and systems, and protection of higher headquarters operations; and

- national missile defense (not considered in this report).

A METHODOLOGY FOR HOMELAND SECURITY

In Chapter Three, the report provides a method for assessing homeland security needs and options. The methodology is organized around a nomogram (Figure S.1) that enables planners to address, in turn, threat and risk assessment, performance levels and needed capabilities, design of cost-effective programs, and budgeting.

The nomogram was designed to address four key questions relating to homeland security:

- What magnitudes of events should the United States plan against for high-explosive, chemical, biological, radiological, nuclear and cyber threats? (Panel I, Threat Analysis)

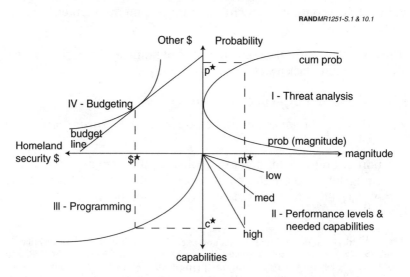

Figure S.1—Nomogram for Assessing Homeland Security Options

- What levels of performance will the nation demand in the national (local, state, and federal) responses to these events? (Panel II, Performance Levels and Needed Capabilities)

- What are the most cost-effective options for providing the capabilities that will address these events at the desired performance levels? (Panel III, Programming)

- What resources will be made available, and will they be sufficient to provide the necessary capabilities? (Panel IV, Budgeting).

Answers to each of these questions are needed to ensure that proper resources will be devoted and the right capabilities will be developed for homeland security. The nomogram shows how decisions taken in each panel contribute to the larger analysis. A decision about the magnitude of the events to be planned against (m*) taken in Panel I is refined when a decision is taken in Panel II to provide a high level of capacity, which establishes performance criteria (c*) for assessing alternatives. The planning magnitude and performance criteria then set the stage in Panel III for designing cost-effective programs, and the total cost of these programs ($*) is traded off against other budgetary claimants in Panel IV. To be sure, behind each panel a great deal of policy discussion occurs, as well as analytic effort in the way of studies and analyses and modeling.

Our analyses suggest that despite a great deal of important work to redress shortfalls in local, state, and federal capabilities to address emerging threats to the homeland, the four key questions—one each associated with a panel of the nomogram—remain substantially unanswered. We believe that if national efforts are to be harmonized and made efficient, it is critical for the Army and others (the DoD, federal civilian agencies, and local and state entities) to collectively, and systematically, address these questions.

DELINEATE ARMY RESPONSIBILITIES

Chapters Four through Seven also delineate, in some detail, the Army responsibilities and capabilities in each of the four homeland security task areas that are the subject of this study.

In three of the task areas (domestic preparedness, continuity of government, and border and coastal defense), the Army is in a supporting role to civil authorities. In domestic preparedness, for example, federal Army participation will take place when the FBI (the lead federal agency for domestic crisis management operations) or the Federal Emergency Management Agency (FEMA) (the lead federal agency for consequence management) requests the Department of Defense to provide military forces and capabilities to assist. National Guard forces also may, of course, participate through the state-level chain of command (the governor and adjutant general).

In domestic preparedness, the Army appears to have the leading military role, based on its deep involvement in all aspects of the task area, including nonproliferation and counterproliferation activities; preparedness activities, such as training first responders; and support to consequence management. In continuity of government (COG) activities, the Army could have the leading military role, although it is difficult to say. In border and coastal defense, there are few indications that the Army would play the leading military role.

In the continuity of operations task area, the Army essentially is responsible for the protection of its own forces, mission-critical facilities and systems, and higher headquarters. Protection of other potential targets seems likely to be on an "as assigned" basis.

General Versus Specialized Forces

One of the questions posed at the outset of this study involves the role of general and more-specialized units in homeland security. Both play important roles, with the specialized units delivering unique capabilities (e.g., medical care; nuclear, biological, and chemical [NBC] identification and decontamination; explosive ordnance disposal). The general-purpose units provide "deep pockets" and personnel for mass response to provide such services as emergency first aid, food, shelter, communications, clothing, and security. As the Army responds to the mandates of the Nunn-Lugar-Domenici legislation and other directives, both its general and specialized units are undergoing additional training to assist in domestic preparedness. For many of the specialized units, this has been a welcome development, because it has meant more opportunities to train in their main competencies. For example, medical units benefit from practicing treating patients whether the victims are combatants or not. For the general-purpose units, the additional training not only provides necessary skills but also represents another demand on their training time. The competition for training time needed for both domestic preparedness and units' other missions requires careful management of mission-essential task lists.

Active-Duty and Reserve Component Forces

The Reserve Component Employment Study 2005 notes that eight Army National Guard (ARNG) divisions are available for employment in warfighting and other missions and suggests that some of them might be assigned to homeland security. The study suggests that, in some specific cases, substituting reserve component for active-duty forces would be a cost-effective solution, although it is not at all clear in which other cases this also might be true.

As argued in this report, however, the current threat levels do not appear to justify the assignment of substantial forces to homeland security missions. It also argues that assignment of missions and allocation of additional forces to homeland security should be based on threat and risk assessments that provide a justification for a given level of effort, and cost-effectiveness and tradeoff analyses that establish that the forces being assigned to the mission are the most effective and efficient solution to the problem, in light of the total pool of local, state, federal, and military capabilities available.

Nevertheless, the probability that threats are increasing does suggest that additional Army preparations for homeland security are warranted.

In Chapter Nine we evaluate the adequacy of current Army doctrine, organizations, training, leadership, materiel, and soldier systems (DOTLMS) for the four homeland security task areas and suggest areas in which short-term improvements can be realized at modest cost.

Additionally, given the poor understanding of the cost-effectiveness of alternative homeland security units or organizations, we also recommend that the Army aggressively explore alternative future operational concepts for homeland security that may be more cost-effective than the current ones (e.g., WMD Civil Support Teams). A combination of experiments and exercises to generate lessons learned, and efforts to design new future operational concepts that can be tested in these exercises and experiments clearly seems warranted.

To accomplish this, the Army might promote the use of joint warfighting experiments to test the likely responsiveness and capacity of the current DoD capabilities to perform homeland security missions. The Army can use the lessons from these experiments to refine its understanding of existing Army capabilities and limitations and thereby refine the WMD CST and other concepts.

The Army also should consider creating a Homeland Security Battle Lab to design and test alternative future Army operational concepts and organizations whose responsiveness and capacity is greater than the present ones. When experimentation and testing have confirmed the cost-effectiveness of these concepts, the Army can begin developing the doctrine, organizational templates, training, and equipment packages needed and, when the threat level warrants, determine the number of units that need to be fielded. Such an approach will improve the Army's ability to provide the necessary capabilities as the threat changes.

DESCRIBE ADDITIONAL FORCE PROTECTION REQUIREMENTS

Although the threats to CONUS-based U.S. forces appear quite low at present, there is reason to remain concerned that adversaries may increasingly plan to use asymmetric attacks to target and disrupt the deployment of U.S. forces. Of particular concern would be a prolonged campaign of such attacks or attacks in numerous locations throughout the United States early in the deployment sequence. Either could severely tax the ability and willingness of commanders to continue the flow of forces to a warfighting theater in the face of threats to deploying forces. Such attacks obviously bring the war to the United States, causing a competition for resources and, essentially, forcing the United States to fight a two-front war.

Planning should focus on additional force protection for early deploying forces (e.g., the Ready Brigade of the 82d Airborne Division), their home stations, fort-to-port movements, and air and sea ports of embarkation. Of particular concern is the potential threat to deploying airlifters and commercial aircraft, where hundreds of troops' lives might be lost in a single incident. Capabilities for ensuring the security of fly-out zones should be assessed and, if necessary, augmented.

The Army also should begin planning now, while the threats are still somewhat remote, for ways to resolve a looming, future conundrum it may face. In the event of an asymmetric campaign of attacks on civilian and military targets in the CONUS during a wartime mobilization, not only could mobilization be disrupted, but fierce competition could arise for low-density units that have the dual mission of warfighting abroad and homeland security. Actions taken now can greatly reduce the possibility and consequences of such competition and better ensure force protection from fort to port and in-theater.

EVALUATE CAPABILITIES, PROVIDE OPTIONS, HIGHLIGHT RISKS

The Army needs to navigate a difficult course. On the one hand, it must avoid overrating the probability and imminence of the threats it faces and doing far too much at too high a cost. On the other hand, it needs to recognize that while the threats are reasonably low now, they are possibly growing, as is the possibility of surprise. While action is warranted, investments should be made strategically and selectively. The Army also needs to avoid taking actions that heighten public sensitivities about the role of the military in domestic law enforcement and in continuity of government.

The Risk of Doing Too Much or Too Little

The best way to negotiate the first two risks is to embrace an adaptive planning framework that bases investments both on an end-to-end analysis of threats and risks, including the potential costs of attacks on high-value targets, and an end-to-end, strategies-to-tasks analysis of what capabilities are needed and the most cost-effective programmatic alternatives for providing those capabilities.

This approach would advocate a focus on low-cost, high-payoff actions. These include detailed studies and analyses, modeling, and simulations to illuminate alternatives and refine doctrine and organizational structures. They also include the design and fielding of prototype units that, once proven to be cost-effective solutions for providing needed capabilities with the desired responsiveness and capacity, can serve as the pattern for fielding additional such units or can be scaled up to larger units providing more substantial capability.

Analysis suggests that although estimating the rate at which the threats might grow is exceedingly difficult, they probably will grow over time, and additional future investments in the homeland security mission accordingly may be necessary. Given that expectation, it would be best for the Army to focus now on refining its concepts, doctrine, organizations, and forces before making additional large-scale investments. For example, on further analysis and reflection, the Army might find that the best concept for its initial response may be a WMD Civil Support Team with a greater emphasis on bringing actual decontamination capabilities to bear than the current concept does.[5] It also may find that the mobility requirements—and costs—associated with making Army contributions responsive enough to affect outcomes could be considerable.

Risks Attendant in Public Concerns About Domestic Military Operations

After a prolonged, hard-fought battle, the Army at the end of the 1990s is held in generally high regard by American civil society. The Army faces some risks to this standing, however, as it addresses the many sensitive issues engendered in homeland security. As Pamela Berkowsky, the Assistant to the Secretary of Defense for Civil Support, recently described the task area of WMD civil support:

> We do not call consequence management "Homeland Defense" but refer to it rather as "civil support." This reflects the fundamental principle that DoD is not in the lead but is there to *support* the lead federal agency in the event of a domestic contingency. Likewise, we

---

[5]"WMD Civil Support Teams" previously were called "Rapid Assessment and Initial Detection (RAID)" teams but were recently renamed. See OASD (Public Affairs) (2000); Bacon (2000); and Berkowsky and Cragin (2000).

are sensitive to the concerns of civil libertarians and others regarding DoD's possible domestic role. (Berkowsky and Cragin, 2000.)

In fact, the role that the Army and the other services play in most of the homeland security task areas is to provide support to civilian authorities, whether local, state, or federal. At the state level, for example, Army National Guard forces work for the governor. At the federal level, the Army works for the National Command Authority (NCA), and, in almost all situations other than civil disturbances when martial law is declared by the President, the Army supports federal departments and agencies.

Although such concerns have not often arisen in disaster responses (perhaps the closest analogy to WMD consequence management activities), using federal military forces in the United States to assist in the maintenance of law and order, for example, is strongly opposed by very vocal segments of the public and their elected representatives. Public concerns about *posse comitatus* and the military role in continuity of government are likely to remain important for the foreseeable future, insofar as they pose two sorts of risk: first, that such concerns, once activated, may interfere in the accomplishment of homeland security missions, and second, that once activated, they can erode public confidence in the Army as an institution.

While we believe that these risks are relatively modest, they need to be considered by the Army, and in any event they can be managed successfully through minor revisions to doctrine, training, and leadership programs and standing public affairs guidance for homeland security operations. Such revisions would help to sensitize future commanders to these larger issues, provide clear guidance on when and how *posse comitatus* and other laws do and do not apply, and provide the elements of broad public affairs guidance that emphasizes the Army's supporting role to civil authority and, whenever it has been disrupted, whether at the local, state, or federal level, Army efforts to effect a speedy restoration of civil authority.

HELPING THE ARMY EXPLAIN ITS ROLE IN HOMELAND SECURITY

Throughout its history, the Army has been involved in homeland security. In other eras, the Army defended the nation's coasts and frontiers, for example, and whenever needed, it has supported civilian authorities in responding to disasters, civil disturbances, and other national emergencies. As the nation's servant, the Army will continue to provide for the nation's defense, both at home and abroad, and the reemergence of homeland security as a serious mission finds the Army well-prepared to provide many of the needed capabilities.

Because the threats seem likely to grow and the missions may turn out to be challenging, the Army will increasingly need to focus on deterring or preventing, preparing for, and mitigating the consequences of attacks on the nation, while seeking to ensure civil authority or assist in its restoration at the earliest opportunity. This dual focus—on improving its performance in the missions it is assigned and on burnishing its image as a protector of the larger constitutional framework—will help ensure the Army's ability to meet the challenges it faces.

The definition and taxonomy of threats described earlier also leads to "bumper stickers" the Army can use to explain its role in the four homeland security task areas that are the focus of this report (the "bumper stickers" are in quotation marks):

- "Protecting Americans at Home" (WMD domestic preparedness and civil support);

- "Ensuring Constitutional Authority" (continuity of government);

- "Protecting Sovereignty" (border and coastal defense); and

- "Ensuring Military Capability" (continuity of military operations).

CONCLUSIONS

Homeland security is a complex, sprawling subject sure to become an increasing topic of deliberation and debate both within government and outside.

Our work suggests that the principal unresolved issues in homeland security can be answered through DoD-wide deliberation over the four core questions of homeland security:

- For what types and magnitudes of events will the defense establishment plan?

- What levels of performance will be demanded of DoD and local, state, and federal actors in their responses to these events?

- What are the most cost-effective options—within DoD and across the entire "layer cake" of local, state, and federal actors— for providing the capabilities that will address these events at the desired performance levels?

- What resources will be made available, will they be sufficient to provide the necessary capabilities, and what opportunity costs or risks will be incurred as a result?

To properly answer these questions and to develop this new mission area, a great deal of analytic, experimental, and planning work clearly needs to be done on each of these questions. Studies and analyses are needed to understand better the risks and cost implications of various "planning magnitudes"; what constitute realistic performance goals for preventing, managing, and responding to various types of threat; what the most cost-effective mix of military and federal, state, and local civilian capabilities to achieve desired performance levels is; and what the opportunity costs and levels of risk incurred with any given set of capabilities and budgets are.

These questions can be explored through the development and use of macro-level simulation, optimization, and other models, and the development of such models should be a priority for the Army and DoD. They could assist in understanding such issues as the optimal number and locations of stockpiles and mobility assets to ensure the desired level of responsiveness and the optimal allocation of resources among military, federal, state, and local entities to ensure the desired level of capacity to deter, prevent, or minimize the consequences of various threats.

It also will be important for the Army and DoD to engage in field experimentation and research and development (R&D). For example, before fielding large numbers of new units, it will be critical to experiment with alternative concepts and organizations—the current proliferation of WMD Civil Support Teams (formerly RAIDs), for example, offers the Army an excellent opportunity to learn lessons and identify best practices that can be used for further refinement of response concepts and organizations. Continued efforts should be directed at identifying the most responsive, most capable, most cost-effective, and most robust contributions that can be made to the larger federal, state, and local response system, and these efforts should include consideration of needed stockpiles and mobility.

Another high priority for Army and DoD-wide R&D will be efforts that aim to reduce the unit costs of advanced capabilities, such as detection and assessment of chemical and biological agents, thereby allowing them to be inexpensively distributed to the local first responders who are likely to be the earliest to arrive at the scene.

As suggested above, Army leaders' efforts would best be directed at ensuring that the capabilities developed by the Army for homeland security are grounded in a solid understanding of the threat (both the likelihood and potential magnitude of different types of attack), the cost-effectiveness of alternative concepts and programs, and the risks and opportunity costs associated with different levels and types of Army preparedness. In particular, although they seem unlikely to be faced with such a dilemma in the near future, Army leaders should begin considering the possibility that in a future mobilization for MTWs, active-duty or reserve component units that have dual missions of warfighting *and* homeland security could be faced with simultaneous taskings, posing a risk to the accomplishment of both the warfighting and the homeland security missions. To avoid such dilemmas, it will be necessary to organize homeland security capabilities in ways that minimize this possibility and to have a robust doctrine for ensuring that both missions receive the appropriate levels and types of forces.

Beyond stating the obvious point that homeland security is likely to grow in importance, it is difficult to say how the issue might evolve in the future. Nevertheless, the Army and DoD will be well-prepared to wrestle with the core issues if they embrace a long-term adaptive approach that ties resources to an understanding of both threat and cost-effectiveness and thereby efficiently provides the capabilities needed to prepare the nation for the emerging threats.

ACKNOWLEDGMENTS

The authors would like to thank a number of individuals for their assistance in the conduct of this research. At RAND, we thank Bruce Hoffman, Maury Eisenstein, and Greg Jones for short papers written at the beginning of the project, and Ted Karasik, Brian Houghton, and Sergej Mahnovsky for longer papers for this study. Thanks also are due to John Pinder for providing data on computer incidents. We also thank Bart Bennett, Jim Dewar, Susan Everingham, Mike Hynes, Dave Kassing, Irv Lachow, and Tom Szayna for their comments over the course of the project and Terri Perkins and June Kobashigawa for their administrative support. We also thank Mike Hynes and Rick Brennan for their thoughtful reviews.

In the Army, we thank LTC Bob Everson, LTC Bob Snyder, and MAJ Joseph Gerard, who served as project monitors, Rich Rinaldo and Larry Heystek of Training and Doctrine Command, and LTC Barbara Goulet, of the Office of the Deputy Chief of Staff, Operations and Plans.

In the office of the Director of Military Support (DOMS), U.S. Army, we would like to thank COL Jay Steinmetz, USAF, and CPT Todd Burton, USA. For providing us with relevant data, we also thank Richard Kaplan of the Land Information Warfare Activity; MAJ Mark Lessig, USA, of Army Program Assessment and Evaluation; Laurie McCray, 3d Chemical Brigade at the Army Chemical School, Fort Leonard Wood; Joe Reap of the State Department's Office of Counterterrorism; and A. Heather Coyne of the Office of Management and Budget.

ABBREVIATIONS

ACERT	Army Computer Emergency Response Team
ACLU	American Civil Liberties Union
ARNG	Army National Guard
ASPG	Army Strategic Planning Guidance
ATF	Bureau of Alcohol, Tobacco, and Firearms
ATID	Advanced Technology Integration Demonstration
CBIRF	Chemical Biological Incident Response Force
CBQRF	Chemical Biological Quick Reaction Force
CBRN	Chemical, biological, radiological, and nuclear
CBRT	Chemical Biological Response Team
C/B-RRT	Chemical/Biological Rapid Response Team
CERT/CC	Computer Emergency Response Team/Coordination Center
CIA	Central Intelligence Agency
CIAO	Critical Infrastructure Assurance Office
CINC	Commander in chief
COG	Continuity of government
COMPIO	Consequence Management Program Integration Office
CONUS	Continental United States
COOP	Continuity of Operations

CTBT	Comprehensive Test Ban Treaty
DARPA	Defense Advanced Research Projects Agency
DII	Defense Information Infrastructure
DoDD	Department of Defense Directive
DOE	Department of Energy
DOJ	Department of Justice
DOMS	Director of Military Support
DOT	Department of Transportation
DOTLMS	Doctrine, organization, training, leadership, materiel, and soldier systems
DP	Domestic Preparedness
DPG	Defense Planning Guidance
EA	Executive Agent
EMI	Emergency Management Institute
EOD	Explosive Ordnance Disposal
EPA	Environmental Protection Agency
ESF	Emergency Support Function
FAA	Federal Aviation Administration
FBI	Federal Bureau of Investigation
FEMA	Federal Emergency Management Agency
FRERP	Federal Radiological Emergency Response Plan
FRP	Federal Response Plan
FTO	Foreign Terrorist Organization
FYDP	Future Years Defense Program
GAO	General Accounting Office
GPRA	Government Performance and Results Act
Hazmat	Hazardous materials
HE	High explosives
HHS	Department of Health and Human Services
IND	Improvised Nuclear Device

IO	Information operations
IRS	Internal Revenue Service
ISAC	Information Sharing and Analysis Center
JOPES	Joint Operational Planning and Execution System
JTF-LA	Joint Task Force–Los Angeles
LIC	Low-intensity conflict
LIWA	Land Information Warfare Activity
MACDIS	Military Assistance for Civil Disturbances
MAGTF	Marine Air-Ground Task Force
Medevac	Medical evacuation
MERS	Mobile Emergency Response Support
MFP	Major Force Program
MMST	Metropolitan Medical Strike Team
MTW	Major theater war
NBC	Nuclear, biological, and chemical
NCA	National Command Authority
NDPO	National Domestic Preparedness Office
NEST	Nuclear Emergency Search Team
NGB	National Guard Bureau
NII	National Information Infrastructure
NIPC	National Infrastructure Protection Center
NMCC	National Military Command Center
NMD	National Missile Defense
NMS	National Military Strategy
NRC	Nuclear Regulatory Commission
NRT	National Response Team
NSS	National Security Strategy
NTSB	National Transportation Safety Board
OMB	Office of Management and Budget

OPLAN	Operations plan
OSC	On-scene coordinator
PCCIP	President's Commission on Critical Infrastructure Protection
PDD	Presidential Decision Directive
PE	Program element
POC	Point of contact
QDR	Quadrennial Defense Review
RAID	Rapid Assessment and Initial Detection
R&D	Research and development
RDT&E	Research, development, test, and evaluation
RPG	Rocket-propelled grenade
RTF	Response Task Force
SBCCOM	Soldier Biological Chemical Command
SHD	Support Homeland Defense
SIED	Special Improvised Explosive Device
SMSA	Standard Metropolitan Statistical Area
SOF	Special Operations Forces
SSC	Smaller-scale contingencies
TEU	Technical Escort Unit
TOA	Total Obligational Authority
TPFDL	Time-Phased Force Deployment List
UCP	Unified Command Plan
USAMRICD	U.S. Army Medical Research Institute for Chemical Defense
USAMRIID	U.S. Army Medical Research Institute for Infectious Diseases
VA	Department of Veterans Affairs
WATS	Wide-Area Tracking System
WMD	Weapons of mass destruction
WMD CST	WMD Civil Support Team

Chapter One

INTRODUCTION

Concern recently has grown within the U.S. national security establishment that the natural protection from attack historically afforded by the nation's enviable geographic isolation—long borders with stable neighbors to the north and south and large oceans to the east and west—may be coming to an end.

One reason can be found in a number of unfavorable long-term trends in the nature of the adversaries of the United States and their potential future warfighting strategies. Future U.S. adversaries, recognizing that they are unlikely to prevail in theater war, it is believed, may instead choose to respond asymmetrically by attacking the U.S. homeland.

The unwillingness of the United States to negotiate with terrorists and its willingness to strike sponsors of terrorism have shaped the environment as well. Contemporary terrorist groups increasingly are more interested in killing than extracting political concessions, and the fear of reprisals has led to an increased desire for covert action and plausible deniability among terrorist groups and their sponsors. The emergence of nonstate and transnational groups accordingly has resulted in adversaries who are more difficult to track and deter than nation states are and who are more interested in creating catastrophic events.

Technology also plays an important role. There are increasing fears regarding the proliferation of weapons of mass destruction (WMD). These include concerns about insecure former Soviet nuclear, biological, and chemical (NBC) weapons and materials or—through efforts by so-called "rogue states" and such well-funded groups as

Aum Shinrikyo and Osama bin Laden's organization—the increasing capacity to develop or acquire such weapons. Similarly, the increasing range and payload of available ballistic missile systems has caused concerns about adversaries' future capacity to attack the United States. Finally, technological advances in information and communication technologies have reduced the importance of geography and made possible attacks on information and communication systems and other computer-dependent infrastructures from anywhere on the globe.

These long-term trends also have been punctuated by a number of attacks at home and abroad that have highlighted the vulnerability to terrorism of advanced societies, such as the United States, and have resulted in widescale death and injury:

- The World Trade Center bombing in 1993, in which six were killed and more than 1,000 injured.

- The bombing of the Murrah federal building in Oklahoma City in 1995, in which 168 were killed and 519 were injured.

- The 1995 use of nerve agents by the Aum Shinrikyo group against the Tokyo subway system, in which 12 were killed and more than 5,000 injured.

- The Centennial Park bombing in Atlanta during the 1996 Olympics, which killed one and injured more than 100.

- The bombing in June 1996 of the Al Khobar barracks in Saudi Arabia, in which 19 servicemen died and more than 300 were injured.

- The simultaneous attacks in August 1998 on U.S. embassies in Nairobi and Dar es Salaam by Osama bin Laden's organization in which 301 died, including 12 Americans.

As described in the Report of the National Defense Panel (1997), the Report of the President's Commission on Critical Infrastructure Protection (1997), the Federal Emergency Management Agency's 1997 assessment of federal consequence management capabilities, and the DoD Tiger Team's report on integration of National Guard and Reserve support for responses to WMD attacks (1998), these developments have motivated policy-level attention to the problem and the identification of numerous shortfalls in the nation's capacity to prevent or mitigate the emerging threats.

The emerging threats and response shortfalls also have led to the allocation of large-scale resources to the prevention and management of the consequences of terrorist attacks against the United States and to serious discussion regarding the parameters of a homeland security (until recently the mission was known as "homeland defense") mission for the Department of Defense (DoD) and U.S. armed forces. This mission would support the national effort to reduce the risks and consequences of future attacks on the United States.

ORGANIZATION OF THIS REPORT

This report seeks to provide an overview of the key policy issues related to homeland security and is organized as follows:

- Chapter Two describes some of the origins of the homeland security mission and provides a definition and taxonomy of tasks.

- Chapter Three provides an analytic framework and methodology for analyzing homeland security options.

- Chapters Four through Seven apply this framework to the four task areas that are the subject of this study: domestic preparedness (Chapter Four), continuity of government (Chapter Five), continuity of military operations (Chapter Six), border and coastal defense (Chapter Seven).

- Chapter Eight provides illustrative planning vignettes that were used to understand potential Army roles in the homeland security task areas.

- Chapter Nine provides an analysis of Army doctrine, organization, training, leadership, materiel, and soldier systems (DOTLMS) for the homeland security task areas.

- Chapter Ten provides conclusions.

- A number of appendixes in this volume provide additional background material. In particular, we draw the readers' attention to the appendixes on threat campaigns (Appendix A), a notional Weapons of Mass Destruction Civil Support Team (WMD CST) tradeoff analysis (Appendix B), and a consolidated list of performance measures that should be considered for use in meeting the reporting requirements of the Government Performance and Results Act (GPRA).

Chapter Two

UNDERSTANDING HOMELAND SECURITY

This chapter places the homeland security mission in the context of the Constitution, the nation's national security, national military strategy, and the Army Strategic Planning Guidance; presents our working definition of homeland security; and describes the task areas that are the essence of the homeland security mission.

THE CONSTITUTIONAL AND LEGAL CONTEXT

The fundamental justification and broader context for homeland security activities can be found in the Preamble; Article I, Section 8; and Article IV, Section 4, of the Constitution of the United States. The Preamble includes the basic "insure domestic tranquility" and "provide for the common defense" justifications:

> [In] Order to form a more perfect Union, establish Justice, insure domestic Tranquility, provide for the common defense, promote the general Welfare, and secure the Blessings of Liberty to ourselves and our Posterity.

Article I, Section 8, elaborates on the circumstances in which the military might be domestically employed:

> Congress shall have Power . . . to provide for calling forth the Militia to execute the Laws of the Union, suppress Insurrections, and repel Invasions.

And Article IV, Section 4, expands on this authority:

> The United States shall guarantee to every State in this Union a Republican Form of Government, and shall protect each of them . . . against domestic Violence.

Federal laws provide the specific mechanisms for federal (including military) support to civil authorities, particularly in the context of "civil emergencies":

> The modern authorization for Federal support to civil authorities is based on the Robert T. Stafford Disaster Relief and Emergency Assistance Act (P.L. 93-288) and the Economy Act. The former enables the Federal Government to "provide assistance to U.S. states, territories, and possessions to alleviate suffering and mitigate damage resulting from major disasters and civil emergencies." The latter empowers Federal agencies to provide routine support to each other under certain conditions if reimbursed. (Grange and Johnson, 1997.)

Homeland security activities are even more apparent in the warrant given the Department of Defense (DoD):

> [DoD] maintains and employs the armed forces to:
>
> - Support and defend the Constitution of the United States against all enemies, foreign and domestic.
>
> - Ensure, by timely and effective military action, the security of the United States, its territories, and areas vital to its interests.
>
> - Uphold and advance the national policies and interests of the United States.
>
> - Safeguard the internal security of the United States. (DoD, 1987, pp. 17–18.)

THE STRATEGIC CONTEXT

The strategic context for homeland security is described well in the report of the National Defense Panel (NDP):

> The United States enters the new millennium as the preeminent political, economic, and military power in the world. Today we are in a relatively secure interlude following an era of intense inter-

national confrontation. But we must anticipate that future adversaries will learn from the past and confront us in very different ways.

We can safely assume that future adversaries will have learned from the Gulf War. It is likely that they will find new ways to challenge our interests, our forces, and our citizens. They will seek to disable the underlying structures that enable our military operations. Forward bases and forward-deployed forces will likely be challenged and coalition partners coerced. Critical nodes that enable communications, transportation, deployment, and other means of power projection will be vulnerable.

Our domestic communities and key infrastructures may also be vulnerable. Transnational threats may increase. As recently stated by [Defense] Secretary [William S.] Cohen, the proliferation of nuclear, chemical, and biological weapons and their delivery means will pose a serious threat to our homeland and our forces overseas. Information systems, the vital arteries of the modern political, economic, and social infrastructures, will undoubtedly be targets as well. The increasing commercialization of space makes it feasible for state and nonstate actors alike to acquire reconnaissance and surveillance services.

In short, we can expect those opposed to our interests to confront us at home and abroad—possibly in both places at once—with asymmetrical responses to our traditional strengths. (National Defense Panel, 1997, p. ii.)

Importantly, the report implies that adversaries may use a range of unconventional weapons (WMD, cyber attacks, etc.) to target both theater forces and the U.S. homeland in future major theater wars (MTWs).

National Security Strategy

In October 1998, the White House released an updated version of the U.S. National Security Strategy (NSS) titled *A National Security Strategy for a New Century*, identified WMD and terrorism as two concerns that transcended national borders:

The possibility of terrorists and other criminals using WMD—nuclear, biological, and chemical weapons—is of special concern.

Threats to the national information infrastructure, ranging from cyber-crime to a strategic information attack on the United States via the global information network, present a dangerous new threat to our national security. We must also guard against threats to our critical national infrastructures—such as electrical power and transportation—which increasingly could take the form of a cyber-attack in addition to physical attack or sabotage, and could originate from terrorist or criminal groups as well as hostile states. (White House, 1998d, pp. 1 and 6–8.)

Potential enemies, whether nations, terrorist groups, or criminal organizations, are increasingly likely to attack U.S. territory and the American people in unconventional ways. Adversaries will be tempted to disrupt our critical infrastructures, impede continuity of government operations, use weapons of mass destruction against civilians in our cities, attack us when we gather at special events, and prey on our citizens overseas. The United States must act to deter or prevent such attacks and, if attacks occurs [sic] despite those efforts, must be prepared to limit the damage they cause and respond decisively against the perpetrators. . . .

Weapons of mass destruction pose the greatest potential threat to global stability and security. Proliferation of advanced weapons and technologies threatens to provide rogue states, terrorists, and international crime organizations the means to inflict terrible damage on the United States, its allies, and U.S. citizens and troops abroad. (White House, 1998d, pp. 1 and 6–8.)

The solution, in the conception of the National Security Strategy, is a broad, national effort that relies on interagency efforts at the federal level and a program that knits these federal capabilities together with local and state capabilities:

At home, we must have effective capabilities for thwarting and responding to terrorist acts, countering international crime and foreign intelligence collection, and protecting critical national infrastructures. Our efforts to counter these threats cannot be limited exclusively to any one agency within the U.S. Government. The threats and their consequences cross agency lines, requiring close cooperation among Federal agencies, state and local governments, the industries that own and operate critical national infrastructures, nongovernmental organizations, and others in the private sector. (White House, 1998d, pp. 1 and 6–8.)

National Military Strategy

The most recent version of the National Military Strategy (NMS) was published in 1997, prior to the current version of the National Security Strategy; this may account for its relative inattention to the issue of homeland security. The 1997 NMS observes:

> Our National Military Strategy depends first and foremost upon the United States remaining secure from external threats. A secure homeland is fundamental to U.S. global leadership.

The NMS nevertheless devotes scant attention to homeland security per se, although it does touch on such threats as state and nonstate actors and asymmetric warfare against the United States. For example, the NMS states:

> Some state or nonstate actors may resort to asymmetric means to counter the U.S. military. Such means include unconventional or inexpensive approaches that circumvent our strengths, exploit our vulnerabilities, or confront us in ways we cannot match in kind. Of special concern are terrorism, the use or threatened use of WMD, and information warfare. These three risks in particular have the potential to threaten the U.S. homeland and population directly and to deny us access to critical overseas infrastructure. . . . We must increase our capabilities to counter these threats and adapt our military doctrine, training, and equipment to ensure a rapid and effective joint and interagency response. (Joint Chiefs of Staff, 1997.)

The Army Strategic Plan

Among the vital interests identified in the 1999 Army Strategic Planning Guidance (ASPG) is "the sovereignty of the United States, to include the safety of the population and the security of critical physical and information infrastructure."[1]

The ASPG envisions a threat environment that contains both transnational and asymmetric threats to the nation. Transnational

---

[1]The list of vital interests identified in the ASPG was extracted from the Defense Planning Guidance.

threats to the homeland include enemies who "use the international telecommunications system to synchronize an impressive set of capabilities to delay or disrupt our military operations or attack the U.S. homeland," while asymmetric threats include the following:

> In the near term, these threats will remain largely limited to traditional concepts and techniques but terrorism and WMD, facilitated by the spread of dangerous technologies, are issues of immediate and special concern. In the mid-term, the United States will face further proliferation of dangerous technologies and expansion of asymmetric concepts and doctrine to include the employment of techniques that exploit social, cultural, technological, and/or environmental change, such as urbanization. The proliferation of information technologies will provide the catalyst for a technologically sophisticated state, group, or individual to target, via computer network attack, the U.S. National Information Infrastructure (NII) or Defense Information Infrastructure (DII). . . . In the long term, we will see the further development of advanced asymmetrical capabilities and significantly more sophisticated capabilities to conduct information operations. (U.S. Army, 1999, p. 8.)

In light of these emerging threats, the ASPG accordingly has a revised set of mission areas that now explicitly includes support to homeland security (U.S. Army, 1999, pp. ii and 52):

> [T]he Army will provide capabilities to conduct operations to *support homeland defense* [emphasis in original]. America's Army must be ready to defend U.S. territory, population, and infrastructure against strategic attack and against emerging transnational threats. Pursuant to Presidential Decision Directive (PDD) 62, these responsibilities will include a growing involvement of the Army, as the Executive Agent (EA) for the Department of Defense (DoD) Domestic Preparedness Program, in supporting domestic authorities in preparation for and execution of crisis response and consequence management with regard to attacks utilizing WMD. The Army will also be involved in supporting PDD 63 to protect and reduce the vulnerability of critical infrastructure including telecommunications; energy; banking and finance; transportation; water; and emergency service facilities. The nature of the emerging threats against the homeland will place a premium on the Army's ability to conduct operations in NBC environments and execute computer network defense while effectively working with sister Services; other federal agencies; state and local governments; and

non-governmental organizations. Finally, the Army is responsible for developing and testing a treaty-compliant, fixed, land-based National Missile Defense (NMD) system, as part of a Joint NMD program, that will provide the option to deploy initial capability in 2003, if so directed. (U.S. Army, 1999, p. 13.)

Thus, although each of the policy documents touches on many of the threats that have led to consideration of a homeland security mission, neither the National Security Strategy, the NMS, nor the Army strategic plan clearly define homeland security as a critical, separate mission consisting of specific task areas or place it in the context of the current defense planning framework of two nearly simultaneous MTWs.[2]

THE DOMESTIC POLITICAL CONTEXT

The response to these emerging threats was three major programs: combating terrorism, enhancing domestic preparedness against WMD, and critical infrastructure protection.

White House Actions

Within the Clinton administration, increasing concern about the proliferation of WMD led, on November 14, 1994, to Executive Order 12938, in which the president declared a national emergency:

> I, William J. Clinton, President of the United States of America, find that the proliferation of nuclear, biological, and chemical weapons ("weapons of mass destruction") and of the means of delivering such weapons, constitutes an unusual and extraordinary threat to the national security, foreign policy, and economy of the United States, and hereby declare a national emergency to deal with that threat. (Executive Order, 1994.)

The Executive Order then went on to enumerate the responsibilities of the departments and agencies in nonproliferation activities. On

---

[2]The NMS does discuss supporting "domestic authorities in combating direct and indirect threats to the U.S. homeland" in a subsection on multiple, concurrent smaller-scale contingency operations but does so only in passing.

November 12, 1998, the President extended the national emergency and amended the original executive order to broaden the types of proliferation activities covered (White House, 1998e).

Two PDDs provided subsequent policy guidance for combating terrorism and WMD:

- PDD 39, June 21, 1995, directed that efforts to combat terrorism include reducing vulnerabilities to terrorism, deterring and responding to terrorist acts, having capabilities to prevent and manage the consequences of terrorist use of NBC weapons, including those of mass destruction (FEMA, 1996).

- The Combating Terrorism directive, PDD 62, May 22, 1998, "highlighted the growing threat of unconventional attacks against the United States and detailed a new and more systematic approach to fighting terrorism by bringing a program management approach to U.S. counterterrorism efforts." (White House, 1998c.)[3]

In a similar vein, concern grew about threats to the nation's physical and electronic critical infrastructures.[4]

Chartered a year earlier, the President's Commission on Critical Infrastructure Protection reported in October 1997 that:

> [W]e found all our infrastructures increasingly dependent on information and communications systems that criss-cross the nation and span the globe. That dependence is the source of rising vulnerabilities and, therefore, it is where we concentrated our effort. We found no evidence of an impending cyber attack which could have a debilitating effect on the nation's critical infrastructures. While we see no electronic disaster around the corner, this is no basis for

---

[3]The directive also established the office of the National Coordinator for Security, Infrastructure Protection and Counter-Terrorism, which oversees policies and programs in counterterrorism, protection of critical infrastructure, and preparedness and consequence management for WMD.

[4]"Critical Infrastructures" are defined as "those physical and cyber-based systems essential to the minimum operations of the economy and government. These systems are so vital that their incapacity or destruction would have a debilitating impact on the defense or economic security of the United States." (White House, 1998b; Executive Order, 1996.)

complacency. We did find widespread capability to exploit infrastructure vulnerabilities. The capability to do harm—particularly
through information networks—is real; it is growing at an alarming
rate; and we have little defense against it. (President's Commission,
1997a.)

The commission accordingly called for a national effort to assure the
security of the nation's increasingly vulnerable and interconnected
infrastructures. And in May 1998, PDD 63 was released, building on
the Commission report, and described as:

[T]he culmination of an intense, interagency effort to evaluate [the
commission's] recommendations and produce a workable and
innovative framework for critical infrastructure protection . . . [PDD
63] sets a goal of a reliable, interconnected, and secure information
system infrastructure by the year 2003, and significantly increased
security to government systems by the year 2000, by immediately
establishing a national center to warn of and respond to attacks . . .
[and] ensuring the capability to protect critical infrastructures from
intentional acts by 2003. (White House, 1998b.)

The PDD also established "a National coordinator whose scope will
include not only critical infrastructure but also foreign terrorism and
threats of domestic mass destruction (including biological weapons)
because attacks on the United States may not come labeled in neat
jurisdictional boxes" (White House, 1998b), as well as a number of
other organizations. These included: a National Infrastructure Protection Center (NIPC) at the FBI, a National Infrastructure Assurance
Council, and a Critical Infrastructure Assurance Office (CIAO) in the
Department of Commerce. Importantly, the directive required each
department and agency to work to reduce its own exposure to new
threats. The PDD also encouraged the private sector establishment
of Information Sharing and Analysis Centers (ISACs) "modeled on
the Centers for Disease Control and Prevention."

Congressional Action

On the congressional front, on June 27, just two days after the
bombing of the Al Khobar barracks in Saudi Arabia in which 19
Americans died, the Senate adopted an amendment aimed at
"preventing terrorist assaults in the United States with nuclear,

chemical, or biological weapons and at helping cities deal with such attacks if they occurred" (*Congressional Quarterly*, 1997, p. 8-8). As described by *Congressional Quarterly*:

> The amendment, sponsored by Nunn, Lugar, and Pete V. Domenici, R-N.M., proposed to authorize $235 million to counter terrorism, including $61 million for research on devices to detect and prevent the spread of "weapons of mass destruction." The Defense and Energy departments would be authorized, under some circumstances, to respond to a domestic terrorist attack that employed nuclear, chemical, or biological weapons and to spend up to $80 million to help local police, fire, and emergency medical service agencies prepare for such an attack. The amendment also included $94 million to expand the scope of the Nunn-Lugar program to include activities such as disposing of spent nuclear fuel from Russian warships and rebuilding some nuclear power plants so they could not produce radioactive material for use in weapons production. (*Congressional Quarterly*, 1997, p. 8-8.)

In September 1996, Congress passed Public Law 104-201, the National Defense Authorization Act for Fiscal Year 1997, Title XIV of which was called the Defense Against Weapons of Mass Destruction Act, also known as the Nunn-Lugar-Domenici legislation. It required DoD to enact:

> [A] program to provide civilian personnel of Federal, State, and local agencies with training and expert advice regarding emergency responses to a use or threatened use of a weapon of mass destruction or related materials.

Specific actions that were authorized included the following:

- Using the National Guard and other reserve components for carrying out the program.

- Establishing "a designated telephonic link (commonly referred to as a 'hot line') to a designated source of relevant data and expert advice for the use of State or local officials responding to such emergencies."

- Loaning appropriate equipment.

- Assisting the Secretary of HHS in the "establishment of metropolitan emergency medical response teams (commonly referred to as 'Metropolitan Medical Strike Force Teams') to provide medical services that are necessary or potentially necessary by reason of a use or threatened use of a weapon of mass destruction."

- Developing and maintaining "at least one domestic terrorism rapid response team composed of members of the Armed Forces and employees of the Department of Defense who are capable of aiding Federal, State, and local officials in the detection, neutralization, containment, dismantlement, and disposal of weapons of mass destruction containing chemical, biological, or related materials."

Taken together, the result of all of this administration and congressional activity has been a dramatic increase in funding for antiterrorism, counterterrorism, critical infrastructure protection, and programs countering WMD, across a broad array of functional areas.[5] Federal spending for combating terrorism in Fiscal Year 2000 is expected to be approximately $10.0 billion, including:

- $8.613 billion for antiterrorism and counterterrorism programs, including $1.385 billion for combating WMD; and

- $1.464 billion for protection of critical infrastructure and computer security, including $500 thousand for R&D efforts.

To provide better oversight of this complex array of programs, Congress enacted subsequent language requiring the President to report annually on governmentwide spending by departments and agencies to combat terrorism and WMD.[6] In 1999, the Senate Armed Services Committee set up the Emerging Threats and Capabilities Subcommittee "to provide a focus for the Department of Defense's efforts to counter new and emerging threats to vital national security interests, . . . such as the proliferation of weapons of mass destruction, international terrorism directed at U.S. targets both at

---

[5]The overall program will be described in Chapter Four.

[6]The Fiscal Year 1998 National Defense Authorization Act (P.L. 105-85) required the President to provide an unclassified report on governmentwide spending to combat terrorism, and Section 1403 of the Fiscal Year 1999 National Defense Authorization Act (P.L. 105-261) required an annex providing information on domestic emergency preparedness programs for response to terrorist incidents involving WMD.

home and abroad, information warfare, and narco-trafficking" (U.S. Senate, 1999, p. 6).

Leadership Statements

In addition to efforts to mitigate the threats through the programs just described, U.S. policymakers have sought to balance the need to alert the public against the desire to avoid creating panic or unfounded fears. For example, in 1999 President Clinton stated:

> I would say that if the issue is how probable [a biological or chemical attack] is in the very near term, an American city or community would be affected, I'd say you probably shouldn't be too worried. But if the issue is, is it a near certainty that at some time in the future there will be some group, probably a terrorist group, that attempts to bring to bear either the use or the threat of a chemical or biological operation, I would say that is highly likely to happen sometime in the next few years. And therefore, I would say the appropriate response is not worry or panic, but taking this issue very seriously . . . and then to try to make sure we are doing everything we can to stop this. ("In the President's Words," 1999.)

> I want to raise public awareness of this, without throwing people into an unnecessary panic . . . [Americans should] not be afraid or asleep. I think that's the trick. (Miller and Broad, 1999.)

When he was asked which threats worried him most, the President answered:

> A chemical attack would be horrible, but it would be finite. You know, it's just like—for the people who went through Oklahoma City, nothing could be more horrible. But it didn't spread. And the thing that bothers people about biological agents is that, unless they're properly diagnosed, contained and treated, that it could spread. For example, we know that if all of us went to a rally on the Mall [in Washington, D.C.,] tomorrow with 10,000 people, and somebody flew a low-flying crop duster and sprayed us all with biological agents from, let's say, 200 feet, that no matter how toxic it were, half of us would walk away for reasons no one quite understands. You know, either we wouldn't breathe it, or we'd have some miraculous resistance to it. And the half of us, somebody would have to diagnose in a hurry and then contain and treat. . . . I'm not

trying to be macabre, but you asked me what keeps me awake at night, and that bothers me. ("In the President's Words," 1999.)

Richard Clarke, National Coordinator for Security, Infrastructure, and Counterterrorism, also stressed the administration's desire to draw attention to the issue without alarming the public:

> The message that we want to get across today is not that we know of an imminent attack—we do not know of any imminent attack being planned on the United States using chemical or biological weapons, or using cyber attack techniques. But we do want to raise consciousness, in the American people, in the scientific community, and in the Congress, that such attacks are growing increasingly likely. And as the President said, we need to be ahead of the power curve; we need to be prepared to defend ourselves against those attacks and, in so doing, perhaps prevent them; at least to be able to mitigate their effects. (White House, 1999b.)

Homeland security has not been free of debate, however. A trial balloon that floated the idea of creating a separate unified command for homeland security was met with visible concern by organizations ranging from the American Civil Liberties Union to conservative groups.[7] There are also indications that the notion of a broader DoD (and Army) role in crisis management has not yet been accepted by key agencies. In short, the evolution of the homeland security problem seems likely to play out in a turbulent political atmosphere.

PUBLIC ATTITUDES

The Commission to Assess the Organization of the Federal Government to Combat the Proliferation of Weapons of Mass Destruction

---

[7]For example, in the words of the American Civil Liberties Union (1999):

> A broad counterterrorism program being considered by the Clinton administration could include measures that severely jeopardize Americans' liberties, the American Civil Liberties Union charged today. The measures include the creation of a domestic military "commandante" responsible for fighting domestic crimes of terrorism.

The proposal also met with criticism from the right. For more on this debate, see Graham (1999) and MSNBC (1999).

stated, "Every American should understand that . . . WMD—nuclear, biological, and chemical weapons and their means of delivery—pose a grave threat to the United States and to our military forces and our vital interests abroad" (Commission, 1999, p. v). As judged by public opinion, the American people seem to have gotten the message. Public opinion data reveal a differentiated set of attitudes that indicate a reasonable level of concern and a strong desire to see action taken against the threats but no expectation that the measures taken can ever eliminate the possibility of attacks:

- Although fewer than 1 percent of Americans think of terrorism when asked to identify the most important problem facing the country,[8] more than half of those polled in September 1996 indicated that terrorism was one of the most important problems for the nation today,[9] and about one in three polled in April 1997 identified terrorism as the greatest threat facing the United States in coming years, and the greatest threat to world peace.[10]

- Nearly three out of four believe that there is a chance that terrorists could attack with WMD, but fewer than one in six said they worried a great deal about this.[11]

---

[8]Polling by Gallup, Pew, CBS/*New York Times*, *Los Angeles Times*, and ABC/*Washington Post*.

[9]Princeton Survey Research Associates asked: "(I'd like you to think about the problems we face as a nation today. As I read you some possible problem areas, please tell me if you think each is one of the most important problems facing this country, important, but not as important, or not too important.) How important a problem for the country is . . . the threat of terrorism?" Another 33 percent said that it was an important problem, but not one of the most important problems facing the nation. PSRA, September 3–15, 1996.

[10]The Pew Research Center for the People and the Press asked two questions about the perceived threat in April 1997. One asked: "In coming years, which one of the following do you think will be the greatest threat to the United States . . . terrorism, international crime and drug rings, illegal immigration, China, Russia, or some other country?" Thirty-five percent identified "terrorism" as the greatest threat in coming years, while 39 percent identified "international crime and drug rings." Each of the other responses elicited less than 10 percent. Also asked was: "Over the next century, which one of the following do you think will be the greatest threat to world peace?" and offered the same options. Thirty-two percent identified "terrorism," while 26 percent identified "international crime and drug rings." Pew Research Center for the People and the Press, April 3–6, 1997.

[11]In March 1996 and April 1997, the Pew Research Center for the People and the Press asked: "Do you think there is much of a chance that terrorists could use a nuclear, chemical, or biological weapon to attack a U.S. city, or don't you think there is much of

- Similarly, nearly six in ten believe that a foreign country could launch a nuclear attack against the United States, although fewer than one in ten said they worried a great deal about it.[12]

- When asked whether they perceive the greater threat of terrorism to come from inside or outside the country, nearly half (47 percent) indicated inside while four in ten said outside, and 11 percent volunteered "both."[13]

- There also were indications at the time of the Oklahoma City bombing in April 1995 that a slight majority of the public believed that bombings like that may become common in the future.[14]

Regarding the government's response to the emerging threat:

- In July 1996, the public was evenly split between those who believed that the U.S. government was doing enough to prevent terrorism in this country (48 percent) and those who did not think so (48 percent).[15]

---

a chance of this?" In March 1996, 72 percent said they believed that there was a chance and, by April 1997, this had risen to 77 percent.

[12]In April 1997, the Pew Center asked: "Do you think there is much of a chance that a foreign country could launch a nuclear attack against the United States, or don't you think there is much of a chance of this?" Fifty-four percent indicated that they thought there was a chance of such an attack.

[13]The question asked was "These days, do you think the greater threat to America from terrorism comes from people outside this country or from people inside this country?" "Inside" was chosen by 33 percent in April 1995 and rose to 39 percent in March 1996 and 40 percent in April 1997. "Outside" was chosen by 40 percent in April 1995 and rose to 49 percent in March 1996 and 47 percent in April 1997. The percent volunteering "both" fell from 21 percent in April 1995 to nine percent in March 1996 and 11 percent in April 1997. The polls were *Los Angeles Times*, April 1995; Pew Research Center for the People and the Press, March 1996 and April 1997. See http://www.people-press.org/apr97que.htm.

[14]The question asked by the *Los Angeles Times* was: "In the future, do you expect attempts at terrorist acts like the bombing in Oklahoma City will be very common, somewhat common, not too common, or not at all common in this country?" Fifty-one percent said that they thought that it would be very (15 percent) or somewhat (36 percent) common. *Los Angeles Times*, April 26–27, 1995.

[15]The question Gallup/CNN/*USA Today* asked was: "Overall, do you think the United States government is doing enough to prevent terrorism in this country or not?" Gallup/CNN/*USA Today*, July 29, 1996.

- More than half of those polled in April 1995 and March 1996 felt that antiterrorism laws were too weak.[16]

- In August 1998, large majorities indicated they were following news reports on government activities to prevent terrorism. A total of 71 percent said that they had followed such reports very closely (33 percent) or fairly closely (38 percent).[17]

- In August 1998, majorities indicated that they had a sober view of the difficulties in preventing terrorist incidents; when asked how many terrorist incidents officials would be able to prevent if they were given the tools they needed, more than half indicated that they would be able to prevent few or none, and fewer than one in 20 thought that all such attacks could be prevented.[18]

- In 1999, substantial majorities indicated that reducing the threat of international terrorism should be a "top priority" of the U.S. government.[19]

The impression one gets from the public opinion data is that the public are concerned about homeland security issues and expect intelligence, law enforcement, and defense officials to engage in the necessary planning and preparations, wherever possible, to prevent

---

[16]The question asked was: "Do you think the federal antiterrorism laws currently on the books in this country are too strong, too weak, or about what they need to be?" Asked by the *Los Angeles Times* in April 1995 and the Pew Research Center for the People and the Press in March 1996. See http://www.people-press.org/terque.htm.

[17]The question the Pew Center asked was: "(I will read a list of some stories covered by news organizations this past month. As I read each item, tell me if you happened to follow this news story very closely, fairly closely, not too closely, or not at all closely.) ... Reports about activities to prevent terrorism both here and abroad." Pew Research Center, August 7, 1998, to September 8, 1998.

[18]The question the *Los Angeles Times* asked was: "If law enforcement officials were given the tools they need, do you think they would be able to prevent all future terrorist attacks here in the United States, or many of them, or only a few of them, or would they be able to prevent none of them?" In August 1998, 54 percent said few or none, while 39 percent said all or many; in April 1995, 56 percent said few or none, while 40 percent said all or many. On both occasions, only 4 percent said they thought that law enforcement officials would be able to prevent all attacks.

[19]Princeton Survey Research Associates asked: "(As I read a list of specific foreign policy problems, tell me whether each one should have top priority in the U.S. (United States) government, a priority but not top priority, or no priority.) How about ... reducing the threat of international terrorism?" Seventy-five percent accorded the problem top priority. PSRA, March 24–30, 1999.

terrorist acts against the United States. Nevertheless, majorities also have a fairly realistic appraisal of the difficulties of preventing terrorist incidents—fewer than one in 20 believe that *all* future terrorist attacks could be prevented if law enforcement officials (and, presumably others) were given the tools they need.

HOMELAND SECURITY TASK AREAS

Our work suggests that homeland security should include at least five task areas. Three of these task areas emerge from the foregoing analysis:

- WMD domestic preparedness (DP) and civil support, ranging from counterproliferation activities to consequence management of incidents involving high explosives (HE), chemical, biological, radiological, and nuclear weapons.

- Continuity of government (COG), i.e., efforts to reestablish at the earliest possible opportunity civilian political and legal authority following a catastrophic incident.

- Continuity of operations (COOP), including force protection against asymmetric homeland attacks during the fort-to-port sequence, critical infrastructure protection of mission-critical facilities and systems, and other activities.

To be complete, two additional task areas also should be included in homeland security:

- Border and coastal defense, the need for which arises from the possible threat of introduction into the United States of WMD or other weapons capable of mass casualties, and the possibility of large-scale refugee flows that could create national security problems and tax available civilian capacity.[20]

---

[20]A recent historical example of this is the flow of refugees from Haiti prior to the U.S. intervention. Possible future scenarios include refugee flows from Cuba in the event that a peaceful transition to a post-Castro Cuba doesn't eventuate or instability at the U.S.-Mexican border.

- Although it is not addressed in the present study, national missile defense.[21]

While overlaps occur among these areas—WMD could be used, for example, against civilian targets, against government targets, or against military mobilization efforts—they collectively seem to capture the essence of the homeland security problem set.

Because at present no agreed-on definition for homeland security exists, the study team developed the following working definition:[22]

> Homeland [security] consists of all military activities aimed at preparing for, protecting against, or managing the consequences of attacks on American soil, including the CONUS and U.S. territories and possessions. It includes all actions to safeguard the populace and its property, critical infrastructure, the government, and the military, its installations, and deploying forces.

While other definitions are certainly possible, the merit of the definition just presented is that it is clear about homeland security's focus on military activities, as distinct from the activities of civilian organizations, its geographic specificity, and the potential targets it seeks to protect.

CONCLUSIONS

This chapter began with necessary background for understanding the broader context in which homeland security programs are being developed. This discussion included a survey of the constitutional, strategic, and domestic political contexts for homeland security and showed not only that homeland security has deep historical roots but also that the homeland security mission is the *fundamental* defense mission. All other military activities are predicated on the notion that the nation's security will be provided for. This analysis also

---

[21]Because this area is heavily studied, we devoted no effort to this area.

[22]We recognize that other departments and agencies have important roles to play in many areas related to homeland security. For example, and most notably, the FBI and FEMA play the key roles in crisis and consequence management. However, we reserve the phrase "homeland security" for the tasks performed by the armed services and the Department of Defense.

showed that the issue of the employment of the military in domestic contingencies can be a divisive one—concerns about the role of the military in civil society greatly shapes and constrains the options. The range of threats to the United States—including actions by terrorists or adversary special operations forces, cyber and other attacks on critical infrastructure, computers and communications networks, and large-scale refugee flows—led to an enumeration of the key homeland security task areas and a definition of homeland security.

The next chapter provides an analytic framework or methodology for thinking about Army homeland security roles and responsibilities in the larger setting of local, state, and federal responders.

Chapter Three

ANALYTIC FRAMEWORK

In a way, homeland security looks like defense analysis probably did before it became analytic, i.e., before the advent of gaming, simulation, cost-effectiveness, and trade-off analyses and the application of other techniques that are, by now, standard tools for assessing options in defense.[1] Most of the work done in the area of homeland security seems to be focused on essentially organizational solutions whose premise seems to be that if only more centralized control of policy were in evidence, the problem would be far more tractable.[2] While more centralized control and policy direction almost certainly would help, we take a somewhat different view of the problem.

To be sure, it is a hard problem to analyze. The data in this area are difficult to obtain and uneven in quality, and no computer or other models can be used to evaluate cost-effectiveness, trade-offs, or robustness. With this in mind, we begin by proposing an analytic framework for assessing homeland security that focuses on four key policy questions that, once answered, provide the necessary information for designing homeland security programs. The questions are:

---

[1]We have not, for example, seen a thorough analysis of the question of the optimal locations for response units for consequence management, what sorts of mobility assets will be necessary to assure their responsiveness, and what sorts of capabilities they should have. In a way, this is not unlike strategic analysis before Albert Wohlstetter's seminal assessment of the optimal basing for strategic aircraft. See Wohlstetter's (1958) classic piece, posted at http://www.rand.org/publications/classics/wohlstetter/P1472/P1472.html.

[2]In this vein, see Carter et al. (1998a, 1998b), and Iklé (1999).

- What types and magnitudes of threat are we planning against, and what risks do we face?

- What level of performance will we demand from our homeland security capabilities?

- What are the most cost-effective program options for providing capabilities with the needed performance levels in incidents of specified planning magnitude?

- What resources will be available for homeland security programs?

Each will be discussed at greater length.

THREAT AND RISK ANALYSES

The first question that needs to be addressed: What types and magnitudes of threats are we planning against, and what risks do we face?

The first element of the analytic framework for analyzing homeland security is thus an assessment of threats and risks. The General Accounting Office (GAO) has strongly and consistently recommended the use of threat and risk assessments in designing programs to combat terrorism. As described by the GAO:

> Threat and risk assessments are widely recognized as valid decision support tools to establish and prioritize security program requirements. A threat analysis, the first step in determining risk, identifies and evaluates each threat on the basis of various factors, such as its capability and intent to attack an asset, the likelihood of a successful attack, and its lethality. Risk management is the deliberate process of understanding "risk"—the likelihood that a threat will harm an asset with some severity of consequences—and deciding on and implementing actions to reduce it. (GAO, 1998b, p. 3.)

> Risk management principles acknowledge that (1) while risk generally cannot be eliminated, it can be reduced by enhancing protection from validated and credible threats; (2) although many threats are possible, some are more likely to occur than others; and (3) assets are not equally critical. (GAO, 1998b, p. 3.)

Threat and risk assessments enable organizations to determine how to prioritize scarce resources across various threats and risks, largely in terms of the conditions—in terms of probability and consequence—under which specific actions are and are not warranted (see Figure 3.1).[3]

The darkest regions in the figure include those cases where the probability/magnitude combination is unacceptable and efforts need to be made to reduce risk through countermeasures. The next two cases are "indeterminate" and require management decision or review. The regions that contain narrow stripes consist of cases that are undesirable but where a management decision is required to determine what if any actions should be taken. The white regions include cases where the combination of probability and magnitude are probably acceptable, although management review is required. Finally, the areas with wider stripes include cases that are acceptable without any management review.

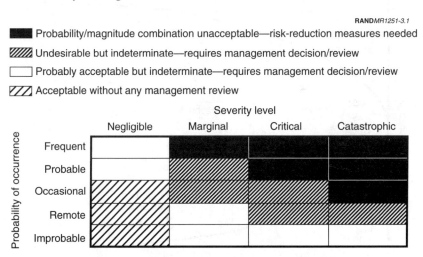

RAND*MR1251-3.1*

■ Probability/magnitude combination unacceptable—risk-reduction measures needed

▨ Undesirable but indeterminate—requires management decision/review

☐ Probably acceptable but indeterminate—requires management decision/review

▨ Acceptable without any management review

Figure 3.1—Risk-Assessment Matrix

---

[3]The figure is adapted from GAO, 1998b, p. 8.

The foregoing suggests that threats and risks can be considered in a systematic framework that uses both probability and severity of consequence as criteria for decisionmaking about whether to take action.[4] The question remains, however, what planning magnitude should we use to size our capabilities?

Not unlike the "spectrum of threat" charts that often accompany defense analyses—where the probability and lethality or consequence of different types of military operations are inversely related—a similar approach can be used for establishing the desirable planning magnitude for a specific type of threat (see Figure 3.2).

The figure is a modified "spectrum of threat" plot, with the consequence or magnitude of events on the x-axis and the probability of

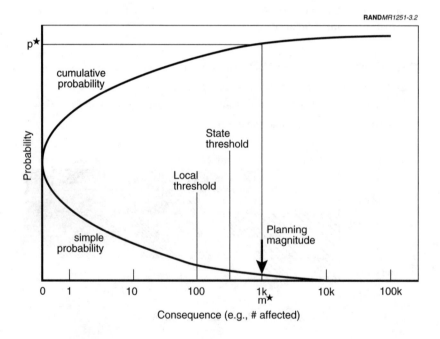

Figure 3.2—Threats in Terms of Probability and Consequence

---

[4]For a particularly good discussion of the importance of considering both probability and magnitude of consequence, see Falkenrath (1998).

the events on the y-axis. The figure portrays two curves. If we focus on the threat of terrorism, the bottom curve would describe the frequency (or probability, if we assume that the distribution of historical incidents also is representative of what we will see in the future) of terrorist incidents of various magnitudes. The upper curve represents the *cumulative* frequency or probability of incidents that are of equal or smaller consequence. In other words, if p* in the figure is assumed to be 90 percent, then programs considered adequate to deal with cases at the ninetieth percentile also would be adequate for all of the smaller terrorist attacks as well. They would, however, only represent partial solutions to the larger 10 percent of cases.[5]

Figure 3.3 plots data on American casualties in terrorist incidents. The number of casualties in each incident (the consequences of these events) is on the x-axis, and the frequency of events is on the y-axis. The figure demonstrates that such curves easily can be constructed from empirical historical data on the past incidence of terrorist or other attacks or on the basis of integrated threat and risks assessments that aim to project the future threat and risk environment.

As shown, the frequency (probability) and consequence of terrorist incidents are inversely related, i.e., injuries are more likely than deaths, small numbers of casualties are more likely than large numbers, and the probability quickly declines as the consequence of the incidents increases.

Two basic methods for establishing the appropriate planning magnitude are suggested. First, based on data from the intelligence and law enforcement community or other sources, we can specify a cumulative probability (p* in the figure) that is sufficiently high that (a) results in a consequence level that is larger than state and local

---

[5]We note that one could also establish planning magnitudes by selecting cases whose consequences are larger than any that have been seen in the past. For example, one might use for a planning magnitude an incident 25 percent, 50 percent, or 100 percent larger than the largest incident that has to date been seen. Indeed, in Chapter Four, we suggest a planning magnitude for chemical incidents (2,500) that is 200 times larger than the number of deaths that occurred in the Aum Shinrikyo sarin attack in Tokyo.

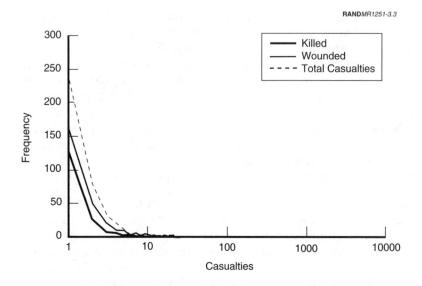

Figure 3.3—American Casualties in International Terrorist
Incidents, 1968–1998

abilities to manage (designated by local and state threshold) and (b) includes a large share of the events we are likely to face in the future (e.g., 90, 95, or 99 percent). Put another way, by choosing to prepare for possible events at the ninetieth, ninety-fifth, or ninety-ninth percentile, we will be prepared for all of the smaller and more probable ones. Of course, we would only be partially prepared for the larger, less likely ones. The second method for establishing a planning magnitude would simply be to establish a consequence severity judged higher than local and state capacity, while possibly providing some additional hedging in light of the possibility of larger incidents. Regardless of the approach taken, such a decision would need to be a collective one, involving expert judgment from the intelligence, law enforcement, and local, state, and federal responders.

The foregoing has demonstrated that empirical data can be used to construct cumulative frequency (or probability) distributions. It will later be shown that, whether one is looking at terrorist incidents or the consequences of cyber attacks, these distributions follow the same pattern: The most likely incidents are the ones that are the smallest in magnitude or consequence, and the largest events are exceedingly rare.

ESTABLISHING DESIRED PERFORMANCE LEVELS

The second question that needs to be addressed: What level of performance will we demand from our homeland security capabilities?

The Government Performance and Results Act (GPRA) of 1993 aims to improve governmental effectiveness by setting program goals, and measuring program performance against those goals. In the National Defense Authorization Act for Fiscal Year 2000, the Senate Armed Services Committee has furthermore directed the Secretary of the Army to review existing modernization programs and provide an assessment not later than February 1, 2000, on how these plans will meet the future challenges associated with, among other mission areas, homeland security (U.S. Senate, 1999, pp. 132–133). Although certain aspects of the Army's homeland security activities have been identified as being in compliance with the Act,[6] each homeland security task area requires different measures of performance.

We now address the issue of measures of performance for homeland security and the establishment of performance levels to guide the development of operational concepts, programs, plans, and budgets.

The previous section suggested that the first step in defining homeland security programs is to undertake threat and risk analyses that specify the types and magnitudes of events against which we will plan. The output of this process was a planning magnitude—designated as m^*—that established the first parameter for sizing homeland security capabilities. The next step in the process is defining the performance levels for responses to homeland security attacks (see Figure 3.4).

As in the previous figures, Figure 3.4 portrays the consequence of an event on the x-axis. The y-axis represents needed capabilities, and

---

[6]The GAO found that Soldier Biological Chemical Command's (SBCCOM's) chemical and biological defense research, development, test, and evaluation (RDT&E) program is quite admirable in this respect.

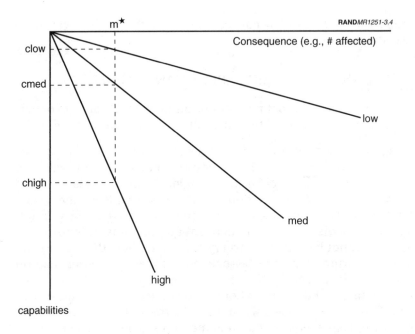

Figure 3.4—Consequence and Performance Levels

the contour lines represent different performance levels (low, medium, and high). Low performance might mean, for example, a capability to save the life of one in 10 who were injured, while a high performance level might mean the capability to save seven out of 10 of the injured.

The figure suggests that needed capabilities to respond to a homeland security attack (on the y-axis) are highly sensitive both to the planning magnitude (m*) established earlier and normative beliefs about desired performance levels (i.e., whether one chooses to be on the low, medium, or high line).

This sensitivity of needed capabilities to planning magnitude for a fixed performance level can be seen by following any one of the three illustrative performance levels (low, medium, or high) from the origin to the bottom right part of the figure: the greater the planning magnitude, the greater the capabilities needed to provide a fixed level performance level.

Sensitivity to performance level can be seen by fixing the planning magnitude at m*, and observing the capability level implied by the three levels of performance (low, medium, and high). For any planning magnitude, the greater the desired performance level, the greater the capabilities implied. As we will see in the next section, with the planning magnitude and desired performance level established, we have sufficient information to begin designing cost-effective programs that provide the needed capabilities.

It also is the case that performance improvements can either be realized by simply increasing the amount of resources allocated to the response or by improving (through improvements in equipment, mobility, or training) the effectiveness of the response capability.

Figure 3.5 illustrates these points by comparing the number of systems of various types needed to yield specific performance levels, here defined in terms of the total number of victims that can be evacuated by litter.

In the figure, the x-axis is the magnitude of the consequence of a disaster or WMD event, in terms of the total number of victims that

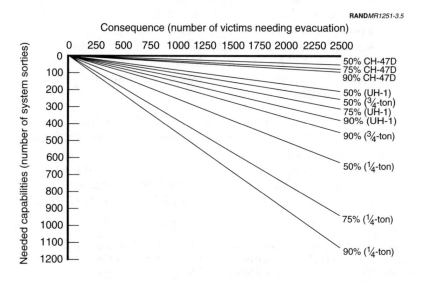

Figure 3.5—Magnitude and Desired Performance Dictate Needed Capabilities

need evacuation on litters (this would be the m* selected earlier). The y-axis is the number of sorties (or trips) by various systems. The lines represent various combinations of performance level (whether we desire a capability for evacuating 50, 75, or 90 percent of the victims) and systems (e.g., CH-47D and UH-1 helicopters and quarter-ton and three-quarter-ton trucks used as ambulances) that can provide the desired capabilities. Thus, each point on a line represents the number of sorties for a specific system that would be required to evacuate a specified percentage of victims for an incident of a given magnitude.[7]

To illustrate, if one wanted the highest level of performance (a capacity to evacuate 90 percent of the victims in a WMD incident), the CH-47Ds can be seen to provide the greatest capacity of the options presented: If our planning magnitude were 1,500, it would take fewer than 60 CH-47D sorties to evacuate the 1,500 victims; if the planning magnitude were 2,500 victims, fewer than 100 sorties would be needed.[8] By comparison, it would take 675 trips by a quarter-ton truck serving as an ambulance to evacuate 1,500 victims, or 1,145 trips to evacuate 2,500 victims.

The main point of the figure is the obvious one that smaller incidents generally require smaller amounts of capability, but also the less obvious points that the needed capabilities are highly sensitive both to the capacity of the units or systems being considered (in this case, UH-1s, CH-47Ds, and quarter-ton and three-quarter-ton trucks), and to the demanded performance levels (a capacity to evacuate 50, 75, or 90 percent of the victims).

These calculations can provide insights into the volumetrics of the capabilities needed, given specified planning magnitudes and desired performance levels. Nevertheless, one needs to impose additional parameters on performance levels (e.g., the ability to evacuate a specified percentage of victims in three hours) or constraints (e.g., no helicopters larger than UH-1s, no more than 120

---

[7]We assumed simply that a quarter-ton truck could carry two litters and a three-quarter-ton truck could carry five litters, a UH-1 could carry six litters, and a CH-47D could carry 24 litters. These numbers are illustrative only.

[8]We assumed that a CH-47D could carry no more than 24 patients on litters.

trucks) to identify the actual numbers of systems (or units) that would need to be deployed to respond adequately to an incident.

Figure 3.6 suggests why this should be the case. In the figure, as we apply additional manpower (labor) and equipment (capital) in balanced combinations, our isoperformance curves shift up and to the right. Additional resources increase the number of victims that can be quickly and effectively located, triaged, evacuated, and medically treated.[9]

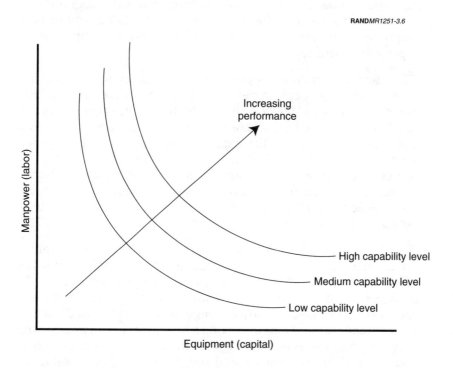

RAND*MR1251-3.6*

Figure 3.6—Higher Performance Through Higher Capability Levels

---

[9]The reason the isoperformance curves have the shape they do is that they are subject to strong assumptions about diminishing returns. For example, if we have only one truck to perform evacuations but keep increasing the manpower associated with that single truck, beyond a certain number of troops, no additional benefits accrue in terms of performance. In fact, at some point, so-called "shoulder space" considerations may begin to apply, where the situation becomes so crowded with personnel that the use of the truck is in fact prevented.

IDENTIFYING COST-EFFECTIVE PROGRAM MIXES

The third homeland security question that needs to be answered: What are the most cost-effective programmatic alternatives for providing capabilities with the needed performance levels for incidents of the type and planning magnitude we specified?

The previous section suggested a number of measures of performance that could be used to establish performance levels for meeting various types of threat. This section addresses programmatic considerations (i.e., the effectiveness and cost of homeland security programs) by describing the Army role in homeland security in the larger federal setting.

The national capabilities for preventing and responding to WMD terrorism—and the capabilities for the other homeland security threats—provides a "layered defense in depth" that cuts across federal departments and agencies and the military services. Throughout this section to simplify the exposition we describe this layered defense in terms of three layers: one focused on preventing attacks, one engaged in preincident activities to prepare for and defend against possible attacks, and one used to respond to attacks and manage their consequences. There are two principal aims in building such a layered defense.

First, the aim of a layered defense in depth is to achieve a robust defense that does not create the possibility of single-point failures by relying solely on the success of any one specific program or solely on the expected effectiveness of prevention or consequence mitigation. Such a robust layered defense can only be achieved by understanding the trade-offs inherent in striking a balance between policies and programs that can provide a high probability of *preventing* acts of WMD terrorism and policies and programs that can *substantially mitigate the consequences* of an act of WMD terrorism.

Figure 3.7 describes notional constant-cost combinations of prevention and consequence reduction capabilities that result in different probabilities of prevention and consequence reduction.[10]

---

[10]As will be described later, for example, federal spending on countering terrorism and WMD is weighted toward prevention.

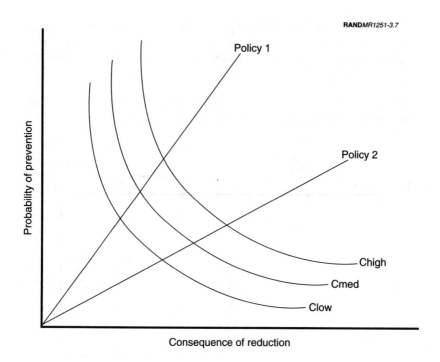

RAND*MR1251-3.7*

Figure 3.7—Trade-Offs Between Prevention and Consequence Reduction

In the figure, the x-axis is the degree of consequence reduction (e.g., the percentage reduction in victims, deaths, or dollar damage) that results from a specific policy. The y-axis is the effectiveness of the prevention efforts in terms of the probability that the policy will prevent the undesired events. The three isocontour curves represent the possible policies, i.e., combinations of prevention and consequence reduction activities, for three fixed budgets (low, medium, and high). Finally, the lines stemming from the origin connote distinct policies: Policy 1 emphasizes prevention at the expense of consequence reduction, and Policy 2 emphasizes consequence reduction.

The second principal aim in building a layered defense is that it should be cost-effective, representing an efficient use of scarce resources to obtain a specified level of performance or effectiveness—i.e., the preferred mix of prevention and consequence reduction—at least-cost.[11] Figure 3.8 presents a curve that traces the most cost-effective programmatic-providing capabilities that yield various performance levels.

The reader will recall that in the previous section, we chose a high performance level that provided a good balance between high assur-

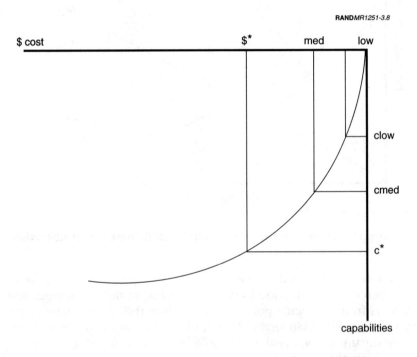

RAND*MR1251-3.8*

Figure 3.8—Cost-Effective Options at Various Performance Levels[12]

---

[11]See Appendix B for an illustration of the sort of notional tradeoff analysis that could help reveal the most cost-effective solution for providing consequence mitigation capabilities.

[12]The figure makes the simplifying assumption that investments exhibit diminishing marginal returns. It also is possible that such a curve would not be a continuous function but would be made up of stair-steps, as the next most expensive cost-effective program options could come at considerable additional cost.

ance of preventing terrorist incidents and high assurance of mitigating the consequences of an event, should prevention efforts fail. This performance mix was shown to lead to a needed capability level of c^*, i.e., a fairly high performance level.

The figure suggests that the higher the performance and capability level established (described in the third panel of the nomogram), the higher the cost. The rationale is that each marginal increase in performance level typically requires an increase in resources, whether in terms of additional labor (personnel), capital (materiel), or other inputs (e.g., enhanced training), and these come at some cost.[13]

To summarize, the national programs that address the homeland security threats—including local, state, and federal actors and a range of activities both at home and abroad—should provide the sort of robust and cost-effective layered defense just described, irrespective of the nature of the threat (e.g., WMD versus "cyber").

BUDGETING AND RESOURCING

The final question to be answered: What resources will be available for homeland security programs?

Once we have identified the most cost-effective mix of programs that meet the needed performance levels for preventing and mitigating the consequences of incidents of specified magnitude, we can examine the budgetary implications of these programs.

As described in Figure 3.9, this exercise essentially involves determining whether the total cost of the program specified in the preceding step is less than or equal to the maximum amount of resources we are willing to allocate to homeland security, in light of warfighting and other obligations.

The figure puts funding for homeland security activities on the x-axis and funding for other activities—generally, in the case of the Army and DoD, warfighting activities—on the y-axis. The straight line rep-

---

[13]Performance increases also could come with the same level of resources, but where processes have been reengineered to be more effective and efficient.

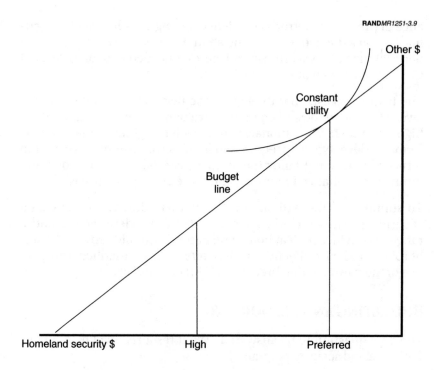

RAND*MR1251-3.9*

Figure 3.9—Budgeting for Homeland Security

resents the total budget that can be allocated among homeland security and other activities. The indifference curve represents combinations of homeland security and other activities where a policymaker has constant utility, i.e., the various combinations along the curve are equally attractive. Finally, the point where the indifference curve touches the budget curve is the optimum or preferred policy, where marginal cost and marginal utility are equal.

PROCESS AND STRATEGY

Each element of the foregoing four-step process has a great deal of activity associated with it—both in terms of analytic work and in terms of decisions that need to be taken—but its proper application also is quite critical, both in the short term and the long term.

Iterative in the Short Term

In the short term, we envision that the Army and DoD would need to iterate a number of times through the entire four-step process described above.

One reason is that empirical data are not routinely collected or reported, and it may take some effort to define the data requirements. In a similar vein, few off-the-shelf tools (e.g., simulation models) are available for doing the underlying analyses, and some effort will necessarily be involved in building and refining these tools to support the larger analytic effort.

Another reason is that the trade-offs between performance and cost—and which planning magnitudes and performance objectives are even deemed feasible from a cost perspective—can only be established by determining the minimum needed response capabilities that meet these objectives and costing them out. Put another way, we believe that attempts to establish exceedingly high planning magnitudes and performance criteria will in fact result in comparably high costs, that these will be seen as prohibitively expensive, and that they will necessitate downward revision to less ambitious short-term objectives, which can then be costed out. Since none of the steps of the process is independent of the others, a substantial number of iterations may be required to build consensus around the planning magnitudes and performance levels that establish needed capabilities and their associated costs. This will not be a strictly analytic enterprise, but will engage value trade-offs made by decision-makers from different disciplines and parts of the defense community, and it may simply take multiple iterations of the process to identify feasible solutions.

Part of an Adaptive Long-Term Strategy

In the longer term, we see the process as embedded in a larger long-term policy development strategy inherently adaptive in nature. Planning magnitudes, for example, would need to be established in large part on the basis of threat and risk analyses that include intelligence, law enforcement, and military personnel, and on the basis of policymakers' desire to hedge against the unexpected. But because the threats and risks may increase or recede over time, these threat and risk analyses would need to be updated periodically, and the suggested planning magnitude revised in light of the increasing (or decreasing) threat. Put another way, any initial numbers selected as planning magnitudes would be "marks on the wall," subject to further refinement or to wholesale change as the threat environment changed or, as described above, if they proved too costly.

This adaptive, long-term strategy would dictate that, for the short term (e.g., one to five years), preparations be made to deal successfully with modest—yet still stressing—threats, rather than less probable, "worst case" scenarios. This will provide a bar high enough to be challenging, without making it impossible to surmount, and will give incentives for the development of the necessary prototype doctrine, organizations, training, and equipment, providing for mobility needs and creating a set of capabilities that can exercise with local, state, and federal civilian responders. If the threat environment has changed enough in three to five years to warrant increased planning magnitudes, then existing organizations can be expanded or new, more capable organizations can be fielded, with a higher degree of confidence that they will be able to address the situations they might encounter. If new capabilities are available at that time that permit much higher performance levels, those can be introduced into the force and tested in the crucible of training and exercises.

In short, the proposed framework is meant to be embedded in a process that involves threat and risk assessments and policy-level decisions regarding what is desirable, what is cost-effective, and, ultimately, what is affordable.

CONCLUSIONS

This chapter has provided a simple analytic framework and methodology that addresses the four key questions that need to be answered in homeland security. The four questions are:

- What magnitudes of events should the United States plan against for high-explosive, chemical, biological, radiological, nuclear, and cyber threats?

- What levels of performance will the nation demand in the national (local, state, and federal) responses to these events?

- What are the most cost-effective options for providing the capabilities that will address these events at the desired performance levels?

- What resources will be made available, and will they be sufficient to provide the necessary capabilities?

Chapters Four through Seven apply the framework to the four homeland security task areas that are the focus of this study and, where possible, populate some of the notional figures presented in this chapter with empirical data.

Chapter Four

PROTECTING AMERICANS AT HOME: WMD DOMESTIC PREPAREDNESS AND CIVIL SUPPORT

The first homeland security task area is domestic preparedness against terrorism and WMD. We conceive of domestic preparedness against WMD terrorism as local, state, and federal activities that aim to improve the ability of the nation as a whole to prevent, prepare for, or respond to such incidents.

THREATS AND RISKS

As was described in Chapter Three, the GAO has called for the use of threat and risk assessments to guide the development of programs for combating terrorism and WMD. The Fiscal Year 1999 National Defense Authorization Act also has called for threat and risk assessments to be used in developing federal, state, and local domestic preparedness programs:

> Requirement to Develop Methodologies—The Attorney General, in consultation with the Director of the Federal Bureau of Investigation and representatives of appropriate Federal, State, and local agencies, shall develop and test methodologies for assessing the threat and risk of terrorist employment of weapons of mass destruction in cities and other local areas. The results of the tests may be used to determine the training and equipment requirements under the program developed under section 1402. The methodologies required by this subsection shall be developed using cities or local areas selected by the Attorney General, acting in consultation with the Director of the Federal Bureau of Investigation

and appropriate representatives of Federal, State, and local agencies.[1]

Although the Department of Justice and the FBI have the lead in this activity, it seems likely that Army—and DoD—activities increasingly will be guided by these sorts of analyses.

While detailed threat and risk assessments are beyond the scope of the present report, this chapter summarizes our principal observations on the threats and risks in the area of domestic preparedness.[2]

Threat Assessment

Public statements have suggested that the threat of WMD terrorism and the risk of surprise are increasing:

- President Clinton has declared it "highly likely" that a terrorist group will launch or threaten a biological or chemical attack on U.S. soil within the next few years.

- Robert Blitzer, former FBI chief of domestic terrorism and counterterrorism planning, said that the number of credible domestic threats involving WMD increased significantly in 1998 and that the FBI opened more than 86 investigations into the threatened use of chemical, biological, radiological, or nuclear materials in the first nine months of 1998. In comparison, only 68 such cases were opened in all of 1997 (Macko, 1998).

- The CIA recently testified that the danger and sophistication of the chemical and biological warfare threat from hostile nations and terrorists is increasing, as is the risk of surprise use.[3]

- But, to reprise the quote from the National Coordinator for Security, Infrastructure, and Counterterrorism: "The message

---

[1]Section 1404, P.L. 105-261, known as the Strom Thurmond National Defense Authorization Act for Fiscal Year 1999, October 17, 1998.

[2]As was described in Chapter Three, under the subhead, "Threat and Risk Analyses."

[3]Four principal reasons were cited: (1) CBW agents could become more sophisticated; (2) CBW programs are becoming more self-sufficient; (3) countries are taking advantage of denial and deception techniques; and (4) advances are occurring in dissemination techniques, delivery options, and strategies for CBW use (Lauder, 1999).

that we want to get across today is not that we know of an imminent attack—we do not know of any imminent attack being
planned on the United States using chemical or biological
weapons, or using cyber attack techniques." (White House,
1999b.)

A number of key events have motivated this policy-level attention
and the allocation of large-scale resources to the prevention and
management of the consequences of terrorist attacks against the
United States:

- The World Trade Center bombing in 1993, in which six were
  killed and more than 1,000 injured.

- The bombing of the Murrah federal building in Oklahoma City in
  1995, in which 168 were killed and 519 were injured.

- The 1995 use of sarin by the Aum Shinrikyo group against the
  Tokyo subway system, in which 12 were killed and more than
  5,000 injured.[4]

More recently, the Centennial Park bombing in Atlanta during the
1996 Olympics, which killed one and injured more than 100, and the
simultaneous attacks by Osama bin Laden's organization on two U.S.
embassies in Africa in which more than 300 died, have reminded the
nation that few sanctuaries from anti-U.S. terrorism exist.[5]

---

[4]The Army also has occasionally provided military assistance for civil disturbances, as
occurred during the riots in Los Angeles in Joint Task Force-Los Angeles (JTF-LA), also
known as Operation Garden Plot, the name given to the generic Operations Plan
(OPLAN) for military support in civil disturbances. This role is guided by DoDD
3025.12, Military Assistance for Civil Disturbances (MACDIS), February 4, 1994, which
pertains to:

> [M]ilitary assistance to federal, State, and local government
> (including government of U.S. territories) and their law enforcement
> agencies for civil disturbances and civil operations, including
> response to terrorist incidents.

See Federation of American Scientists, "Operation Garden Plot/JTF-LA Joint Task
Force in Los Angeles, at http://www.fas.org/man/dod-101/ops/jtf-la.htm.

[5]The September 1999 terrorist attacks against apartment buildings in Moscow by pre-
sumed Dagestani or Chechen sympathizers further suggests the willingness of motivated groups to target noncombatants.

Nevertheless, the actual incidence of terrorism remains quite low. Although 1998 saw 741 people killed and 5,952 injured in international terrorist incidents—a record toll—the number of international terrorist attacks worldwide in 1998 was the lowest level since 1971. In 1998, according to the State Department, no international terrorist attacks took place on U.S. soil (U.S. Department of State, 1999), and, according to the FBI, only two domestic terrorist incidents occurred in the United States in that year (FBI, 1999; GAO, 1999a, p. 4). In fact, in all years except 1992, terrorist incidents in the United States numbered fewer than five.[6]

Further, an analysis of data on chemical and biological attacks,[7] as well as news reporting, suggests that hoaxes and idle threats of chemical and biological attacks predominate.[8] The problem had evidently become so acute by December 1998 that the FBI put out an advisory on anthrax scares caused by hoax letters.[9] In short, there is something of a disconnect between the experience of actual WMD terrorism incidents and the level of policy interest in the issue.

Threats. Although such estimates are highly problematic,[10] as many as a hundred terrorist threats to U.S. interests currently are being

---

[6]In 1992, there were 12 domestic terrorist incidents counted (GAO, 1999a, p. 4).

[7]See the data posted at Monterey Institute, 1999.

[8]For example, Congress reported that "in the first four months of 1999 there have been close to 100 RF threats made alleging anthrax possession. Fortunately, anthrax was not actually used in any of those cases." (U.S. Senate, 1999, p. 351).

[9]The advisory read, in part:

> Recently, there have been numerous anthrax scares caused by hoax letters advising the reader (victim) that anthrax was contained within the envelope. Some of these letters were found to contain a form of inert powder (such as baby powder, detergent, or other common household materials) with an accompanying note advising the recipient that he or she had been exposed to anthrax. Other notes have merely contained the written statement advising the reader of the presence of anthrax, although no foreign substance was contained within the envelope. The reaction to these events by WMD first responders has resulted in quarantine, evacuation, decontamination, and chemoprophylaxis efforts. All cases thus far have been hoaxes.

"Anthrax Advisory from WMD Operations Unit of the Federal Bureau of Investigation," December 1998, http://www.emergency.com/fbiantrx.htm.

[10]The numbers are problematic primarily because only open sources were used; reliance on classified sources would enable a more accurate accounting.

tracked closely.[11] Of these, some groups (e.g., Osama bin Laden's organization, which is waging a highly publicized *jihad* against U.S. interests) are of greater concern than others.

While only a subset of this collection are of concern now in the context of domestic preparedness against WMD, proliferation or learning-curve phenomena could increase this number. The intersection between active WMD programs and sponsorship of state terrorism provides one window into the potential sources of future WMD threats to the U.S. homeland (see Table 4.1).[12]

As shown in the table, a small number of "rogue states" are involved in terrorism, and a smaller number are pursuing WMD programs. In addition to these nations, about a dozen terrorist groups have expressed an interest in or have sought chemical, biological, radiological, and nuclear (CBRN) agents (Lauder, 1999), including a number of domestic groups who have exhibited interest in WMD.[13]

---

[11]In the event, we derived the figure of 100 as follows. The State Department has identified seven states (Cuba, Iran, Iraq, Libya, North Korea, Sudan, and Syria) as state sponsors of terrorism, and 28 organizations as Foreign Terrorist Organizations (FTOs). The intelligence community reportedly focuses its collection and analysis on about 10 states, with another 50 also of proliferation concern, for a total of 60. Assuming that the intelligence community list includes the state sponsors, this brings the total to perhaps 88 foreign terrorist organizations and states of interest. Because only a subset of the FTOs historically have attacked U.S. interests, the number is probably lower. The FBI, meanwhile, appears to be most concerned about up to two dozen foreign and domestic terrorism groups. In 1997, there were two terrorist incidents in the United States, two suspected incidents, and 21 terrorism preventions. Assuming a unique group for each incident or prevention leads to 25 organizations of key concern in 1997. Again, the number is probably lower because of multiple incidents by some groups. This leads to a total of 113 organizations or states of concern. This suggests that the total number of interest is perhaps as high as 100, but the number of highest threat to the United States is possibly much lower. See Department of State, Patterns of Global Terrorism 1999, Washington, D.C., 2000, at http://www.state.gov/www/global/terrorism/1999report/patterns.pdf. For the FBI numbers, see FBI, Domestic Terrorism in the United States, 1997, at http://www.fbi.gov/publish/terror/terr97.pdf.

[12]The Defense Against Weapons of Mass Destruction Act of 1996 (P.L. 104-201, also known as the Nunn-Lugar-Domenici legislation) provided a good synopsis of the threats facing the nation, particularly the potential for the proliferation of WMD (chemical, biological, radiological, and nuclear) technology and know-how to adversaries of the United States. The text of the Act's threat findings are included in Appendix D.

[13]In 1984, two members of the Rajneesh religious sect in Oregon produced and dispensed salmonella in restaurants to influence the outcome of a local election—715

Table 4.1

State Sponsors of Terrorism and WMD Programs

Country	State Sponsor	Not Cooperating	Chemical Program	Biological Program	Nuclear Program
Afghanistan		X			
Cuba	X	X			
Iran	X	X	X	X	X
Iraq	X	X	X	X	Limited
Libya	X	X	X	X	Limited
North Korea	X	X	X	X	Limited
Sudan	X	X			
Syria	X	X	X	X	

NOTE: State Sponsor = state sponsor of terrorism. Not Cooperating = "Not cooperating fully" with U.S. antiterrorism efforts pursuant to Section 40A of the Arms Export Control Act (P.L. 90-629), as added by the Antiterrorism and Effective Death Penalty Act of 1996 (P.L. 104-132) (22 U.S.C. 2771 et seq.) and Executive Order 11958, as amended.

SOURCES: U.S. State Department (1997, 1999); Department of Defense (1996).

Additionally, a small number of nonstate actors—we would include the Aum Shinrikyo and the Osama bin Laden organizations in this group—appear to have access to substantial resources that could be used to acquire WMD.[14]

Weapons. In spite of the potential future danger posed by WMD, the weapons of choice for terrorists remain firearms and high explosives.[15] A recent report by the GAO described the intelligence community's view of terrorists' preferred weapons as follows:

---

persons were affected. There were no fatalities. In April 1991, several members of a domestic extremist group called the Patriot's Council in Minnesota manufactured the biological agent ricin from castor beans and discussed using it against federal law enforcement officers. The group was arrested before executing an attack and convicted in 1995.

[14]Of course, Aum Shinrikyo was able to manufacture chemical and biological WMD, although it was manifestly incapable of successfully employing them. According to a statement to the Commission to Assess the Organization of the Federal Government to Combat the Proliferation of Weapons of Mass Destruction by the Central Intelligence Agency's senior nonproliferation official, at least a dozen terrorist groups have expressed an interest in or have actively sought NBC weapons capabilities (Commission, 1999, p. 1).

[15]For example, both of the terrorist incidents in the United States in 1997 involved conventional weapons.

The U.S. intelligence community continuously assesses both the foreign-origin and the domestic terrorist threat to the United States and notes that conventional explosives and firearms continue to be the weapons of choice for terrorists. Terrorists are less likely to use chemical and biological weapons than conventional explosives, although the possibility that they may use chemical and biological materials may increase over the next decade, according to intelligence agencies. (GAO, 1999a, pp. 1–2.)

According to intelligence agencies, conventional explosives and firearms continue to be the weapons of choice for terrorists. Terrorists are less likely to use chemical and biological weapons at least partly because they are more difficult to weaponize and the results are unpredictable. However, some groups and individuals of concern are showing interest in chemical and biological weapons. Chemical and biological agents are still less likely to be used than conventional explosives. (GAO, 1999a, p. 3.)

Other recent analyses have concluded that terrorist groups are generally uninterested in biological agents, although that may be changing.[16]

The potential for mass casualties in WMD incidents is staggering, if the results historically have fallen short of the perpetrators' hopes. For example, the perpetrators of the World Trade Center attack hoped to topple one of the towers into the other, ultimately killing 250,000 people. Instead, six people died and more than 1,000 required medical treatment. Similarly, Aum Shinrikyo hoped to kill thousands with their sarin attack but instead killed 12 while injuring over 5,000.

One reason for these failures to date is that the barriers to manufacturing, weaponizing, and employing WMD weapons appear to be rather higher than is often understood or acknowledged. Consider the case of biological weapons, as viewed by the GAO:

---

[16]Seth Carus (1997), for example, concluded that: "A review of past incidents suggests limited interest on the part of terrorist groups in biological agents. While some have explored biological weapons as a potential terrorist tool, only a handful have attempted to acquire agents, and even fewer have attempted to use them. Yet, there is strong reason to worry that bioterrorism could become a much greater threat."

We are looking into the scientific and practical feasibility of a terrorist or terrorist group improvising a biological weapon or device
outside a state-run laboratory and program, successfully and effectively disseminating biological agents, and causing mass casualties.
Much of the information we have obtained is sensitive, classified,
and in the early stages of evaluation. Overall, our work to date suggests that, for the most part, there are serious challenges at various
stages of the process for a terrorist group or individual to successfully cause mass casualties with an improvised biological or chemical weapon or device.

More specifically, our preliminary observations are that: a terrorist
group or individual generally would need a relatively high degree of
sophistication to successfully and effectively process, improvise a
device or weapon, and disseminate biological agents to cause mass
casualties; a weapon could be made with less sophistication, but it
would not likely cause mass casualties; some biological agents are
very difficult to obtain and others are difficult to produce; and effective dissemination of biological agents can be disrupted by environmental (e.g., pollution) and meteorological (e.g., sun, rain, mist,
and wind) conditions. (GAO, 1999b, pp. 2–3.)

Finally, it is important to note that efforts to prevent or disrupt terrorist action frequently are successful, and these activities have
reduced the number of terrorist incidents that would have occurred
in the absence of these activities:

- Disruption of terrorist events by working with foreign intelligence and law enforcement services has proved profitable: U.S.
  intelligence agencies prevented Osama bin Laden's organization
  from carrying out at least seven vehicle bomb attacks on U.S.
  facilities since August 1998 (Kelly, 1999, p. 1A), and U.S. intelligence had conducted successful disruption operations in as
  many as 10 countries in the six months up to March 1999
  (Associated Press, 1999).

- The State Department offers rewards up to $7 million for infor-
  mation preventing acts of international terrorism. Since the ini-
  tiation of the program in 1984, rewards totaling millions of
  dollars have been paid in dozens of cases.

- Nevertheless, while military action against terrorists may reduce
  their capabilities, it also may backfire by resulting in greater

efforts to target Americans, as was seen in Muammar Qaddafi's call for attacks on Americans after the 1986 U.S. bombing of Tripoli, and in Osama bin Laden's recent death threats against Americans.

The conclusion we draw from this anecdotal, empirical, and analytic evidence is that:

- high-consequence incidents of terrorism are fundamentally low-frequency/low-probability phenomena;

- there are indications, largely on the basis of terrorists' increasing use of high explosive bombs, that the lethality of terrorism *may* be increasing;[17]

- while the barriers remain fairly high, there is evidence of growing interest in acquiring WMD;

- even under modest (i.e., optimistic) assumptions about the ability of U.S. adversaries to acquire WMD, over an extended span of time the issue appears to be one of "not if, but when." (See the sidebar)

- given the growing possibility of surprise—i.e, that a group of terrorists overcomes the barriers to using WMD and actually successfully employs it in a mass casualty terrorist incident—the probability could be even higher.

In short, WMD terrorism deserves policy attention and resources. Nevertheless, it is not at all clear either what the optimal level of resources might be or what the optimal mix of program options should be. These issues will be discussed later in this chapter.

Risk Assessment

We now provide our observations on risk assessment, focusing on targets whose selection could result in catastrophic losses.

---

[17]The noisiness of the data makes it difficult to speak of trends in this regard. Based on available data, it seems more accurate to us to say that the variance is increasing than that the average lethality is increasing. For another view, see U.S. State Department (1999) and the work of RAND colleague Bruce Hoffman.

"Not If But When"

Although the probability of successfully acquiring or manufacturing, weaponizing, and employing WMD is presently low, the probability of an attack increases over a longer time span.

An illustration:

- Assume that 25 terrorist groups are seeking to acquire and employ WMD.

- Assume furthermore that each group has an independent probability of .01 annual chance of acquiring and successfully employing WMD.

- The probability of a successful attack in the next year is $(1 - (1 - 0.01)^{25}) = 0.222$, or a little over one in five.

- The probability of a successful attack in the next 10 years is $(1 - (1 - 0.01)^{25 \cdot 10}) = 0.918$, or about nine in 10.

- If one assumes that the probability of success is increasing each year (e.g., through a learning curve phenomenon or through diffusion of learning among WMD-intent groups), the probability is even higher.

By the very nature of the choice of weapon, it seems likely that terrorists who seek to use WMD will target either population centers, facilities with high numbers of potential victims, or, in the case of biological weapons, targets more likely to foster epidemics or pandemics through transmission from victim to victim:

- A nuclear incident or large radiological incident near a population center, if it were on the order of Chernobyl, could result in large numbers of victims, at the very least in terms of the numbers who need to be relocated.[18]

- High explosives, chemical weapons, biological weapons incapable of transmission from victim to victim, and smaller radiological weapons, all would be most useful against facilities containing high numbers of potential victims. Such targets include

---

[18]Even in cases where the actual threat is less grave, such as the Three Mile Island incident, the possibility of panic and large-scale evacuations may be encountered.

auditoriums, theaters, sports arenas, and stadiums, and such other large-capacity structures as skyscrapers, as well as crowded streets and sidewalks in urban centers during rush hour.

- Biological weapons capable of transmission from victim to victim (e.g., smallpox) also would be quite suitable against high-density targets and also against such transportation hubs as airports and subway stations, where victims can efficiently expose others as well.

Planning Magnitudes

To develop and assess options for addressing various threats, policymakers need to have in mind numbers that specify the scale or magnitude of the events for which response capabilities will be sized.

Planning magnitudes appropriate for sizing national prevention and response capabilities should meet a number of criteria. First, they should be large enough to include historically observed experience, as well as providing some additional hedging against the possibility of larger attacks.

Second, planning magnitudes should be low enough to challenge existing or planned capabilities without creating an unreachable goal for them. This will facilitate planning as well as the development of doctrine, organization, training programs, and equipment that can later be expanded, should the need arise, with high confidence that the capabilities being developed will be adequate to the tasks they will face.

Finally, as described in Chapter Three, the planning magnitudes initially selected constitute only "marks on the wall" that may subsequently be revised up or down on the basis of threat and risk assessments or on the basis of affordability. In a sense, initial planning magnitudes are not unlike an initial seed number in simulation modeling that is close to the central tendency of a distribution but is only one number used in a larger parametric or sensitivity analysis.

While the actual number ultimately chosen for a planning magnitude could, in practice, well turn out to be lower or higher, we now suggest notional planning magnitudes that can be used as initial "seeds" and subsequently adjusted up or down, depending on threat and risk assessments or cost-effectiveness or budget criteria. Although they are offered as "marks on the wall," these magnitudes appear consistent with available open-source data on past experience and the current threat and generally are consistent with the sorts of numbers that we believe are being discussed in the Army, DoD, and in the broader federal setting:

- For attacks with chemical weapons, an illustrative planning magnitude might be to prepare for incidents in which 5,000 people are exposed, with 2,500 receiving a dose that requires treatment to prevent their deaths.[19]

- For biological attacks, an illustrative planning magnitude might be to prepare for incidents in which 5,000 people could die from exposure if left untreated.[20]

- For radiological incidents, a capability to evacuate up to 25,000 people from the areas adjacent to the incident might be a reasonable illustrative planning magnitude.[21]

- For nuclear incidents involving an improvised nuclear device, an illustrative planning magnitude with as many as 100,000 who might be killed might be a reasonable illustrative planning magnitude.[22]

---

[19]In terms of possible deaths, this planning magnitude is more than 200 times larger than the 12 people who died in the March 20, 1994, Aum Shinrikyo sarin attack on the Tokyo subway, and is equal to the number 5,000 who sustained injuries in the attack. According to data from the Monterey Institute for International Studies, it also is 2,500 times larger than the largest number of deaths (one) sustained in the most deadly chemical attack in the United States from the 1960s to the present.

[20]This is far more deadly than the largest biological attack in the United States, which occurred as a result of the Rajneeshee sect dispensing salmonella in a salad bar in Oregon in September 1984, and in which 751 people were made ill (none died).

[21]This would appear to be well within the range of historical experience. In the September 1999 nuclear accident in Japan, for example, local residents simply were told to stay indoors and the only evacuees were employees at the nuclear plant. In the Three Mile Island incident, on the other hand, although only children and pregnant women were ordered to be evacuated, this order prompted an exodus of 140,000 from the immediate area. See PBS, "Meltdown at Three Mile Island."

[22]We assumed a 15-kiloton weapon. Smaller weapons of one kiloton to 10 kilotons also are possible, but these would be more sophisticated and probably would not be improvised nuclear devices. For example, according to PBS's "Frontline" series, a Russian-style suitcase nuclear bomb would have a yield of perhaps one kiloton. We infer from recent intelligence community statements regarding the community's abil-

To emphasize, the aim in each case is to provide an illustrative example of a planning magnitude that is high, yet generally comports with experience and intelligence or technology forecasts.[23]

In practice, and as described in Chapter Three, we would hope that more reliable planning magnitudes would be established by intelligence and law enforcement personnel, in conjunction with planners and policymakers, and that these magnitudes would be increased when the threat is deemed to have increased or in light of changes in cost-effectiveness or available budgets. Put another way, the numbers proposed above appear to be in the right neighborhood, but serious analytic and policy effort should be put into their refinement.

MEASURES OF PERFORMANCE

The GPRA of 1993 aims to improve effectiveness by setting program goals, and measuring performance against those goals.[24]

The measures of performance that should be considered for the domestic preparedness task area break out into three classes: those

---

ity to monitor compliance with the Comprehensive Test Ban Treaty (CTBT) that a one-kiloton bomb might be developed without the U.S. intelligence community's becoming aware of its testing, at least through seismic instruments. U.S. construction practices also would reduce the scale of the firestorms that resulted from the atomic bombings of Japan. In short, a planning magnitude of 100,000 casualties may well be toward the high end. Estimates of the total fatalities from the bombings of Hiroshima and Nagasaki vary widely. The Avalon Project at Yale Law School reports that the Manhattan Engineer District's best available figures were that 66,000 were killed in Hiroshima, and 39,000 killed in Nagasaki, for a total of 105,000 deaths. The Australian Uranium Information Centre Ltd. reports comparable numbers: 45,000 killed on the first day at Hiroshima, with another 19,000 dying in the next four months, and 22,000 dying on the first day at Nagasaki, with another 17,000 dying in the next four months. Nevertheless, according to John Dower, deaths are now estimated by the Japanese government to have been between 300,000 and 350,000, presumably including radiation-related deaths in the years following. See PBS, "Russian Roulette," and the Avalon Project website, Uranium Information Centre Ltd., (1999), and Dower (1995).

[23]U.S. construction practices would be expected to lead to greater mitigation than the modest protection offered by Japanese buildings at the end of World War II.

[24]In the area of domestic preparedness, performance measures can be derived in part from the 1997 Counterproliferation Program Review Committee report, which provides potential measures for proliferation prevention; strategic and tactical intelligence; battlefield surveillance; NBC/M counterforce; active defense; passive defense; and countering paramilitary, covert delivery, and terrorist NBC threats. See Counterproliferation Program Review Committee, 1997, Table 1.1, reproduced as Table K.4.

associated with prevention activities, with preparedness, and with response.[25] Each is discussed separately.

Prevention Activities. Performance in terrorism and WMD prevention activities could be quantified by such measures as:

- terrorist incidents prevented;
- ratio of known preventions to known incidents;
- deaths possibly prevented;
- amount of damage possibly prevented;
- arrests/extraditions of terrorists; and
- proliferation incidents prevented.

These measures would have to be considered in the context of the base rate of terrorist and WMD-related activity:

- terrorist plans detected;
- domestic terrorist incidents;
- suspected incidents;
- deaths due to domestic terrorism; and
- damage sustained in domestic terrorism.

They also would have to be considered in the context of hoaxes, idle threats, and other "noise."

Preparedness Activities. Preparedness and response activities could be assessed by any number of measures.[26] To illustrate, consider the following:

---

[25]The Commission to Assess the Organization of the Federal Government to Combat the Proliferation of Weapons of Mass Destruction posited four national goals, for each of which required operational capabilities were identified. The national goals were: proliferation prevention/denial; WMD deterrence (short of military action); WMD military action (including active defenses and/or retaliation); and WMD consequence management. See Commission (1999), Appendix H, pp. 155–167.

[26]As a practical matter, many preparedness and response activities blend together— the preparedness training and equipping that occurs well in advance of an actual incident favorably affects performance when employed.

- estimated responsiveness, i.e., time until specific capabilities can be at the scene of an incident or increase in responsiveness since last employment or exercise;

- estimated capacity of specific response units or overall response system to mitigate consequences (e.g., deaths and injuries) or increase capacity;

- assessed overall performance of response capabilities in training and field exercises;

- number of hazardous materials (hazmat) (or other first responder teams) trained to a high level of capability for WMD;

- number of U.S. cities trained to a level that provides highly responsive and capable WMD actions; and

- percentage of U.S. population covered by highly responsive and capable WMD preparedness.

Response Activities. Response activities could be assessed by such measures as the following:

- percentage of mitigation attained, i.e., the number of deaths or injuries that otherwise would have occurred in an incident prevented as a result of response capabilities;

- responsiveness, i.e., time until specific capabilities can be at the scene of an incident or increase in responsiveness since the last exercise or employment; and

- actual capacity of specific response units or overall response system to mitigate consequences (e.g., deaths and injuries) or increase capacity since the last exercise or employment.

Redundancy for Robustness. Although we have no basis for establishing a priori what level of redundancy is desirable, policymakers should consider how much robustness is desired for the total national response capability—local, state, and federal—and what this means in terms of redundant capabilities. Without explicit consideration of this issue, policymakers face the risks and opportunity costs, whether they have underinvested in needed capabilities or have overinvested in capabilities already sufficiently robust.

NOTIONAL PERFORMANCE LEVELS

Like the planning magnitudes, specified performance levels should meet some basic criteria. For example, they should be ambitious enough to make a difference to the outcome (e.g., by reducing by a nontrivial fraction the number of injured or dead from an incident), without being so ambitious that they are impossible to achieve or can only be achieved through unrealistically high funding levels.

In the same spirit that we offered "marks on the wall" in the earlier discussion of planning magnitudes, we now discuss some notional performance levels that might be used as initial "seeds" for policy deliberations. In practice, the performance levels chosen through policy deliberations could be lower or higher. In the Domestic Preparedness arena, notional performance levels for immediate planning purposes might resemble the following:

- *For chemical WMD attacks*, a national response capability (including local, state, federal, and military contributions) to prevent a high percentage (e.g., 95-plus percent) of attacks, while providing a combined capacity to address up to three separate attacks on cities with 5,000 victims in each city. The response should be sufficient to place all necessary capabilities, including responders, equipment, transportation and medevac, vaccines, and other elements, at the scene of each incident in time to reduce by 50 percent the mortality rate—from 2,500 to 1,250— the number of victims who actually die from lethal doses.

- *For biological WMD attacks*, a national response capability to prevent a high percentage (e.g., 95-plus percent) of attacks, while providing a combined capacity to address three separate attacks with 10,000 victims in each city and reduce by 90 percent the number of deaths that would otherwise occur.

- *For radiological and nuclear attacks*, a national response capability to address one or more separate attacks each of which involves the evacuation, housing, feeding, clothing, and medical treatment of up to 250,000 victims.

While they do not provide worst-case estimates, the performance levels described provide a planning basis certain to reveal shortfalls, while setting a reasonably high bar for each type of event, although not so high that it will be unachievable.

These performance levels should be increased if the threat increases but might have to be reduced if cost-effectiveness and budget analyses, described below, suggest that such objectives are unacceptably costly. In the event, we would expect that performance measures and desired performance levels would be established by planners and policymakers, in interaction with programmers, who can describe the realm of the possible, and cost analysts or budgeteers, who can illuminate the costs of various alternatives.

PROGRAM DESIGN ISSUES

As discussed in the introduction to this chapter, we conceive of domestic preparedness against WMD terrorism as local, state, and federal activities that aim to improve the ability of the nation as a whole to prevent, prepare for, or respond to such incidents. These three layers in turn consist of a much richer set of activities undertaken by federal, state, and local actors.

Prevention includes

- nonproliferation activities that can reduce the risks of WMD availability to terrorists or other U.S. adversaries;

- intelligence operations abroad, and domestic law enforcement intelligence operations, that can provide warning, enhancing the prospects for prevention or consequence mitigation;

- law enforcement, intelligence, and diplomatic cooperation abroad that can lead to the prevention by U.S. friends and allies of terrorist acts against U.S. targets;

- various military capabilities, including direct action by special operations forces and strikes, that may be employed in counterterrorism actions abroad to disrupt and prevent terrorist operations; and

- law enforcement assets, including special operations capabilities residing in the U.S. law enforcement community, that can be employed domestically in the same role.

Preparedness activities consist of preincident activities that can improve crisis and consequence management in terrorist events, including hardening potential targets at home and abroad, training and equipping of first (and other) responders, exercises, and stockpiling. Response activities consist of the employment of robust local, state, and federal capabilities for response and recovery that can mitigate the consequences of an act of WMD terrorism.

Although states and localities have primary responsibility for managing incidents, the federal responders have two critical roles to play. The first is that, in catastrophic incidents, local and state capacity may be exceeded and a federal response may be necessary. The second is that individual states and localities generally face a low probability of being the victim of a WMD attack, while the federal government's national security responsibilities give it a more diversified portfolio of potential risks (see the sidebar). As a result, the federal government is the natural source for funding.

This range of activities suggests that the federal role in domestic preparedness is complex, not least because it requires balancing issues of national security against issues of federalism. As one FEMA official put it:

> From its earliest beginnings, the United States has operated on two fundamental principles. The first is that State and local governments have the primary responsibility for disaster assistance. The second is that the Federal Government is responsible for the collective defense or national security of the respective states. (Goss, 1997.)

The Army has a role to play in many of the layers of the layered defense described above—in prevention, preparedness, and response—but these roles need to be considered in the context of the broader federal enterprise that supports state and local responders.

The Federal Setting

Table 4.2 presents data from the Office of Management and Budget (OMB) on the proposed Fiscal Year 2000 U.S. government budget for combating weapons of mass destruction, broken out by function and department or agency.

"Why a Federal Role?"[27]

The first reason is that this is a national security issue.

The second reason is that cities and localities face smaller incentives to prepare than the federal government does:

- Assume 120 cities, each with a .01 chance (independent probabilities) of being the target of a WMD attack in the next 10 years with at least d level of damage

- From the cities' perspective, there is slight risk:

    —.01 probability of attack, so expected damage is (.01•d)

    —Assuming dollar-for-dollar cost-effectiveness in mitigation, incentive is to invest up to .01•value of d to mitigate consequences

- From the federal perspective, there is a broader portfolio of risk:

    —With 120 cities there is a $(1 - (1 - 0.01)^{120}) = 0.70$ chance of at least one city being attacked, assuming independence

    —Assuming dollar-for-dollar mitigation, incentive is to invest 0.70•value of d to mitigate consequences.

A third reason is that the federal government provides a coordination element that enables local and state governments to pool resources during emergencies.

Bottom line—The U.S. government will be a (or the) principal source of resources for domestic preparedness.

The question is how to optimally allocate these resources.

The table breaks federal spending into five broad functions and by subfunction within each functional area. The five broad functions are as follows:

- Law enforcement and investigative activities: activities to reduce the ability of groups or individuals to commit terrorist acts and investigation and prosecution of terrorist acts when they occur.

---

[27]The reader also should note that other investments based on risk-pooling, e.g., compacts between collections of states, also make a great deal of sense.

(Includes intelligence collection activities and programs to detect and prevent the introduction into the United States of WMD.)

- Preparing for and responding to terrorist acts: planning, training, equipment, and personnel directed at incident response.

- Physical security of government facilities and employees: activities to protect federally owned, leased, or occupied facilities and federal employees, including high-ranking officials, from terrorist acts. Includes protection for foreign embassies, dignitaries, and others as authorized by federal law or executive order.

- Physical protection of the national populace and national infrastructure: activities related to physical protection of the national infrastructure, including air traffic, railroad, highway, maritime, and electronic distribution systems; physical protection of energy production, distribution, and storage (electrical, natural gas, petroleum); physical protection of vital services, including banking and finance, water, and emergency services; and protection of telecommunications systems.

- Research and development (R&D): R&D activities to develop technologies to deter, prevent, or mitigate terrorist acts.

Only the first function—law enforcement and investigative activities—is predominantly offensive, counterterror, or preventive in nature, while the others are defensive, antiterrorism programs that fall into the category of preparedness or response programs.

Prevention Programs

Prevention activities constitute the first layer of the layered defense described earlier and reduce the *probability* of terrorist incidents.

These include antiterrorism activities aimed at preventing terrorist acts, as well as counterterrorism and counterproliferation activities.[28] These prevention programs, including law enforcement and

---

[28]The Senate version of the National Defense Authorization Act authorizes $740 million for DoD and DOE nonproliferation activities for the former Soviet Union alone (U.S. Senate, 1999, p. 7).

Table 4.2

Proposed Fiscal Year 2000 Spending on Combating WMD

	DOC	NSC	DOE	HHS	DOJ	DOT	TREAS
Combating WMD (total)	4	196	538	230	284	2	95
WMD figure for law enforcement and investigative activities		20	3		44		19
WMD figure for preparing for and responding to terrorist acts		115	109	158	195	2	55
Public health infrastructure/ surveillance				65			
Stockpile vaccines, antidotes, antibiotics				53			
Planning/exercises		1	13	4	1		
Training of first responders		31	2		39	2	
Protective equipment for first responders			5	2	82		
WMD detection equipment			31	35	51		46
Medical responder training			1				
State and local planning and assistance		70	2		6		4
Other		12	55		17		5
WMD figure for physical security of government facilities/employees	4		188				12
WMD figure for physical protection of national population and infrastructure					26		
WMD figure for research and development		62	238	73	18		9
Pathogen genome sequencing		4	10	14	3		
Vaccines/therapeutics							
Vaccines				43			
Therapeutics				7			
Detection/diagnostics		34	13	8			
Personal and environmental decontamination		12	3				
Modeling, simulation, systems analyses			7	1			
Other		12	205		15		9

Table 4.2—continued

	VA	EPA	FEMA	NRC	USG FY 00	USG FY 99	99–00 Change
Combating WMD (total)	[1]	2	31	3	1,385	1,227	158
WMD figure for law enforcement and investigative activities				1	87	87	0
WMD figure for preparing for and responding to terrorist acts	[1]	2	29		664	629	35
Public health infrastructure/ surveillance					65	44	21
Stockpile vaccines, antidotes, antibiotics	[1]				53	51	2
Planning/exercises			4		22	24	–2
Training of first responders			12		87	90	–3
Protective equipment for first responders			7		95	101	–6
WMD detection equipment					128	105	23
Medical responder training							
State and local planning and assistance			7		123	113	10
Other		2			91	101	–10
WMD figure for physical security of government facilities/employees			2		206	223	–17
WMD figure for physical protection of national population and infrastructure				2	28	30	–2
WMD figure for research and development					400	258	142
Pathogen genome sequencing					28	16	12
Vaccines/therapeutics					50	9	41
Vaccines							
Therapeutics							
Detection/diagnostics					58	23	35
Personal and environmental decontamination					15	2	13
Modeling, simulation, systems analyses					8	4	4
Other					241	204	37

NOTE: NSC = National Security Community (i.e., primarily DoD and the intelligence community).

SOURCE: Office of Management and Budget (1999a, 1999b).

investigative activities to combat terrorism and WMD, are performed by the national security community (predominantly DoD, the services, and the Intelligence Community) and a number of other departments and agencies (see Table 4.3).

DOJ's efforts are directed at the investigation of extraterritorial acts of terrorism against U.S. persons and property overseas and all domestic acts of terrorism. The FBI has lead responsibility for investigating and preventing violent acts by terrorists and their organizations operating in this country. Activities include apprehending and prosecuting those responsible for terrorist acts.

According to OMB, these activities in DoD include military police, Defense Protective Service, and special military forces as well as defense criminal investigations, vulnerability assessments, terrorism investigations, antiterrorism training, surveillance and counter-surveillance teams, protective service details, and route surveys. Also included in this category are the significant resources the Intelligence Community devotes overseas and at home to identify terrorist capabilities.

Anecdotal and empirical evidence suggests that federal prevention programs are reasonably effective. For example, the GAO has recently noted that federal agencies have successfully participated in many counterterrorist activities:

> In actual operations and special events, agencies generally coordinated their activities. For example, we examined several overseas counterterrorist operations and found that agencies generally followed the draft interagency International Guidelines. DoD, the FBI, and the Central Intelligence Agency (CIA) performed their respective roles in military planning, law enforcement, and intelligence gathering under the oversight of the State Department (e.g., the ambassador). Minor interagency tensions or conflicts during these operations were resolved and did not appear to have posed risk to the missions.[29]

---

[29]Among the operations GAO examined were the arrests of Ayyad Namin (July 1995), Wahli Khan (December 1995), Tsutomo Shirasaki (September 1996), Matwan Al-Safadi (November 1996), Mir Aimal Kansi (June 1997), and Mohamed Said Rasheed (June 1998). Other operations that were not examined by GAO but were also successful

Table 4.3

Key Federal Departments and Agencies Involved in Counterterrorism

International Counterterrorism	Domestic Counterterrorism
Department of State (lead)	Federal Bureau of Investigation (lead)
Department of Justice	Department of the Treasury
Federal Bureau of Investigation	U.S. Secret Service
Department of Defense	Bureau of Alcohol, Tobacco, and Firearms
Central Intelligence Agency	U.S. Customs Service
Others	Internal Revenue Service (IRS)
	Federal Emergency Management Agency
	Department of Defense
	Department of State
	Bureau of Diplomatic Security
	Department of Energy (DOE)
	Nuclear Regulatory Commission (NRC)
	Department of Health and Human Services
	Department of Transportation
	Federal Aviation Administration (FAA)
	U.S. Coast Guard
	Department of Veterans Affairs
	Department of Agriculture
	Department of Interior
	Environmental Protection Agency (EPA)
	General Services Administration

NOTE: Criteria used were receipt of funding for law enforcement and investigative activities function of combating terrorism or participation in counterterrorist exercises, as described in GAO, 1999c, pp. 1–8, 11.

In a similar vein, FBI data on terrorism in the United States suggest a reasonably high degree of success in terrorism prevention activities at home—only a small annual number of actual terrorist incidents occurred in recent years,[30] and more preventions of terrorist incidents than actual incidents.[31]

---

arrests included Ramzi Yousef (February 1995) and Mohamed Sadeck Odeh and Mohamed Rasheed Daoud Al Awhali (August 1998).

[30]According to the FBI, five or fewer incidents occurred in each of the years 1994–1998.

[31]According to the FBI, the ratio of terrorism preventions to actual known incidents was 2.00 in 1995, 1.67 in 1996, 10.5 in 1997, and 2.4 in 1998.

GAO has noted that the DoD-sponsored program for international counterterrorism exercises appears to be more effective in integrating key players than the domestic exercise program:

> International counterterrorism exercises, sponsored for many years by [DoD], are relatively comprehensive in that they include many federal agencies and test tactical units along with State Department's leadership role and DoD's command and control. In contrast, domestic exercises sponsored by the FBI and the Federal Emergency Management Agency (FEMA)—the lead federal agencies for domestic operations—are not as comprehensive. (GAO, 1999c, p. 2.)

Nevertheless, GAO also has noted some problems within DoD's command and control, already under review:

> DoD needs to clarify its internal command and control structure for domestic operations. Although not a lead federal agency, DoD could have a major supporting role in any federal response to terrorist incidents in the United States, particularly those involving WMD. In reviewing DoD's participation in domestic support operations, special events, and exercises, we found several command and control issues where guidance was either confusing or conflicting. To resolve these issues, DoD is undertaking a high-level review of its support to civilian authorities, generally under the rubric of "homeland security." (GAO, 1999c, p. 9.)

Nor have the Domestic Guidelines of the FBI and the International Guidelines of the State Department been coordinated with all federal players. Put another way, although prevention programs appear to be reasonably effective both at home and abroad, their cost-effectiveness is not known, and there are opportunities to improve coordination.[32]

The Army Role in Prevention Activities Abroad. Civilian antiterrorism capabilities that operate abroad, including intelligence, law en-

---

[32]In addition to real-world experience, federal agencies participate in counterterrorism exercises, which also would be expected to improve coordination and overall performance. For example, 201 counterterrorism exercises took place in the three years following PDD 39, more than two-thirds of which had WMD scenarios; half of these used scenarios involving chemical agents (GAO, 1999g, p. 2).

forcement, and diplomatic assets, are extensively—and successfully—used in terrorism prevention activities.[33] These include sharing
intelligence and cooperating with allies and friends in law enforcement and diplomatic efforts to reduce the threat of terrorism.[34]

The U.S. Army and other services have a number of capabilities that
may be employed in activities to deter, prevent, respond to, or otherwise combat WMD terrorism. Perhaps the most obvious are the
special operations capabilities available from force providers in the
CONUS, and from the combatant commanders in chief[35] that can be
used in counterterrorism and counterproliferation missions and for
direct action against terrorist and WMD facilities.

Although Army counterterrorism and counterproliferation capabilities can make important contributions in this layer of the layered
defense, as a practical matter they tend to be used only *in extremis*
and, therefore, somewhat sparingly.[36]

The Army Role in Prevention Activities at Home. The Army has even
more limited opportunities to play a direct role in law enforcement
and intelligence activities at home. In part, this is because at the fed-

---

[33]Antiterrorism is defined by the *Joint Doctrine Encyclopedia* (Joint Chiefs of Staff,
1997b) as "Defensive measures used to reduce the vulnerability of individuals and
property to terrorist acts, to include limited response and containment by local military forces." These include training and defensive measures that strike a balance
among the protection desired, mission, infrastructure, and available manpower and
resources. Counterterrorism is "offensive measures taken to prevent, deter, and
respond to terrorism" and provides response measures that include preemptive, retal-
iatory, and rescue operations.

[34]Nonproliferation activities abroad also include many of these same actors, as well as
participation from the U.S. armed forces. Although we note that the Army participates
in inspection, intelligence collection, and other activities related to the nonproliferation mission, assessing the Army role in nonproliferation was well beyond the
scope of our study. For readers interested in nonproliferation capabilities, see the
report of the Commission to Assess the Organization of the Federal Government to
Combat the Proliferation of Weapons of Mass Destruction (1999).

[35]The U.S. Army Special Operations Command (USASOC) defines counterterrorism as
"offensive measures taken to prevent, deter, and respond to terrorism" (Joint Chiefs of
Staff, 1997b). Direct action is "either overt or covert action against an enemy force.
Seize, damage, or destroy a target; capture or recover personnel or material in support
of strategic/operational objectives or conventional forces." (USASOC, 1999.)

[36]In part, this is because covert actions require a presidential finding and prior
reporting to Congress. It also is because objectives sometimes can be accomplished
through other means, e.g., cruise missile strikes.

eral level primary responsibility rests with the FBI and other domestic law enforcement organizations.[37] It also is because important legal restrictions on the use of the military in domestic law enforcement activities exist, although it is often ignored that governors can use National Guard units in such a role, and the federal restrictions often are misunderstood or overstated.[38] Nevertheless, the Army can provide important support to civilian law enforcement organizations, including intelligence, surveillance and reconnaissance, transportation, and logistics support under many circumstances.[39]

Preparedness Programs

Preparedness activities can be undertaken in advance of an actual incident, but these activities seek to reduce the *consequences* of an incident by reducing risks to high-value targets, for example, and equipping, training, and exercising effective response capabilities. These programs tend to focus on the later, defensive, layers of the layered defense described earlier.

As seen in Table 4.1, federal activities include a broad range of functions and performers, including (federal performers are in parentheses) public health infrastructure and surveillance (HHS); stockpile of vaccines, antidotes, and antibiotics (HHS, VA); planning and exercises (national security community, DOE, HHS, DOJ, FEMA); training of first and medical responders (DOJ, DoD, FEMA, DOE, DOT); providing protective equipment for first responders (DOJ, FEMA, DOE,

---

[37]For example, among the federal agencies sending teams to the Atlanta Olympic Games were the Treasury Department's U.S. Secret Service, FBI, FEMA, DoD, DOE, HHS, EPA, CIA, the State Department's Bureau of Diplomatic Security, the ATF, the U.S. Customs Service, the Internal Revenue Service, and the NRC. Such agencies as the U.S. Secret Service and the ATF also play key roles in certain circumstances. Federal agencies conducted eight exercises specific to the games (GAO, 1999c, p. 7).

[38]A number of authors recently have argued that it is common to overstate the importance of the Posse Comitatus Act (18 U.S.C. Section 1385 et seq.), given that important exceptions are granted by the Constitution and by congressional action. Among these are Lujan (1997), Byrne (1999), and Iklé (1999, especially pp. 16–18). See Appendix D for an overview of the Posse Comitatus Act restrictions.

[39]Nevertheless, the federal investigation into military support to the FBI and ATF operation against the Branch Davidian compound outside of Waco, Texas, could result in the imposition of further clarification or additional restrictions on the military role in support of law enforcement.

HHS); acquiring WMD detection equipment (DOJ, Treasury, HHS, DOE); state and local planning and assistance (national security community, FEMA, DOJ, Treasury, DOE); and other, unspecified activities (DOE, DOJ, national security community, Treasury, EPA).

DoD activities include planning and exercises, training of first responders, state and local planning and assistance, and such other activities as chemical/biological agent detection, individual and collective protection, decontamination, vaccines and antidotes, and providing storage for disaster supplies.[40] Next described is the Army's critical role in domestic preparedness training.[41]

The Army Role in Domestic Preparedness Training. Two types of domestic preparedness training are of interest. First, is the training of military forces for civil support activities. Second, is the suite of training programs for first responders.

Joint Forces Command is now responsible for providing military support to civilian authorities in all circumstances and will be in charge of the U.S. military response rather than simply serving as a force provider. To accomplish this mission, JFC recently created a Joint Task Force for Civil Support headed by a Brigadier General to train and equip that force and to provide the command and control of all federal uniformed military forces that respond.[42]

Another of the primary Army roles in these activities is the training of first responders.[43] Through the Nunn-Lugar-Domenici legislation,[44]

---

[40]Through interagency agreement, the Army Corps of Engineers also provides storage space for the Disaster Response Support Facilities for the Mobile Emergency Response Support (MERS) detachments.

[41]Because RDT&E for all DoD chemical and biological defense programs (except those in DARPA) has been consolidated into six defensewide program element (PE) funding lines and procurement funds also have been consolidated, the issue of WMD-related Army R&D will not be discussed further.

[42]Admiral Harold W. Gehman, Jr., Commander, U.S. Joint Forces Command (USJFC), quoted in Peterson, 2000, p. 9.

[43]The DoD's Domestic Preparedness Program received $36 million in FY 1997, $43 million in FY 1998, and $50 million in FY 1999, with the FY 2000 budget request set at $31 million.

[44]FY 1997 Defense Authorization Bill, Public Law 104-201, September 23, 1996, commonly called the Defense Against Weapons of Mass Destruction Act of 1996, or the Nunn-Lugar-Domenici legislation.

DoD was given the responsibility to train state and local first responders in the largest U.S. cities and cities identified by the FBI as being at particularly high risk for incidents of WMD terrorism. The Anti-Terrorism and Effective Death Penalty Act required the Department of Justice to work with the 120 largest metropolitan areas, with a focus on preincident training, prevention, and awareness (Goss, 1997).

At present, the Department of Justice (DOJ), Department of Defense (DoD), Federal Emergency Management Agency (FEMA), Department of Energy (DOE), and Department of Transportation (DOT) are all involved in training local responders. However, DoD responsibility for training first responders will move, in FY 2001, to DOJ's expanded train-and-equip program, managed by the National Domestic Preparedness Office (NDPO).[45]

In the meantime, the Army's role in WMD training programs derives from the Secretary of the Army's role as Executive Agent for the Secretary of Defense on Domestic Preparedness. The executive agency is exercised through the Director of Military Support (as Action Agent for the Secretary of the Army), who has responsibility for overseeing DoD's domestic preparedness training responsibilities.[46]

Of the DoD-sponsored WMD training courses, all but six are sponsored by Army organizations, and one of these is sponsored by the National Guard Bureau, which includes Army National Guard capabilities.[47]

The Army's Soldier Biological Chemical Command (SBCCOM) is providing, under Nunn-Lugar-Domenici, the lion's share of DoD's domestic preparedness training to first responders.[48] Of the 120

---

[45]The proposed Fiscal Year 2000 budget for training first responders includes $39 million for DOJ, $31 million for DoD, $12 million for FEMA, and $2 million each for DOE and DOT. DOE is slated to receive another $1 million for training medical responders. OMB (1999a, 1999b).

[46]Funding for first responder training by DoD was $50 million in FY 1999 and is expected to be $31 million in FY 2000. State and local planning assistance, however, is expected to grow over the same period, from $49 million to $70 million.

[47]See Table H.1 in Appendix H.

[48]SBCCOM is "the lead DoD agency charged with enhancing existing metropolitan response capabilities to include nuclear, chemical, and biological incidents. Six sepa-

cities where the Army Domestic Preparedness Team was scheduled to provide training,[49] nearly half of the cities (58) have already received their training.[50] As the program is completed, the principal source of first responder training is expected to shift further to DOJ.[51]

Other Army Preparedness Activities. Nunn-Lugar-Domenici also authorized funds for DoD to assist with four other elements of domestic preparedness. First, DoD was to assist the Secretary of Health and Human Services in establishing Metropolitan Medical Strike Teams (MMST) to help improve local jurisdictions' medical response capabilities for a WMD incident.[52] Second, DoD was to set up a telephonic link to provide data and expert advice for the use of state and local officials responding to emergencies involving WMD. In response, DoD established a hot line for reporting incidents and requesting technical assistance through the existing National Response Center for hazardous materials spills, and a help line was established through which SBCCOM experts can provide information and advice. Third, DoD was to create a chemical/biological rapid response team (C/B-RRT), a unit based on the deployable chemical biological response teams of the Army Technical Escort Unit (TEU).

The Secretary of the Army also is Executive Agent, and the Director of Military Support (DOMS) his action agent, for Consequence Management Program Integration, i.e., the integration of the Guard into consequence management activities. The flagship of this effort is the WMD Civil Support Team (formerly Rapid Assessment and Initial Detection—RAID), described in more detail below. DOMS also is Action Agent for the Secretary of the Army, who is Executive Agent

---

rate training courses have been developed to accomplish this task: Awareness, Operations, Technician-Hazmat, Technician-Emergency Medical Service, Hospital Provider, and Incident Command." SBCCOM, "Domestic Preparedness Fact Sheet."

[49]See Table H.2 in Appendix H.

[50]See Table H.3 in Appendix H.

[51]DOJ funding for training of first responders is expected to grow from $29 million in FY 1999 to $39 million in FY 2000, while training provided by the national security community is expected to fall over the same period from $50 million to $31 million.

[52]There are an estimated 27 MMSTs at present, although the Public Health Service plans to establish MMSTs in all 120 program cities. Each MMST is required to have sufficient pharmaceutical stocks to initially treat at least 1,000 casualties. See GAO, 1998d, p. 6.

for support to Special Events such as the 1996 Olympics and the NATO fiftieth anniversary, where terrorism and WMD-related capabilities may be predeployed as a deterrent and hedge against terrorism incidents (DOMS, undated).

Observations. The Domestic Preparedness training program's train-the-trainer approach is, generally speaking, a highly cost-effective means of delivering training,[53] and cities that have received training under the Domestic Preparedness Program have a greater awareness of how to respond to a potential chemical or biological terrorist incident (GAO, 1998d, p. 4).

However, the parallel training programs by other departments and agencies and the focus on cities rather than on states' existing emergency and training structures may have, according to the GAO, resulted in a less cost-effective program than otherwise might have been the case (GAO, 1998d, pp. 2, 8–17). Although about half of the 120 cities already have been trained, the Army should assess whether the benefits of a shift to a focus on Standard Metropolitan Statistical Areas (SMSAs), counties, response regions, mutual aid arrangements, or other collectivities—namely, greater population coverage and better integration—are sufficient to justify advocating such a shift in focus.[54] If not, it still might be desirable for the Army—or DOJ, because it will be taking over the training program in FY 2001—to advocate that the city-based train-the-trainer program provide a core capability for training responders in surrounding jurisdictions, thereby ensuring that all partners in local response communities get trained.

The effectiveness of the current domestic preparedness training program is exceedingly difficult to measure at the federal level because, according to DOMS, the results of the tabletop and field exercises are retained by the city and are not released to SBCCOM. At the very

---

[53]In train-the-trainer programs, the only cost incurred by the sponsoring organization is the cost of training the initial cadre of trainers. This cadre subsequently trains others at little or no cost to the initial sponsoring organization.

[54]GAO estimates that the current program of 120 cities covers 22.0 percent of the country, while a focus on SMSAs would cover 64.1 percent. No estimates of cost were given for the SMSA-based program, which would presumably need to train more trainers and provide more equipment sets. GAO reports that DoD already has rejected such a change.

least, further action should be taken to facilitate the compilation of these data to provide at least aggregated measures of progress resulting from the training and equipment loan program.[55]

Response Programs

Response programs also mitigate the consequences of incidents, although these programs do this through the application of local, state, and federal (including military) capabilities that may vary in terms of their responsiveness and capacity.

Tables 4.4 and 4.5 summarize key federal "operational" and "reachback" capabilities that can be employed in WMD attacks using HE, chemical, biological, radiological, and nuclear weapons.

Table 4.4

Operational Capabilities for Domestic Preparedness

	Type of Event					
	HE	CHEM	BIO	RAD	NUC	CYBER
Department of Defense						
Joint						
JTF–Civil Support	X	X	X	X	X	
JTF–Computer Network Defense[a]						X
U.S. Army						
Response Task Force–East	X	X	X	X	X	
Response Task Force–West	X	X	X	X	X	
USAR Regional Support Commands (10)	X	X	X	X	X	
Army SOF capabilities	X	X	X	X	X	
52d Ordnance Group						
Special Improved Explosive Device (SIED) companies (4)	X	X	X	X	X	

---

[55]An Advanced Technology Integration Demonstration (ATID) program also is being conducted by the Consequence Management Program Integration Office (COMPIO) in DOMS. See DoD Tiger Team, 1998.

Table 4.4—continued

	HE	CHEM	BIO	RAD	NUC	CYBER
		Type of Event				
NBC companies and platoons (270), including:		X	X	X	X	
11th Chemical Company (AC)[b]		X				
310th Chemical Company (AC)[b]		X				
416th Chemical Detachment (Recon), 81st RSG (USAR)		X	X	X	X	
704th Chemical Company (Recon) (USAR)		X	X	X	X	
806th Chemical Detachment (NBCC) (USAR)		X	X	X	X	
Biological Integrated Detection System (BIDS) Teams (35)[c]		(X)	X			
Technical Escort Unit Chemical-Biological Response Team (4)[d]	X	X	X			
WMD CSTs (10+)		X				
WMD CSTs (Light) (44)		X				
Edgewood Research, Development, and Engineering Center Mobile Analytical Response System		X	X			
Soldier Biological Chemical Command (SBCCOM) U.S. Army SBCCOM 24-hour hot line		X	X			
Army Materiel Command Chemical Treaty Laboratory[d]		X				
Edgewood Research Development, and Engineering Center Real-Time Analytical Platform (RTAP) (5)		X				
Mobile Environmental Analytical Platform (MEAP) (1)		X				
Madigan Army Medical Center	X	X	X	X	X	
Disaster Assistance Response Team (DART)		X	X	X	X	
Guard/Reserve WMD Patient Decontamination Teams		X	X	X	X	
U.S. Army Medical Research Institute for Infectious Diseases (USAMRIID)			X			

Table 4.4—continued

	HE	CHEM	BIO	RAD	NUC	CYBER
			Type of Event			
Aeromedical Isolation Team			X			
Army Regional Medical Centers		X?	X	X?	X?	
Specialty Response Teams		X?	X	X?	X?	
U.S. Air Force						
Air Force Radiation Assessment Team				X	X	
Air National Guard Prime BEEF civil engineering units (89)		X	X?			
Air National Guard Prime BEEF fire-fighting units (78)		X	X?			
Air National Guard Explosive Ordnance Disposal units (10)[c]	X					
U.S. Navy						
Naval Medical Research Institute Bio-Defense Research Program (BDRP) bio field laboratory		X	X			
Naval Research Laboratory		X	X			
U.S. Marine Corps						
USMC Chemical/Biological Incident Response Force (1)		X	X			
Civilian						
Defense Coordinating Officials	X	X	X	X	X	
Federal Coordinating Centers (with Veterans Affairs) (72)			X			
Department of Energy						
Nuclear Emergency Search Team				X	X	
Department of the Treasury						
Bureau of Alcohol, Tobacco, and Firearms (ATF)	X					
U.S. Secret Service	X	X	X?	X	X	
U.S. Customs Service	X	X	X?	X	X	
Department of Transportation						
U.S. Coast Guard						
Marine Safety Officers (44)		X	X	X	X?	
U.S. Coast Guard National Strike Force Teams (3)		X	X	X	X?	
Federal Aviation Administration (FAA)	X	X	X	X	X?	
Federal Emergency Management Agency						
Federal Coordinating Officials	X	X	X	X	X	

Table 4.4—continued

	Type of Event					
	HE	CHEM	BIO	RAD	NUC	CYBER
Urban Search and Rescue Task Forces (27)	X	X?	X?	X?	X?	
Department of Health and Human Services						
National Medical Response Team		X	X	X		
Chemical-Biological Rapid Deployment Team		X	X			
PHS-1 Disaster Medical Assistance Team (DMAT)	X?	X?	X?	X?	X?	
Department of Justice						
FBI Command Post (or Joint Operations Center, JOC)	X	X	X	X	X	
FBI Hazardous Materials Response Unit (HMRU)	X	X	X	X		
FBI Evidence Response Teams	X	X	X	X		
FBI Critical Incident Response Group	X	X	X	X		
Hostage Rescue Team (HRT)	X	X	X	X		
Crisis Management Unit (CMU)	X	X	X	X		
Crisis Negotiations Unit (CNU)	X	X	X	X		
Aviation and Special Operations Unit (ASOU)	X	X	X	X		
Domestic Emergency Support Team (DEST) (under FBI OSC)	X	X	X	X	X	
Intelligence Collection and Analysis cell	X	X	X	X		
10-man FBI Field Office hazmat teams (15)		X	X			
4-man FBI Field Office hazmat teams (41)		X	X			
Environmental Protection Agency						
EPA On-Scene Coordinators (270)	X	X	X	X	X	
Environmental Response Teams (2)	X	X	X	X	X	
Superfund Technical Assessment and Response Teams (10)		X?				
EPA Research Laboratory mobile units (5)		X	X			
Radiological response capabilities				X	X	

Table 4.4—continued

	Type of Event					
	HE	CHEM	BIO	RAD	NUC	CYBER
Regional, State, and Local						
Regional poison control centers		X	X			
Regional public health laboratories		X	X			
State departments of emergency services	X	X	X	X	X	
State departments of public health		X	X			
State/local hazardous materials units (hazmat) (600)[f]		X	X			
Metropolitan Medical Strike Teams (10/25+)[g]		X	X	X	X	
Disaster Medical Assistance Teams (60)[h]	X?	X?	X?	X?	X?	
Community Emergency Response Team (CERT)[h]	X?	X?	X?	X?	X?	

[a]Includes service contributions, e.g., Army A/CERT and LIWA teams.
[b]Tapped for domestic preparedness missions by DOMS.
[c]Basic mission in support of warfighting; capabilities severely degraded in urban environment.
[d]Comprises DoD Chemical/Biological Rapid Response Team (C/B-RRT).
[e]NBC-capable.
[f]120 receiving training through the federal domestic preparedness program.
[g]One established (D.C.); 10 standing up; 25-plus planned.
[h]Trained for natural disasters.

The capabilities described in the table vary in their responsiveness and capacity in responding to WMD events. Variations in responsiveness result from differences in the readiness and location of operational units (whether military or civilian) at the time of the incident and as a result of the readiness, location, speed, and capacity of the mobility assets needed to transport these assets to the scene of the incident. Variations in capacity result from differences in the sizes of units that can be deployed, their basic capabilities and equipment sets, and their actual level of training and operational experience.

Although the FBI is federal lead agency for domestic crisis management, and FEMA is federal lead agency for domestic consequence management,[56] the table suggests that the Army can provide a wide range of reachback and operational capabilities that can be employed in incidents of WMD terrorism as well.

Among these are Army capabilities that can support FBI-led domestic crisis management activities and those that support FEMA-led consequence management activities, including support to technical operations in a terrorism incident, and the Reserve Component WMD Civil Support Teams (formerly RAID). Next discussed is support to crisis management and consequence management.

Table 4.5

Reachback Capabilities for Domestic Preparedness

	Type of Event					
	HE	CHEM	BIO	RAD	NUC	CYBER
Department of Defense						
U.S. Army						
Soldier Biological Chemical Command (SBCCOM)		X	X	X	X	
Army Research Laboratory		X				
U.S. Army Medical Research Institute for Infectious Diseases (USAMRIID)			X			
U.S. Army Medical Research Institute of Chemical Defense (USAMRICD)		X	X			
Deployable Chemical- Biological Advisory Team		X	X			
U.S. Army Radiological Advisory Medical Team				X	X	
U.S. Army Radiological Control Team				X	X	
Chemical Stockpile Emergency Preparedness Program (CSEPP)		X				
Army Chemical School		X				
CWC Treaty Lab		X				

---

[56]For a review of FBI capabilities in this arena, see Freeh, undated. The respective roles of the various federal agencies for WMD events are described in FEMA, 1999b and 1998c.

Table 4.5—continued

	Type of Event					
	HE	CHEM	BIO	RAD	NUC	CYBER
Edgewood R&D Engineering Center	X	X	X			
Land Information Warfare Agency						X
Army Computer Emergency Response Team (A/CERT)						X
Army Computer Science School						X
U.S. Air Force						
Air Force Technical Applications Center				X	X	
Air Force Information Warfare Center						X
U.S. Navy						
Naval Medical Research Institute		X	X			
U.S. Navy Environmental and Preventive Medicine Unit		X	X			
Other DoD						
Armed Forces Radiobiology Research Center				X	X	
Defense Information Security Agency						X
Department of Justice						
Federal Bureau of Investigation	X	X	X	X	X	X
FBI Strategic Information Operations Center (SIOC)	X	X	X	X	X	X
National Domestic Preparedness Office (NDPO)		X	X			
National Infrastructure Protection Center (NIPC)						X
Federal Emergency Management Agency		X	X	X	X	
Department of Health and Human Services						
Centers for Disease Control and Prevention			X			
Agency for Toxic Substance and Disease Registry		X	X			
Food and Drug Administration			X			
Substance Abuse and Mental Health Services Administration		X?	X?			
Environmental Protection Agency						

Table 4.5—continued

	HE	CHEM	BIO	RAD	NUC	CYBER
			Type of Event			
Radiological Environmental Laboratories				X	X	
EPA Research Laboratories (12)		X	X			
National Enforcement Investigations Center		X	X			
Department of Commerce						
Critical Infrastructures Assurance Office (CIAO)						X
Department of Energy						
Chemical Stockpile Emergency Preparedness Program (CSEPP)		X				
Federal Radiological Monitoring and Assessment Center				X	X	
Atmospheric Release Advisory Capability				X	X	

Support to Crisis Management. In the context of the Terrorism Incident Annex (see Appendix G), "crisis management" is defined by the FBI as "measures to identify, acquire, and plan the use of resources needed to anticipate, prevent, and/or resolve a threat or act of terrorism." The FBI is the lead federal agency for all federal crisis management activities.

The specific DoD and Army roles in domestic crisis management activities are likely to be conditioned by the FBI on-scene coordinator's (OSC) assessments of which capabilities are needed and the desirability of the military providing those capabilities. The OSC's judgments regarding which supporting military (including Army) capabilities are desirable are in turn influenced by other considerations, including the availability of comparable civilian capabilities, the legal constraints associated with the specific presidential authorities that apply,[57] and the OSC's judgments about

---

[57]For example, while the Posse Comitatus Act of 1878 imposes restrictions on the use of the Army for civil law enforcement activities in peacetime, the act does not apply when an emergency arising from a civil disturbance is declared by the President. Many DoD lawyers believe that the constraints imposed by Posse Comitatus in WMD incidents are illusory and that Presidents have wide latitude in the use of the Army

public sensitivities to employment of the military in various supporting roles.[58]

As in the discussion of preventive antiterrorism activities at home, there appears to be only a modest and fundamentally supporting role for the Army in domestic crisis management activities, such as intelligence, surveillance and reconnaissance, transportation, and logistics support, unless a President declares a state of emergency or imposes martial law in a particular locale.

Support to Consequence Management. DoD defines WMD Consequence Management as "emergency assistance to protect public health and safety, restore essential government services, and provide emergency relief to those affected by the consequences of an incident involving WMD agents, whether they are released deliberately, naturally, or accidentally" (Berkowsky and Cragin, 2000).

In the context of the Terrorism Incident Annex, "consequence management" activities are defined by FEMA as "measures to protect public health and safety, restore essential government services, and provide emergency relief to governments, businesses, and individuals affected by the consequences of terrorism."

Support to Technical Operations. According to the Terrorism Incident Annex of the Federal Response Plan (FRP), the Department of Defense role in terrorist incidents is predominantly one of providing support to technical operations:

> As directed in PDD-39, the Department of Defense (DoD) will activate technical operations capabilities to support the Federal Response to threats or acts of WMD terrorism. DoD will coordinate military operations within the United States with appropriate civilian lead agency(ies) for technical operations. (FEMA, 1999c.)

The principal mechanism for providing DoD support to technical operations for chem-bio incidents is the C/B-RRT. The principal

---

after declaring an emergency or imposing martial law. The authors are grateful to one of this report's reviewers, Rick Brennan, for clarifying this point.

[58]A good recent example of this is the congressional and media concern about reports that the Army played an Army advisory role in the Waco incident in 1993, and if so, whether this role was consistent with federal law.

building-block of the C/B-RRT is the Chemical Biological Response Team, the deployable element of the Army's TEU. Other Army capabilities also appear capable of providing support to technical operations, however. These include the Army's 52d Ordnance Group (EOD), which has four Special Improvised Explosive Device (SIED) companies, and Army Chemical Companies that have been trained and equipped for reconnaissance or decontamination in support of the WMD mission.

Emergency Support Functions (ESFs). Shifting from the Terrorism Incident Annex to the larger FRP, the Army can expect to provide support to many of the ESFs. Perhaps foremost among these are Public Works and Engineering (ESF #3) and Energy (ESF #12, under DOE), where the Army Corps of Engineers has the DoD lead,[59] and Information and Planning (ESF #5) and Urban Search and Rescue (ESF #9), where the DOMS plays this role, under FEMA's lead.[60]

The Reserve Component Employment Study 2005 notes that eight ARNG divisions are available for employment in warfighting and other missions and suggests that some of them might be missioned to homeland security. The study suggests that in some cases, substituting reserve component for active-duty forces would be a cost-effective solution, although it is not at all clear in which other cases this also might be true. However, as detailed in this report, assignment of missions and allocation of additional forces to homeland security should be based on threat and risk assessments that provide a justification for a given level of effort and on cost-effectiveness analyses that establish that the forces being assigned to the mission are the most cost-effective solution to the problem.

WMD Civil Support Teams. Another deployable Army asset is the WMD CSTs, formerly known as RAID Teams.[61] These 22-member Guard teams—10 currently standing up with another 44 possible—

---

[59]DoD is the lead agency for ESF #3, Public Works and Engineering, so the importance of the Army Corps of Engineers is assumed to be higher.

[60]See Appendix G, Table G.1. We believe that the DoD previously was the responsible agency for Urban Search and Rescue.

[61]The recent study of reserve component employment also promotes the use of RAID-like teams in the Air National Guard. See Department of Defense, 1999b, p. 4. RAIDs also may be created within the Air National Guard. See U.S. Senate, 1999, p. 298.

will be available for employment either at the state level (as the result of an order by a state governor or adjutant general) or federal level (as a result of their employment through the federal chain of command for responses to WMD terrorism incidents).[62]

While the details regarding the effectiveness of the WMD CSTs are limited to their postulated ability to be at the scene of an incident within four hours, some data are available on their notional costs that suggest that the costs for 54 WMD CSTs over 10 years could amount to more than $1.5 billion.[63] A recent study suggests that remissioning reserve component units for WMD consequence management could be cost-effective (DoD, 1999b, pp. 3–4), as could converting Air National Guard Bare-Base Air Wings to teams resembling WMD CSTs (DoD, 1999b, pp. 4–5), and increasing reserve component participation in a Joint Task Force (JTF) Headquarters for homeland security (DoD, 1999b, pp. 6–7),[64] although more-detailed analyses are required. For example, the estimated cost of retraining and equipping 76 company-sized Army organizations (with 131 soldiers per company) for homeland security-related chemical specialist tasks recently was estimated to be $200 million (10-year costs are not available). Although the sustainment costs for 76 companies might be more costly than the WMD CSTs, including their sustainment and mobility costs, they would have more substantial decontamination capabilities that would be useful in an actual incident (DoD, 1999b, Appendix C, p. 3).

Further, unlike the Army capabilities for support to technical operations described above—which are codified in the Terrorism Incident

---

[62]The numbers continue to change, but 10 RAID teams were being created in FY 1999, with another 44 less-capable RAIDs (Lights) also being created. The President's FY 2000 budget request asks for five more RAIDs, but the Senate Armed Services Committee is pressing for the establishment of an additional 17 teams in FY 2000. In any case, the potential total of 54 RAIDs is based on the assumption of one RAID element for each state and territory or possession. As stated in the Senate Armed Services Committee report on the defense authorization bill: "It is the intent of the committee to ultimately provide for the establishment of 54 RAID teams—one for each state and U.S. territory" (U.S. Senate, 1999, p. 288).

[63]The 10-year total costs of a RAID team are estimated in Appendix C, in the context of a notional tradeoff analysis.

[64]A JTF headquarters using 100 percent active-duty personnel was estimated to cost $18 million, while the two options that relied more heavily on reserve component manning were in the $13.3 million to $13.5 million range.

Annex and widely regarded as constituting an important part of DoD's contribution to the federal response to a WMD terrorism incident—the role of the WMD Civil Support Team in the larger federal response remains unclear.[65] Congressional concerns have arisen about the lack of established procedures by which states can employ WMD CSTs based in other states and the readiness of active-duty and reserve component units and particularly decontamination units (U.S. Senate, 1999, p. 358).

Observations. Both generalized and specialized units play important roles, with the specialized units delivering unique or highly specialized capabilities (e.g., medical care, NBC identification and decontamination, EOD). The more general-purpose units contribute "deep pockets" and personnel to provide such services as emergency first aid, food, shelter, clothing, and security. As the Army responds to the mandates of Nunn-Lugar-Domenici and other directions, both its general and specialized units are undergoing additional training to assist in domestic preparedness. For many of the specialized units, this has been a welcome development, because it has meant more opportunities to train in their main competencies. For example, medical units benefit from treating patients whether the victims are combatants or not. For the general-purpose units, the additional training requirements not only provide the necessary skills but also represent another demand on their training time. The competition for training time for both domestic preparedness training and the units' other missions will require careful management of mission-essential task lists.

At the policy level, Congress appears to be increasingly focused on a perceived lack of coordination in the overall federal program and increasingly concerned that the overall program may be less effective and efficient than is desirable. Consider the following congressional language:

> In light of the continuing potential for terrorist use of weapons of mass destruction against the United States and the need to develop a more fully coordinated response to that threat on the part of Federal, State, and local agencies, the President shall act to increase the

---

[65]We will return to this issue later in this chapter.

effectiveness at the Federal, State, and local level of the domestic emergency preparedness program for response to terrorist incidents involving weapons of mass destruction by utilizing the President's existing authorities to develop an integrated program that builds upon the program established under the Defense Against Weapons of Mass Destruction Act of 1996. (Public Law 105-261, 1998, Section 1402.)

The report of the House Armed Services Committee for the National Defense Authorization Act for Fiscal Year 2000 contains even stronger language:

Unfortunately, despite the federal government's attempts to consolidate and better coordinate counterterrorism efforts among the various federal, state, and local agencies involved in this mission, substantial confusion remains over the appropriate agency roles. As a November 1998 report by the General Accounting Office (GAO) concluded, the individual efforts among federal agencies to coordinate an effective approach to consequence management "are not guided by an overarching strategy." The result has been an apparent piecemeal, uncoordinated approach to this issue.

. . . Although the committee has encouraged the Department of Defense to accelerate its efforts to build a comprehensive and coordinated plan for integrating its program into the overall federal counterterrorism effort, progress has been slow. . . . The committee believes that the Department should continue to play a critical support role in the overall counterterrorism effort, but remains troubled by the difficulties in coordination and implementation as noted above. The committee encourages the Secretary of Defense to make greater efforts to ensure that the Department's support to this effort is thoroughly coordinated and effective. (U.S. House of Representatives, 1998b, pp. 390–391.)

The Senate's Committee on Armed Services likewise has complained about the transparency of DoD programs to combat terrorism and the inability to assess the cost-effectiveness of these programs:

[DoD] has numerous programs to combat terrorism divided among scores of offices, agencies and services, the funding for which is buried in the overall budget submission. The committee has tried unsuccessfully for months to gather accurate and complete information on the specific budget and programs that comprise the Department's efforts to combat terrorism. The committee believes that the Department's efforts in this critical area should be more visible, and organized in a coordinated and coherent fashion. With current budget submissions, it is difficult for the committee to determine the scale of the Department's effort to combat terrorism, the effectiveness of the effort, how well the Department's efforts respond to the threat, and how the DoD programs fulfill the overall government policy and strategy in this area. (U.S. Senate, 1999, p. 353.)

This suggests to us that transparency, coordination, integration, effectiveness, and efficiency increasingly will become the criteria by which DoD and Army programs to combat terrorism and WMD will be judged and that efforts are needed to relate programs and budgets to effectiveness measures.[66]

These integration issues are arising in programs in which the Army has a compelling interest. For example, although the DoD has disputed the reasoning behind the finding, concern is apparently increasing about whether the WMD CST elements fit into the larger local, state, and federal response.[67] GAO reported local and state concerns regarding the WMD CSTs as follows:

State and local officials and some national firefighter organizations also raised concerns about the growing number of federal response elements being formed, including the new initiative to train and equip National Guard units for WMD response role. These officials did not believe specialized National Guard units would be of use because they could not be on site in the initial hours of an incident and numerous other military and federal agency support units can already provide assistance to local authorities as requested. These units include the Army's Technical Escort Unit, the Marine Corps' Chemical Biological Incident Response Force, and the [Public Health Service's] National Medical Response Teams. State and local officials were more supportive of the traditional National Guard role in providing requested disaster support through the state governor. (GAO, 1998d, p. 21.)

---

[66]The Act calls on DoD, beginning in FY 2001, to "set forth separately all funds for combating terrorism within its overall budget request to Congress."

[67]See GAO, 1998d, p. 21; 1999c; and 1999e.

Differing views also exist at the state level. Officials in states without a RAID team do not see how the teams can benefit their states' response capabilities because of the time it takes the RAID teams to respond. (GAO, 1998d, p. 21; and 1999e, p. 2.)

GAO further reported that neither the FBI, the lead federal agency for domestic crisis management, nor FEMA, the lead federal agency for consequence management, could see a role for the WMD CSTs.

Officials with the two agencies responsible for management of the federal response to terrorist incidents—the Federal Bureau of Investigation and the Federal Emergency Management Agency—do not see a role for the RAID teams in the federal response. Instead, they see the National Guard, whether in state or federal status, providing its traditional assistance in emergencies. (GAO, 1998d, p. 21; and 1999e, p. 2.)[68]

The solution to this, i.e., to avoid disputes with the FBI and FEMA about the role of the WMD CST in federal responses, was to make it a state-level asset:

The WMD Civil Support Teams are unique because of the federal-state relationship. They are federally resourced, federally trained, and federally evaluated, and they operate under federal doctrine. But they will perform their mission primarily under the command and control of the governors of the states in which they are located. They will be, first and foremost, state assets. Operationally, they fall under the command and control of the adjutant generals of those states. As a result, they will be available to respond to an incident as part of a state response, well before federal response assets would be called upon to provide assistance. (Berkowsky and Cragin, 2000).

Another opportunity for improving the WMD CST's utility is to integrate it into state-level responses to all hazards, both WMD and hazmat:

[O]ne state official does see the RAID team bringing some expertise that could be useful. Officials in Pennsylvania, a state with a RAID

---

[68]This appears to be an instance of a broader debate over the roles and missions of DoD in consequence management. See Windrem (1999).

team, plan not only to fully integrate its team into the state's weapons of mass destruction response plan, but also use it to respond to more common hazardous materials emergencies.[69]

Thus, while the cost-effectiveness of the WMD CST team concept in the larger context of the local, state, and federal response architecture is not yet proved, the Army has some opportunities to influence its future direction in ways that could satisfactorily resolve these questions.

Domestic Preparedness-Related R&D

Most of the homeland security–related R&D activities in the federal government seem to be related to chemical and biological defense, although there is a small amount of modeling and simulation, particularly in the DOE and in the area of modeling weapons effects.

Four federal programs currently fund R&D of nonmedical chemical-biological defense technologies. They are the Department of Defense's Chemical and Biological Defense Program;[70] DARPA's Biological Warfare Defense Program; DOE's Chemical and Biological Nonproliferation Program; and the Counterterror Technical Support Program conducted by the Technical Support Working Group.

The GAO has criticized these programs for a lack of coordination, although they noted that efforts to improve coordination already were under way.[71] GAO also singled out the U.S. Army's SBCCOM for

---

[69]The official is from Pennsylvania, whose program therefore provides a good model (GAO, 1998d, p. 21; and 1999e, p. 2).

[70]The National Defense Authorization Act for Fiscal Year 1994, Public Law No. 103-160, Section 1703 (50 USC 1522), mandated the coordination and integration of all DoD chemical and biological (CB) defense programs.

[71]GAO stated:

> The current formal and informal program coordination mechanisms may not ensure that potential overlaps, gaps, and opportunities for collaboration are addressed. Coordinating mechanisms lack information on prioritized user needs, validated [chemical-biological] defense equipment requirements, and how programs relate R&D projects to these needs. . . . Agency officials are aware of the deficiencies in the existing coordination mechanisms and some have initiated additional informal contacts in response. (GAO, 1999j, pp. 2–3.)

being the only RDT&E organization to apply the GPRA principles to its efforts in RDT&E for biological and chemical defense (GAO, 1999j, p. 9). Put another way, Army homeland security–related R&D efforts are being undertaken in the context of a federal framework, and using a methodology for evaluating RDT&E performance, that should enhance the prospects for cost-effective outcomes.[72]

BUDGETING AND RESOURCING ISSUES

The critical issues in budgeting and resourcing issues is making tradeoffs across desirable goals and objectives. The key tradeoff issues that arise in the area of domestic preparedness appear to be those associated with the budget shares that will be allocated to supporting homeland security activities and how these activities will be integrated into defense planning, programming, and budgeting. Each is discussed.

Budget Shares

A total of $10 billion will be spent on federal programs to combat terrorism in FY 2000—$11.4 billion if critical infrastructure protection also is included. Nevertheless, domestic preparedness activities comprise a very modest share of DoD and Army budget aggregates:

- Proposed FY 2000 funding for the national security community (including defense and intelligence activities) to combat terrorism is set at $5.052 billion, less than 2 percent of DoD budget aggregates, of which funding to combat WMD comprises $196 million, or less than 0.1 percent of DoD budget aggregates.

- As a share of budget aggregates, the Army's equities in homeland security appear to be quite a bit higher. According to the Army draft estimates of total obligational authority (TOA) by mission area for FY 2001 through FY 2005, support to homeland security will constitute approximately 6.4 percent of Army spending.

---

[72]For a review of RDT&E and procurement in the broader counterproliferation context, see the tables in Appendix C of CPRC (1997).

The overall program to combat terrorism and WMD appears to be reasonably well-balanced between offense and defense—both offensive (counterterrorism) and defensive (antiterrorism) activities are reasonably well-funded. The balance between current capability development and longer-range R&D also appears to be reasonably well-balanced—R&D activities will yield more effective and less costly capabilities that should be useful in both civilian and military spheres. Whether the balance between military and civilian spending—$1.385 billion for combating WMD terrorism by civilian agencies and less than $1 billion for military-related WMD spending—is correct is more difficult to judge because it could be argued that battlefield employment of WMD is more likely than employment at home. The Army should examine this issue more closely to assure itself that this investment mix is in balance.

Spending for key Army operational capabilities, such as WMD CSTs and the TEU, also appears to be growing.[73] For example, although the numbers are uncertain, additional WMD CSTs will be authorized for FY 2000,[74] Army chemical units continue to be trained for WMD incidents, and spending on the TEU has increased from $7.7 million in FY 1998 to $9.4 million in FY 1999.[75] As suggested elsewhere, however, the Army should closely examine whether WMD CSTs will be responsive and capable enough to provide the most useful and cost-effective capabilities for WMD incidents or whether further enhancement of the TEU or chemical units might make a greater difference in mitigating the consequences of these incidents.

As was argued earlier, the current threat of WMD appears to be low but possibly growing, and the risk of surprise also may be growing. Nevertheless, a number of issues need to be addressed to improve

---

[73]Unfortunately, the Army budget does not provide very much visibility into WMD-related programs. See Assistant Secretary of the Army for Financial Management and Comptroller (1999).

[74]The numbers vary depending on the source, but, according to the Army's Justification of Estimates for FY 2000, Army AGRs for the WMD program are due to increase from 223 in FY 1999 to 267 in FY 2000 and FY 2001, while the National Defense Authorization bills have included five new WMD CSTs, and some in Congress have been discussing even more WMD CSTs.

[75]The $7.7 million comprised $5.6 million in direct funds and $2.1 million in reimbursable funds, and the $9.4 million comprised $5.9 million in direct funds and $3.5 million in reimbursable funds.

the adequacy of resourcing. First, a failure to use threat and risk assessments or, when used, to use them consistently, has resulted in a failure to identify specific, analytically based planning magnitudes for the threats of concern. Second, overall performance levels have not been established for the total national response capability, consisting of local, state, and federal responders, including contributions by the services. Finally, to our knowledge, the federal program has not been assessed in terms of its cost-effectiveness, or whether the overall architecture of local, state, and federal capabilities is either the most effective capability possible for current funding levels or the least expensive set of capabilities for a desired level of effectiveness. Until these issues are better understood, it is impossible to answer the question, "how much is enough?"

Planning, Programming, and Budgeting

With its draft effort to understand TOA by mission area, the Army appears to be making great strides in establishing processes and data sources that will enable it to understand the Army activities that provide support to homeland security. The larger DoD and federal arenas are more problematic. Neither the current Defense Planning Guidance (DPG) nor the current planning, programming, and budgeting process adequately address homeland security needs.

Current defense planning appears to treat threats to the homeland as modestly complicating factors, rather than in terms of their potential to seriously disrupt mobilization and deployment activities.[76] In cases where combat, combat support, or combat service support capabilities have dual missions—i.e., identified both for warfighting abroad and for homeland security activities—attacks on the homeland during a deployment easily could lead to difficult decisions regarding which set of missions had precedence. Given the atten-

---

[76]Nor does Nunn-Lugar-Domenici (P.L. 104-201, 1996) resolve this issue. Section 1416, Military Assistance to Civilian Law Enforcement Officials in Emergency Situations Involving Biological or Chemical Weapons, amends Chapter 18 of title 10, U.S. Code, to allow for DoD to provide resources in the event of an emergency situation involving a biological or chemical WMD, but only if "the Secretary of Defense determines that the provision of such assistance will not adversely affect the military preparedness of the United States." In cases where attacks are made against mobilizing or deploying forces, military preparedness easily could be impaired.

dant constitutional and political issues, it is not at all clear that warfighting abroad would be given the highest priority.

Competition between warfighting and homeland security needs could be especially fierce among the key capabilities likely to have dual missions, e.g., chemical units and the TEU. Even in the case of capabilities earmarked for homeland security, such as the WMD CSTs, problems might arise. For example, it is not clear that the WMD CSTs have sufficient personnel for 24-hour-a-day, seven-day-a-week responses; that their personnel and the mobility assets needed to transport them are to be maintained at a sufficient state of readiness to have a substantial impact in WMD incidents; or that they would fare well in a competition for mobility assets during a simultaneous mobilization for warfighting. At the very least, it appears necessary to develop notional Time-Phased Force Deployment Lists (TPFDLs) that rationalize and deconflict homeland security assets and their associated mobility and other support assets.

DoD's budget process does not provide a reliable means for understanding which programs contribute directly or indirectly to homeland security activities. The Commission to Assess the Organization of the Federal Government to Combat the Proliferation of Weapons of Mass Destruction, for example, has advocated the creation of a budget subfunction to include most of the relevant areas of domestic preparedness (Commission, 1999, Appendix G, pp. 147–152). This cross-cutting budget function would include all federal defense threat reduction, nonproliferation, and counterproliferation activities and for WMD would include antiterrorism and counterterrorism, infrastructure protection, emergency response/management capabilities, domestic preparedness activities, export control efforts, and epidemiological activities (e.g., biosurveillance/early warning).

The Army should, of course, continue to refine its efforts to track funding for support of homeland security activities. It also should begin considering the benefits of promoting more systematic DoD-wide efforts to track these activities, possibly including the creation of such a budget subfunction and possible creation of a new Major Force Program (MFP) for homeland security activities that includes an appropriate taxonomy of supporting PEs.

CONCLUSIONS

This chapter has characterized the threats of WMD terrorism, delineated Army responsibilities in the larger federal response framework for the domestic preparedness task area, and evaluated key Army capabilities. Five principal conclusions derive from this analysis.

First, the threat of WMD terrorism, while currently relatively low, is probably growing, as is the risk of being surprised. Nevertheless, the Army should press forward with formal threat and risk assessments to prioritize threats and risks and remediation measures.

Second, the Army should press within DoD and the larger federal setting to establish measures of performance appropriate to the threat of WMD terrorism and to establish performance levels that will guide Army, DoD, and other federal planning to prevent or mitigate the consequences of such incidents.

Third, the Army should use tradeoff and cost-effectiveness analyses to guide its investment in additional capability and should press for such techniques to be used DoD-wide and in all federal departments. Decisions regarding investment in additional capacity for domestic preparedness should be based predominantly on the criteria of cost-effectiveness, and robustness.

Fourth, our analyses of federal operational and reachback capabilities and budget data suggest that the Army has a greater investment—and therefore greater equities—in the domestic preparedness task area than do the other services. The Army also has key executive agency responsibilities in this task area. Put another way, it is plausible that, although all service activities ultimately are in support of civilian authorities, the Army has the leading military role in domestic preparedness.

Nevertheless, our illustrative analysis of the WMD CSTs suggests that the Army's leading military role in domestic preparedness activities will rely to a great extent both on actual capacity to mitigate the consequences of WMD incidents and on the availability of air mobility assets from the active-duty, Guard, or Reserve Air Force. The Army should examine closely the WMD CST concept to ascertain whether its responsiveness and capacity meet the criteria of cost-effectiveness and robustness when compared with other options.

Fifth and finally, it is not at all clear that the larger local, state, and federal domestic preparedness program is either the most effective program mix for its $1.385 billion budget or the lowest-cost program for a fixed level of effectiveness. It is, furthermore, impossible to assess the level of redundancy that exists across the local, state, and federal programs or how much of this redundancy represents unnecessary duplication of effort. The Army should press to ensure that responsiveness, capacity, cost-effectiveness, and robustness are the guiding criteria for fielding domestic preparedness capabilities.

Chapter Five

ENSURING CONSTITUTIONAL AUTHORITY: CONTINUITY OF GOVERNMENT[1]

The continuity of government (COG) task area of homeland security includes providing for the continuity and restoration of all levels of government—federal, state, and local.[2] For a host of reasons the importance of COG is difficult to overstate:

- At the federal level, COG ensures the integrity of constitutional authority.

- At the state and local level, COG operations can facilitate the quick restoration of civilian authority and essential government functions and services.[3] This can greatly reassure citizens and can minimize the risks that military support to consequence management activities is misperceived as an imposition of mar-

---

[1]See Appendix A for a list of the Department of Defense Directives (DoDDs) relevant to continuity of government activities.

[2]See Federation of American Scientists, 1999a. Press interest in federal COG programs increased after the cold war. See Emerson (1989) and Gup (1991, 1992).

[3]Article IV, Section 4, of the Constitution seems to provide the constitutional authority for military activities in support of the state under conditions of domestic violence, terrorism, and the like:

> The United States shall guarantee to every State in this Union a Republican Form of Government, and shall protect each of them against Invasion; and on Application of the Legislature, or of the Executive (when the Legislature cannot be convened) against domestic Violence.

The authors are grateful to RAND colleague Michael Hynes for bringing this to our attention.

tial law.[4] It also can reduce the undesirable burdens that can be imposed on the military in attempting to carry out traditional civilian functions, ranging from law enforcement to garbage collection.

This chapter will argue that the concept of COG needs to be broadened in three important ways. First, where past COG planning has concentrated on actions that might mitigate the impact of a strategic nuclear missile strike aimed at decapitating federal civilian and military authority, we argue that other means of delivery and other WMD should be considered in planning. Second, we argue that Army and DoD COG operations also should address disruptions to state and local governments and should consider the range of actions that can facilitate restoration of civil authority in the wake of WMD attacks. Third, we argue that public and congressional sensitivities in this area need to be carefully considered in reviewing doctrine and standing public affairs guidance for Army activities in this area.

THREAT AND RISK ANALYSES

Threats and Weapons

The same threats described in Chapter Four probably apply in the COG task area: adversaries of the U.S. government, whether state, nonstate, or domestic actors. And the weapons they choose could range from small arms to WMD.[5]

Targets

The potential target set in COG activities are government facilities attacked by design or incidental casualties of a larger attack:

- At the federal level, these could range from national icons, such as the White House, Capitol building, Supreme Court, or Federal

---

[4]The reader is reminded of the criticism that resulted from the trial balloon of a potential "CINC Homeland Security," described in Chapter Two; such risks can easily be avoided by remaining attentive to these latent concerns.

[5]For example, in 1954, Puerto Rican nationalists attacked the floor of the U.S. House of Representatives with small arms.

Reserve Board, to headquarters of federal departments and agencies, to federal buildings nationwide.[6] Of these, some targets already are known to be of long-standing interest to domestic groups.[7]

Although the threats seem more remote, emergencies could disrupt COG at lower levels as well:

- Although such attacks seem less likely than attacks on federal facilities, at the state level, the governor's offices and mansion and capital buildings housing state legislatures and their offices, as well as buildings housing state-level departments and agencies, could be targets.

- Still less likely are attacks on government offices at the local level, although city government buildings in the larger U.S. cities probably face a somewhat higher risk than the facilities of smaller localities.

Nevertheless, in a WMD attack, federal, state, or local government facilities might be destroyed of disrupted.

Available documentation suggests that the justifications for federal COG activities may have been adapted to address the recent changes in the threat environment and have shifted from an earlier focus on COG in the context of a nuclear exchange to continuity in a more diverse threat environment:

> The changing threat environment of recent emergencies, including localized acts of nature, accidents, technological emergencies, and military or terrorist attack–related incidents, have shifted awareness to the need for COOP capabilities that enable agencies to continue their essential functions across a broad spectrum of emergencies. Also, the potential for terrorist use of weapons of mass destruction has emphasized the need to provide the President a capability [that] ensures continuity of essential government functions across the Federal Executive Branch. (FEMA, 1999d.)

---

[6]For example, the Murrah building primarily housed federal offices.

[7]For example, the ATF and the IRS are seen as threats to liberty by domestic militias and tax foes.

PERFORMANCE MEASURES AND NOTIONAL PERFORMANCE LEVELS

A recent FEMA circular suggests a number of relevant performance measures in its discussion of the objectives and planning considerations for COG activities. Stated objectives include the following:

- Ensuring the continuous performance of an agency's functions/operations during an emergency.

- Protecting essential facilities, equipment, records, and other assets.

- Reducing or mitigating disruptions to operations.

- Reducing loss of life, minimizing damage and losses.

- Achieving a timely and orderly recovery from an emergency and resumption of full service to customers.

And planning considerations suggest that a viable COG capability

- must be maintained at a high level of readiness;

- must be capable of implementation both with and without warning;

- must be operational no later than 12 hours after activation;

- must maintain sustained operations for up to 30 days; and,

- should take maximum advantage of existing agency field infrastructures.

Generally speaking, then, the key performance measures for COG are the degree to which the consequences of emergencies can be mitigated and the speed with which government functions and services can be restored. Our recommendation is that in cases where civil government and services have been disrupted, that planning should aim to reestablish a sort of nominal or basic level of civil authority within 12 hours, as suggested by FEMA.[8]

---

[8]As in the discussion of performance levels for domestic preparedness activities, policymakers might set lower or higher performance criteria.

PROGRAM DESIGN ISSUES

Federal COG

According to press reporting, for many years the federal government had a robust COG program aimed at ensuring the survivability of constitutional authority in the event of a decapitating strike in a general nuclear exchange.[9] Reporting now suggests that much, perhaps most, of this program has been discontinued.[10]

Federal COG activities generally fall into the broader category of federal emergency management, overall policy guidance for which is provided in Executive Orders and other presidential policy documents, as well as FEMA circulars.[11] As a matter of policy:[12]

> It is the policy of the United States to have in place a comprehensive and effective program to ensure continuity of essential Federal functions under all circumstances. As a baseline of preparedness for the full range of potential emergencies, all Federal agencies shall have in place a viable COOP capability which ensures the performance of their essential functions during any emergency or situation that may disrupt normal operations. (FEMA, 1999d.)

PDD 67 established FEMA as the Executive Agent for Executive Branch COG activities. Within FEMA, the Office of National Security Affairs is responsible for COG activities:

---

[9]Weiner (1994) reports that approximately $8 billion was spent on COG activities over the 11 years up to 1994. Weiner reported that: "The Doomsday Project, as it was known, sought to create an unbreakable chain of command for military and civilian leaders that would withstand a six-month nuclear war, which was regarded as a plausible length for a controlled conflict."

[10]For example, Mount Weather, widely reported to have been a relocation site for national leaders in the event of a nuclear site, is now "a hub of emergency response activity providing FEMA and other government agencies space for offices, training, conferencing, operations, and storage." See Weiner (1994) and FEMA, 2000a.

[11]For example, Executive Order 12656, "Assignment of Emergency Preparedness Responsibilities, November 18, 1988; PDD 67, "Ensuring Constitutional Government and Continuity of Government Operations," October 21, 1998; FEMA (1990); and FEMA (1999d). The following additional Executive Orders EOs (listed in the bibliography) also apply: 10222; 11179; 11795; 12127; 12148; 12241; 12472; and 12657.

[12]At the federal level, the terms "continuity of government" (COG) and "continuity of operations" (COOP) are used somewhat interchangeably.

The Office of National Security Affairs coordinates activities in support of FEMA's roles and responsibilities in terrorism preparedness, planning, exercises and response, particularly those involving coordination among multiple program offices within FEMA and with other departments and agencies. It is also responsible for activities related to planning with regards to Continuity of Government (COG), Continuity of Operations (COOP), and Critical Infrastructure Protection (CIP).[13]

The Federal Preparedness Circular on Federal Executive Branch Continuity of Operations describes the broad parameters of the federal COG program, which are applicable to all Executive Branch departments, agencies, and independent organizations. For example, FEMA identifies the following minimal elements of agency COG programs:[14]

- Plans and procedures.

- Identification of essential functions.

- Delegations of authority.

- Orders of succession.

- Alternative facilities.

- Interoperable communications.

- Vital records and databases.

- Tests, training and exercises (FEMA, 1999d).

Federal departments and agencies are responsible for making their own COG preparations, consistency with the broad guidelines established by FEMA and higher authority.[15]

COG planning generally envisions three distinct phases:

- Phase One: Activation and relocation (0–12 hours).

---

[13]FEMA website, at http://www.fema.gov/about/nsa1113.htm.

[14]We consider the continuity of higher headquarters operations in another section of this report.

[15]For example, the U.S. Agency for International Development's COG plan is described at http://www.info.usaid.gov/pubs/ads/100/106.htm.

- Phase Two: Alternative facility operations (12 hours–termination).

- Phase Three: Reconstitution (termination and return to normal operations) (FEMA, 1999d).

Using these three phases to frame the potential Army roles in COG activities, it can be seen that the Army role could range from such general activities as securing relocation sites and providing assistance in relocating government operations and personnel, to more specialized activities, such as providing continuous secure communication capabilities and provisioning alternative operation sites.

While it appears that the federal programs may have successfully adapted to the new threat environment, the Army should review these programs to ensure that they adequately address the relevant threat scenarios and to determine what, if any, modifications might still be warranted. The Army also should review its own participation in these programs to ensure that it contributes where it has the greatest comparative advantages.[16]

State and Local COG

Some states and cities appear to have plans for COG that would be exercised in an emergency or disaster, and federal training is available.[17] However, it is not at all clear the degree to which these state and local plans anticipate the possibility and nature of a military role in consequence management activities or the possibility that military forces temporarily might need to provide services normally provided by civilian authorities. As a result, three Army actions are suggested:

- First, the Army should establish that domestic preparedness planning assistance to states and localities also includes planning for the quick reestablishment of government authority at

---

[16]According to Weiner (1994), the Army had a substantial role in the earlier COG program.

[17]For example, the plan of the city of Yonkers, New York, is at http://www.ci. yonkers.ny.us/code/chptr8continuity.htm, and the city of Malibu, California's plan is at http://www.ci.malibu.ca.us/sems-04.htm. Florida's COG statute, Statute 22, is at http://www.leg.state.fl.us/citizen/documents/statutes/1995/CHAPTER_22.html.

the state and local level and the restoration of key government services, whenever this is necessary. It is not clear to us whether this is explicitly covered in existing domestic preparedness training programs.[18]

- Second, it may be desirable for the Army to develop procedures, protocols, and doctrine for expediting the reestablishment of civilian authority at the state or local level when this is necessary and for making this a high priority in consequence management and reconstitution.[19] As mentioned earlier, the sooner civilian authority is reestablished, the quicker that unfounded concerns about the military's role will be resolved.

- Finally, education modules for leadership education programs and standing public affairs guidance should be developed to prepare Army officers for the close congressional, press, and public scrutiny (and potential) criticism that could accompany Army COG activities.[20]

BUDGETING ISSUES

If the threat of terrorism is of sufficient gravity to justify $10 billion in federal spending (about $1.4 billion of which is related to WMD terrorism) then, a fortiori it should be sufficient to justify some level of effort to ensure COG in the face of a determined adversary's campaign of chemical, biological, radiological, or nuclear incidents directed against the nation's constitutional leadership or against state or local governments. The Army should press to ascertain—

---

[18]For example, FEMA's Emergency Management Institute (EMI) has a workshop called "Continuity of Operations (COOP): Workshop in Emergency Management."

[19]We note that in the wake of disasters, the U.S. Army Corps of Engineers often has been tasked to establish and manage public works and other, normally civilian, services and to manage the transition back to civilian provision of these services.

[20]To be clear, we believe that as a practical matter the possibility of "usurpation" of civilian authority by the military in homeland security operations is infinitesimal. And even in cases where the military is asked temporarily to provide what are normally civilian services and functions, we believe that most victims would be more inclined to express gratitude than concern about larger civil-military issues. Nevertheless, we believe that the Army would do well to take some modest actions to minimize the potential that statements or actions are misinterpreted or lead to unnecessary criticism or micromanagement of homeland security response activities.

through the framework described earlier—whether the current funding levels are appropriate, given the current and emerging threats and risks.

CONCLUSIONS

This chapter has described the COG mission area and suggested, in general terms, the wide range of roles that the Army might assume in supporting these operations. The principal conclusions that emerge from the analysis are as follows.

First, because of the tremendous changes in the threat environment over the last decade and because of the evident changes to federal COG activities, the Army should seek to reacquaint itself with the program as it currently stands and to ensure that the current program is responsive to the emerging threat environment. Of greatest importance may be the shift from the threat of attack by nuclear missiles to a broader range of WMD attacks using less exotic, and potentially less easily detected, delivery means.

Second, the Army should ensure that planning with local and state governments for emergency and disaster preparedness also includes COG issues and that Army doctrinal, procedural, and other guidance is available to help commanders facilitate the continuity or restoration of civilian authority at the local and state level, just as guidance is available at the federal level.

Finally, because of the scrutiny given military activities in the CONUS, the Army must remain equally mindful of the contributions it can make to ensuring the COG at the local and state as well as the federal level. It should review its doctrine and other preparations to ensure its capacity to assist in restoring civilian authority at the earliest possible opportunity when it has been disrupted.

Chapter Six

ENSURING MILITARY CAPABILITY:
CONTINUITY OF OPERATIONS

This chapter addresses the third homeland security task area—the continuity of military operations in the United States, its territories, and its possessions.

As distinct from the COG operations, discussed in Chapter Five, this task area of homeland security consists of the continuity of *military* operations, including

- force protection, primarily for deploying units;

- critical infrastructure protection, i.e., the protection of mission-critical facilities and systems, i.e., the infrastructure necessary for the Army to carry out its missions; and

- protection of higher headquarters operations, which will help to ensure the integrity of the military chain of command.

The importance of this task lies in the following simple truth: Unless the Army and other military organizations can ensure the continuity of their own operations, they will be incapable of defending the United States and its vital interests at home and abroad and providing military capabilities for other purposes.

THREAT AND RISK ANALYSES

Threats

Conventional and WMD Attacks. Many of the threats requiring domestic preparedness described in Chapter Four probably apply here as well, although in this task area one would anticipate a higher probability of involvement by state actors attempting to wage asymmetric war on the United States by attempting to hobble its ability to deploy military forces, rather than by nonstate or domestic actors.[1]

Our analysis suggests that we would expect such threats to attack in breadth rather than depth. What this means is that attacking multiple targets separated in time and space could psychologically create the appearance of a far more formidable adversary than is actually the case. To be more explicit, a single 12-man team of terrorists inserted into the United States with four Stinger missiles would appear to be less formidable and have a lower shock value than if the team divided into four groups, each of which simultaneously attacked civilian or military aircraft in four different locations.[2]

Cyber Attacks. One also should add to the list of threats state and nonstate actors inimical to the United States who possess no known WMD programs or aspirations but appear to have active programs to develop offensive information capabilities that might be used against the U.S. military.[3] This is a very dynamic and complex area, and our analysis accordingly only can skim the surface. Accordingly, the analysis that follows will address the issue in relatively broad strokes, supplying data where they are available.

The unclassified literature is somewhat contradictory on the degree of threat of cyber attack. Our reading is that catastrophic cyber

---

[1]One can construct scenarios, however, in which right-wing groups attack U.S. military capabilities in the belief that they are in fact attacking efforts to impose a "new world order" by UN forces about to impose martial law on the United States.

[2]The potential for this type of asymmetric attack against deploying forces has been demonstrated in numerous war games conducted over the past decade. In fact, in every Army After Next war game conducted that "played" homeland security, adversaries consistently attempted to deter, degrade, and disrupt the flow of deploying forces to prevent the U.S. military from arriving in time to accomplish its mission. For a more detailed review of how potential adversaries might asymmetrically attack U.S. forces during deployment, in transit, and in theater, see the Joint Strategic Review for 1999. We are grateful to Rick Brennan for suggesting these points.

[3]Former Director of Central Intelligence John Deutch warned in 1996 that "[w]e have evidence that a number of countries around the world are developing the doctrine, strategies and tools to conduct information attacks," and the *London Sunday Times* reported in July 1999 that Russian hackers were stealing U.S. weapon secrets (Deutch, 1996; Campbell, 1999).

attacks are not an imminent threat, but over time—and if actions are not taken to protect against them—the threat could grow.

Consider the transmittal letter of the President's Commission on Critical Infrastructure Protection, which noted that:

> We found no evidence of an impending cyber attack which would have a debilitating effect on the nation's critical infrastructures. While we see no electronic disaster around the corner, this is no basis for complacency. We did find widespread capability to exploit infrastructure vulnerabilities. The capability to do harm—particularly through information networks—is real; it is growing at an alarming rate; and we have little defense against it. (President's Commission, 1997a.)

And more recently, Willis Ware of RAND noted:

> There is no evidence that the "sky is falling in"; the country is not in imminent danger of massive disruption through infrastructure cyber-attacks. In part, this stems from the natural resilience the country has evolved from having to deal with natural disasters and man-caused events of various kinds and magnitudes; in part, from the natural responses of organizations to protect themselves against anything that causes operational intrusions or upsets. (Ware, 1998, p. vii.)

According to the commander of DoD's Joint Task Force–Computer Network Defense:

> The odds of the U.S. being attacked on line by a foreign nation state in some kind of cyber war in the near future are probably pretty low. But the odds of foreign nation states wanting to develop capabilities to help them if and when we are adversaries are probably pretty high. We need to have the same capability or better. (Wolfe, 1999, p. 1.)

Nevertheless, according to a 1996 study by GAO, the computer systems of the Department of Defense have come under increasing attack over the last several years:

> The Department of Defense's computer systems are being attacked every day. Although Defense does not know exactly how often hackers try to break into its computers, the Defense Information

Systems Agency (DISA) estimates that as many as 250,000 attacks may have occurred last year [i.e., in 1995]. According to DISA, the number of attacks has been increasing each year for the past few years, and that trend is expected to continue. Equally worrisome are DISA's internal test results; in assessing vulnerabilities, DISA attacks and successfully penetrates Defense systems 65 percent of the time. Not all hacker attacks result in actual intrusions into computer systems; some are attempts to obtain information on systems in preparation for future attacks, while others are made by the curious or those who wish to challenge the Department's computer defenses. For example, Air Force officials at Wright-Patterson Air Force Base told us that, on average, they receive 3,000 to 4,000 attempts to access information each month from countries all around the world.

Many attacks, however, have been very serious. Hackers have stolen and destroyed sensitive data and software. They have installed "backdoors" into computer systems which allow them to surreptitiously regain entry into sensitive Defense systems. They have "crashed" entire systems and networks, denying computer service to authorized users and preventing Defense personnel from performing their duties. These are the attacks that warrant the most concern and highlight the need for greater information systems security at Defense. (GAO, 1996a, p. 2–3.)[4]

FBI Director Louis Freeh has indicated that cases of commercial, military, and infrastructure-related computer systems hacking incidents have doubled every year (Freeh, 1998). On July 25, 1999, Deputy Secretary of Defense John J. Hamre was quoted by the *London Sunday Times* as saying: "We're in the middle of a cyber war."

Anecdotally, in the spring of 1998, during the deployment of forces to the Persian Gulf in response to Iraqi provocations, Department of Defense networks reportedly experienced their most widespread and systematic attacks to date, with 20 major installations' networks compromised.[5] Teenage hackers were behind attacks on Air Force

---

[4]See also Campbell (1999).

[5]During the attacks, dubbed "Solar Sunrise":

> [T]he defense community and law enforcement agencies struggled to understand the nature of the attacks and identify the threat. The attacks were launched from computers within the United States and overseas. As it turned out, this incident involved a couple of Califor-

systems in February 1998 (Graham, 1998; CNN, 1998). The 1999 "Solar Sunrise" exercise also showed the potential consequences of cyber attacks, although these were "attacks" carried out by DoD players in a larger war game (CNN, 1999b). The trashing of web sites apparently has become a part of the larger battle for public opinion, although its consequence for military operations seems dubious.[6] Nevertheless, attacks in March 1999 were traced to computers in Russia (CNN, 1999a), and attacks that resulted in stolen military secrets also have been reported (Agence France-Presse, 1999).

Thus there seems little doubt that defense computers are under *increasing* risk of attack, although the evidence on the frequency and severity of past and current attacks is generally anecdotal rather than statistical and therefore difficult to assess.[7] Put another way, the unclassified public statements, anecdotal evidence, and empirical data in this area are somewhat contradictory.[8] One suspects the existence of a gap between rhetoric and actual experience, in part stemming from the tension, described in Chapter Four, between the need to prudently alert the public so that they are not complacent about the threat and the desire to avoid frightening the public.[9]

An analysis of open-source data on computer incidents revealed that the distribution of frequency versus magnitude for cyber attacks taken as a whole follows the by-now familiar pattern of an inverse relationship (See Figure 6.1), with incidents of small or modest con-

---

nia teenagers. But "Solar Sunrise" demonstrated an enormous vulnerability in our unclassified computer systems which nevertheless play a critical role in management and moving U.S. armed forces all over the globe. (U.S. Senate, 1998.)

[6]Attacks on web sites presenting the public case in crises and conflicts have been observed in India and Pakistan and during the war in Kosovo, which included denial-of-service attacks against the White House website. See Varma (1999) and Messmer (1999).

[7]Or, in the case of the widely cited figure of 250,000 attacks in 1995, the result of somewhat liberal interpretations of what constitutes an attack, and a potentially questionable extrapolation on the basis of the experience of a rather small number of defense systems

[8]We believe that the Army could make quite good use of classified data, however, if used as we describe in our methodology.

[9]In any case, we detect more than a little hyperbole in many of these statements.

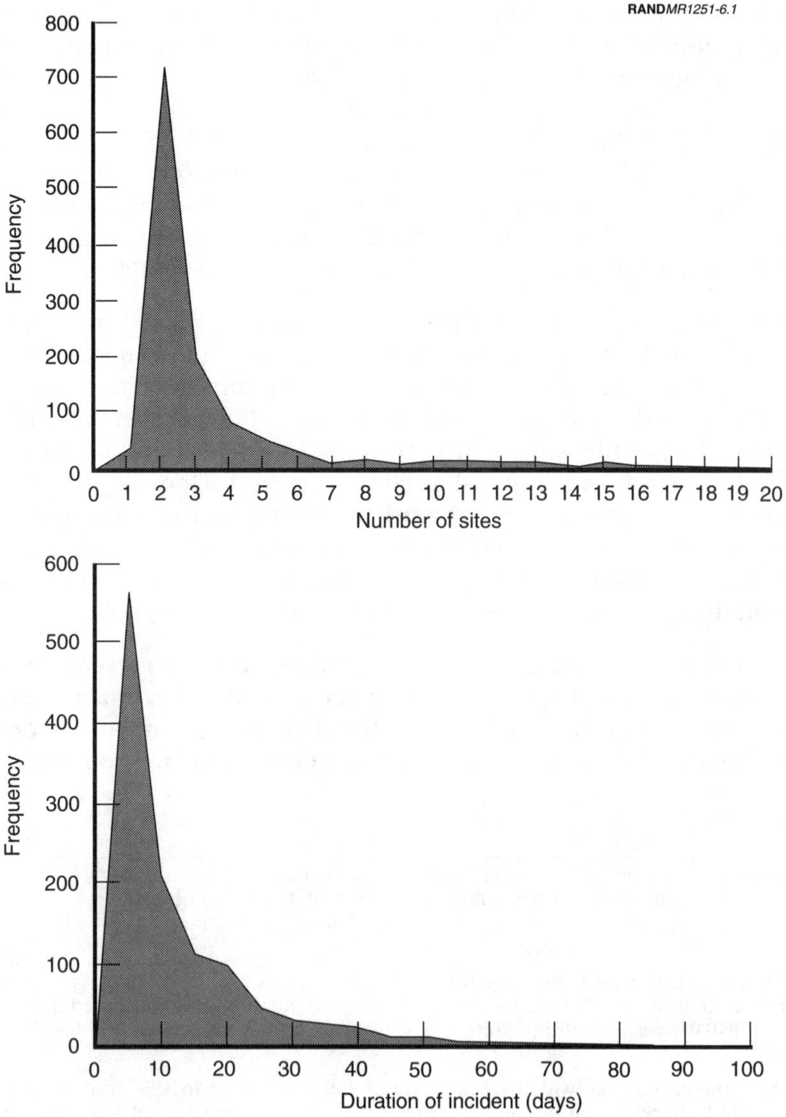

Figure 6.1—Two Measures of Consequence for Cyber Attacks (CERT/CC)

sequence predominating but with long tails containing occasional incidents of much greater consequence.

The two panels of the figure are built from data from the Computer Emergency Response Team Coordination Center (CERT/CC) for 1995 and convey two different measures of consequence.[10]

The top panel uses the number of sites involved in an incident to connote the magnitude of consequence, while the bottom panel uses the duration in days of incidents.[11]

The trend data suggest a growing threat.   Figure 6.2 presents CERT/CC trend data on computer incidents, showing the number of incidents handled, the number of hot line calls received, and the number of mail messages handled.

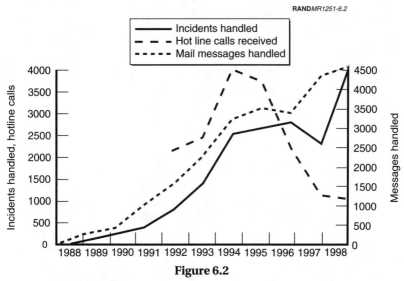

RAND*MR1251-6.2*

Figure 6.2

SOURCE: CERT/CC, 1999.

Figure 6.2—Various CERT/CC Measures of Cyber Attacks, 1988–1998

---

[10]The authors wish to thank RAND colleague John Pinder for providing these data, which were used in Howard (1997).

[11]Of course, we would want to monitor a number of other, more-specific measures of consequence, such as the number of incidents involving the destruction or theft of critical files.

Two of the measures (incidents handled and mail messages received) show fairly consistent annual growth, while the third (hot line calls) shows a decline. How much of the growth results from increases in the number of attacks and how much it reflects an increasing ability to detect or willingness to report such attacks is unclear.

Data from the Federal Computer Incident Response Capability (FedCIRC, see Figure 6.3) suggest the number of federal computer security incidents has generally been below 100 per month, but these incidents vary greatly in the number of affected sites, apparently stemming, in the main, from such computer viruses as Melissa and ExploreZip.[12]

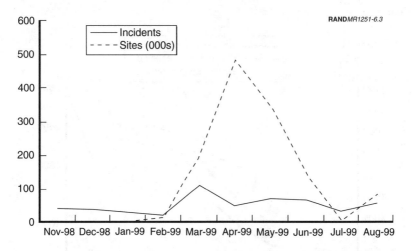

Figure 6.3—Federal Computer Security Incidents and Sites[13]

---

[12]We suspect that the increase over March–April 1999 is attributable to the Melissa virus. According to *U.S. News and World Report*, hundreds of thousands of computers were infected by Melissa. To aid in interpretation, CERT/CC's advisory on Melissa is dated March 27, 1999, while its advisory for the ExploreZip virus is dated June 10, 1999. Of the 59 incidents reported in August 1999, 23 were attributed to reconnaissance efforts, 10 were of unknown type, nine were information requests, six were root compromises, five were viruses, four were denials of service, two were user compromises. See Mitchell (1999).

[13]Monthly data are available from http://www.fedcirc.gov.

Data from the Army's Land Information Warfare Activity's (LIWA's) Army Computer Emergency Response Team (ACERT, see Figure 6.4) show an increasing frequency of attacks, although again, it is impossible to separate actual increases from improved detection and reporting capabilities.

Taken together, while the open-source data are somewhat incomplete, relatively compelling evidence suggests increasing incidents and numbers of affected sites.

Weapons

Conventional Weapons and WMD. It is entirely possible that WMD could be used, but significant impact could be felt even in uses of small arms or other portable weapons. In particular, because of their portability and lethality, three types of threats would seem particularly attractive to enemy special operations forces or saboteurs bent on disrupting U.S. military operations, facilities, or systems:[14]

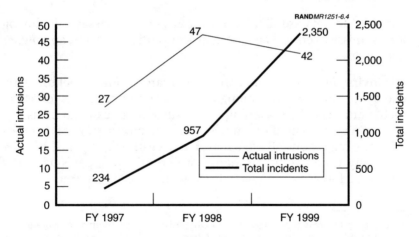

Figure 6.4—Incidents and Actual Intrusions of Army Systems[15]

---

[14]Some attacks on the United States may not be terrorism but rather acts of war brought to the U.S. homeland.

[15]Year-to-date data for 1999 are as of June 1999.

- Man-portable air defense missiles, such as Stingers, are of significant concern, since they could be used either against deploying airlifters or commercial carriers, and in either case result in hundreds of victims.[16]

- Rocket-propelled grenades (RPGs), which also could be used against low-flying aircraft as well as against troop convoys.

- Mortars, which were used effectively in an attack on a Sarajevo marketplace and could easily be used against a fort or Air Force base or against a port facility.

Cyber Attacks. While mission-critical systems could be attacked by conventional means, it seems more likely to us that, with the proper training, planning, and preparation, a committed adversary could launch computer attacks on mission-critical computer systems and networks.[17]

Potential Targets

Potential targets are divided into four general classes: deploying forces, mission-critical facilities, mission-critical systems, and higher headquarters.

Deploying Forces. In the context of a larger military action, early deploying forces will be among the most attractive targets for asymmetric attacks. The reasoning is that such forces can halt invasions and stabilize the situation on the ground in anticipation of counteroffensive operations. By this reasoning, a campaign against deploying Army units would probably preferentially target such early deploying forces as the Ready Brigade of the 82d Airborne Division

---

[16]According to press reporting, in 1989 DoD estimated that between 200 and 500 Stinger missiles were in the hands of the Afghan mujahedin (Weiner, 1994a).

[17]The reason we judge cyber attacks on critical computer systems and networks as more likely than conventional attacks is that the difficulties and costs of mounting computer attacks appear lower than conventional attacks on critical nodes and communications systems, and the opportunities for deception and deniability appear higher. Indeed, recent experience suggests that cyber attacks are far more prevalent than conventional attacks on mission-critical systems and networks. In the event that an adversary were willing to use special operations forces or terrorist capabilities for conventional attacks on military targets in the United States, however, mission-critical computer systems and networks could prove to be attractive targets.

and advance echelons of mechanized and armored forces.[18] These attacks probably would be directed at such power projection platforms as airfields where U.S. forces are deploying and probably would aim to kill large numbers of troops through such actions as downing one or more airlifters.

Mission-Critical Facilities. For the Army's purposes, continuity of operations in the sense of force protection and the continuous operation of mission-critical facilities and systems seems most likely to be placed at risk by attacks on the forts that maintain deployable forces, the air and sea ports of embarkation (APOEs/SPOEs), and key depots and ammunition facilities.[19]

Mission-Critical Systems. Continuity of operations, in the sense of Critical Infrastructure Protection of mission-critical systems (computers, networks, and communications systems), could be jeopardized either by attacks using small arms and other light weapons, those using mortars or RPGs, or through the use of so-called "cyber attacks."[20]

The Year 2000 remediation problem provides insight into the nature of the potential target set of mission-critical systems. According to Secretary of Defense William S. Cohen, the DoD has

> 10,000 separate computer systems involving 1.5 million individual computers which are spread at hundreds of locations across the globe. Of these, over 2,000 systems are so-called mission-critical— communication, navigational, targeting systems—that absolutely must work for the military to meet its missions on January 1, the year 2000. In fact, over one-third of the government's critical systems are in the Department of Defense.[21]

---

[18]By the same logic, Air Force and other early deploying airpower will be preferred targets, since they will be essential to the halt phase of a major theater war. Marine Air Ground Task Forces (MAGTFs) also could be attractive targets for asymmetric attacks.

[19]See Appendix I for a listing of illustrative mission-critical facilities. The Army should evaluate the list to determine priorities, e.g., on the basis of whether units or facilities are critical to early deployments.

[20]See Appendix I for a listing of illustrative Army mission-critical systems that could come under attack. The list might be too inclusive. The Army should constantly evaluate which systems are mission-critical ones.

[21]Of these, 198 are mission-critical, nuclear-related systems (DoD, 1999d).

According to the GAO, as of February 1998, the Army had 376 mission-critical systems and nearly 20,000 nonmission-critical ones;[22] DoD mission-critical systems totaled 2,915, and DoD non-mission-critical systems totaled 25,671, and total networks were estimated at 10,000 (GAO, 1998a, pp. 1 and 10).

Higher Headquarters. To be sure, the continuity of higher head-quarters operations ensures the integrity of command and control, but it also provides the connecting link between the continuity of military operations and the continuity of government.[23] For both reasons, threat and risk assessments should be used to establish what actions should be taken to assure the continuity of headquarters operations.

Net Assessment

With the possible exception of cyber threats—where attacks appear already to be under way but where data on the frequency and magnitude of consequence of these attacks are notably lacking—we believe that most threats to continuity of operations are at best future, not imminent ones.

As described in Chapter Four, the bars to WMD appear to be rather higher than often is acknowledged, but it seems probable that U.S. adversaries at some point will acquire these weapons. Although such weapons could be used to disrupt U.S. future military operations, other weapons, ranging from small arms to man-portable missiles, rocket-propelled grenades, and mortars appear more likely.

Thus, as with the domestic preparedness task area and as will be discussed in the remainder of this chapter, our recommendation is that efforts should begin to, at a minimum, assess more carefully and plan against these threats, while making selected investments to mitigate the threats to key warfighting and supporting units,

---

[22]The GAO reported that the Army had a total of 18,731 nonmission-critical systems. See GAO (1998c, p. 8).

[23]We consider higher headquarters to include OSD and OJCS; Headquarters, Department of the Army; the headquarters of the various CONUS armies; the head-quarters of CONUS-based CINCs; and other, comparable high-level commands.

mission-critical facilities and systems, and higher headquarters. Larger investments should await more complete analysis.

Threat Campaigns

If one takes seriously the possibility of asymmetric attacks against the homeland in response to the deployment of U.S. conventional military capabilities or in an act of regime preservation to coerce the United States to cease military operations before the total defeat of the adversary, then it is relatively easy to envision a determined adversary undertaking an extended campaign against the United States.

In such a situation, it is possible to envision simultaneous attacks on multiple military targets, a sequence of attacks against such high-payoff targets as deploying airlifters, or a differentiated strategy in which attacks on military targets are interspersed with attacks on civilian targets. Such a campaign could easily tax civilian and military capacity. It might do this, for example, by requiring extended alerts or by exhausting one-of-a-kind capabilities.[24]

Put another way, although the threats and risks now seem relatively remote and with the capacity for the use of WMD yet to be proved, a future, sustained conventional campaign against U.S. military forces could prove quite stressing.

PERFORMANCE MEASURES

Performance measures for continuity of operations and COG activities appear to be somewhat similar, although the specific activities depend on which aspect of this problem set is considered.

Prevention Activities

Because the threats are assumed to overlap with those in the domestic preparedness task area—state and nonstate sponsors of terrorism and disaffected domestic groups—the same sorts of prevention-

---

[24]For example, there is only one USMC Chemical Biological Incident Response Force (CBIRF).

based performance measures apply, e.g., the number of actual attacks, the number of known, credible attack plans discovered, and the number of preventions.

Preparedness Activities

Threat and risk analyses would lead to a prioritization of potential mission-critical targets, whether focused on the continuity of headquarters operations, critical facilities, or critical systems and networks. A wide range of preparedness activities could then be undertaken, including improving defenses (e.g., hardened facilities, improved network security for systems) and contingency planning for relocation.

Measures for preparedness activities would aim to reduce the level of damage and the time that any set of mission-critical assets was unavailable. These measures could include

- percentage of mission-critical facilities that have a high capability to withstand attack (e.g., blast effects or introduction chemical or biological attack);

- expected maximum time that normal operations of mission-critical organizations or facilities are likely to be disrupted;

- expected maximum time mission-critical facilities are unavailable; and

- expected maximum time until mitigation or reconstitution capabilities are deployed.

Response and Reconstitution Activities

Some of the operational measures associated with responses in the domestic preparedness area also would apply to response activities. Added to these, however, would be the speed at which headquarters could be relocated to areas of lower risk.

In addition to response performance, planners also need to consider performance in terms of the speed with which basic functions and services can be restored. Perhaps the best measure would be time, i.e., the time until operations can resume at their normal tempo.

Threat Campaigns

An additional measure of performance would be the ability to sustain the full range of continuity operations over a sustained threat campaign that involved multiple attacks in dispersed locations.

NOTIONAL PERFORMANCE LEVELS

We believe technical analyses and policy deliberations could lead to lower or higher levels than those suggested below but offer the following notional performance levels for the continuity of operations task area to provide a flavor of the levels we have in mind:

- For Force Protection of deploying forces, the capability of deploying forces to suffer no more than one half-day delay in mobilization and deployment as a result of attacks on fort-to-port movements or mission-critical facilities and systems. We believe that limiting delays to a half day would minimize the flow of forces to a military contingency.

- For mission-critical facilities, the ability to reconstitute and restore operations within one day.

- For mission-critical systems, networks, and communications systems, an ability to detect and isolate or terminate all external intrusions within minutes of penetration and an ability to reconstitute mission-critical systems, networks, and databases within three hours of penetration.

- For Continuity of Headquarters Operations, an ability to recover and reconstitute headquarters and mission-critical functions within 12 hours of an attack.

- For threat campaigns, an ability to sustain continuity operations activities over at least 60–90 days in the face of enemy attacks.

PROGRAM DESIGN ISSUES

Force Protection

In most cases, force protection is organic to units and their bases, i.e., the commander for each unit and base is responsible for meeting force protection needs.[25] Table 6.1 describes the sorts of capabilities available to support enhanced force protection activities.

The DoD, furthermore, has embarked on a DoD Force Protection Initiative:

> The Secretary of Defense has tasked the [Chairman of the Joint Chiefs of Staff] to review the force protection capabilities of U.S. forces worldwide. Several DoD Agencies and OSD organizations are actively involved in this initiative. Currently, each Service is responsible for protecting its own personnel and facilities. Near-term force protection enhancements are being fielded through the Physical Security Equipment Action Group under the guidance of the Physical Security Equipment Steering Group (chaired by the Director of Strategic and Tactical Systems, PDUSD (A&T) (S&TS)) and funded under the OSD Physical Security Equipment Program.

Table 6.1

Force Protection Capabilities

	Type of Event					
	HE	CHEM	BIO	RAD	NUC	CYBER
Operational Capabilities						
Installation alert system and physical security measures	X	X	X	X	X	
Installation military police	X	X	X	X	X	
Tenant units and their security SOP	X	X	X	X	X	
Local police, fire, and rescue services	X	X	X	X	X	
Local FBI	X	X	X	X	X	X
ATF	X	X		X	X	
Civilian port and airport police	X			X	X	
Reachback Capabilities						
USACOM J-2						
Installation G-2	X	X	X	X	X	X
DIA	X	X	X	X	X	X
FBI intelligence	X	X	X	X	X	X
State and local police	X	X	X	X	X	

_____

[25]The dictum of "mission first, people always" applies.

These efforts are being coordinated with the technology develop-ment activities of the [Technical Support Working Group Counter-terrorism Technical Support] TSWG/CTTS. DSWA is supporting the initiative by conducting force protection assessments of facilities worldwide, fielding assessment teams to identify and evaluate force protection shortfalls, and assisting commanders in rectifying the identified shortfalls. The CBD Program is also assisting in this effort. The CJCS has approved DSWA's proposed methodology and concept of operations for conducting the assessments. Using ideas and inputs to fulfill CINC and Service requirements to address force protection shortfalls. Key milestones are to i) complete 50 assess-ments by the end of calendar year 1997 and complete 100 assess-ments by the end of 1998; ii) continue to apply the latest technology to achieve enhanced force protection; and iii) define a prioritized technology R&D plan to address key force protection shortfalls. (CPRC, 1997, Section Eight, "DoD, DOE, and U.S. Intelligence Pro-grams for Countering Paramilitary and NBC Threats.")

Although the threat of such an eventuality is currently judged to be low, in an asymmetric enemy campaign against deploying forces and their power project platforms, the organic assets that provide force protection could easily prove inadequate. As described above, par-ticular concern is warranted about the vulnerabilities and force pro-tection of early deploying forces, particularly when they are massed at air bases or seaports, or on board airlifters.

The Army should work with the other services, predominantly the Air Force and Navy, to establish what sorts of enhanced force protection might be possible to reduce the vulnerability of deploying forces and to clarify the respective roles of the services for providing this pro-tection. Particular attention should be given to the vulnerability of APOEs and SPOEs and to the vulnerability of airlifters as they egress fly-out zones adjacent to air bases. The Army and Air Force should jointly explore the trade space associated with alternative concepts for enhancement of force protection (e.g., additional security forces versus equipping airlifters with decoys, chaff, or other counter-measures).

Continuity of Operations

Table 6.2 describes what appear to us to be the key continuity of operations capabilities in the National Capital area.[26] These capabilities include a host of DoD, joint, and service activities that could play important roles in the continuity of operations task area.[27]

Although these capabilities are judged to be adequate under normal circumstances, it seems likely that they would be greatly stressed by a prolonged enemy asymmetric campaign against deploying forces and mission-critical facilities.

Mission-Critical Facilities

In 1997, DoD-wide efforts to improve the security of mission-critical facilities included an OSD Joint Physical Security Equipment Program that aimed to undertake RDT&E that would enhance the security of forces and mission-critical facilities:

> This program consolidates related DoD Joint Service and Agency RDT&E programs developing advanced technologies for protecting critical, high-value military assets from paramilitary, terrorist, intelligence, and other hostile threats. Efforts focus on protecting personnel, facilities, and high-value weapon systems, including nuclear and chemical weapon systems and storage facilities. This program is serving as the focal point for near-term upgrades to U.S. facilities under the Force Protection initiative discussed above.
>
> Key accomplishments since last year's report include: i) completion of numerous qualification tests and evaluations of integrating video motion detection capabilities into the Tactical Automated Security System; ii) installation of an interior Mobile Detection Assessment Response System in a Naval facility for operational evaluation; iii) installation of a Waterside Security System at Submarine Base Kings Bay, Georgia; iv) testing of promising commercial off-the-shelf technologies for the Portable Explosive Detection project; and v)

---

[26]Many of these are deployable to locations outside of the District of Columbia.

[27]Service headquarters also should be included.

Table 6.2

Continuity of Operations Capabilities in the National Capital Area

	Type of Event					
	HE	CHEM	BIO	RAD	NUC	CYBER
Operational Capabilities: DoD						
Defense Protective Service	X	X	X	X	X	
Defense Information Systems Agency					X	X
Defense Communications Agency	X	X	X	X	X	X
Criminal Investigation Command	X	X	X	X	X	X
Military District of Washington MPs	X	X	X	X	X	
Army Computer Emergency Response Team (ACERT)						X
USMC/Navy security detachments	X	X	X	X	X	
Other Operational Capabilities						
National Capitol Region hospitals and clinics	X	X	X	X	X	
Reachback: DoD						
INSCOM	X	X	X	X	X	X
DIA	X	X	X	X	X	X
JTF-CND	X	X	X	X	X	X
Walter Reed AMC	X	X	X	X	X	
Criminal Investigation Command	X	X	X	X	X	X
Defense Information Systems Agency					X	X
Defense Communications Agency	X	X	X	X	X	X

NOTE: This chart treats only those Military District of Washington assets and National Capitol Region assets that might be involved. From the perspective of an outsider, any of the physical attacks and the responses to them would involve the agencies that normally respond to a domestic preparedness event.

demonstration of prototype sensor hardware for various detection systems. (CPRC, 1997, Section Eight, "DoD, DOE, and U.S. Intelligence Programs for Countering Paramilitary and NBC Threats.")

The Army should perform the necessary threat and risk assessments to assist in developing formal risk management programs that can be used as a basis for prioritizing and allocating resources, and these assessments probably should focus on mission-critical facilities at home, such as power projection platforms.

Mission-Critical Systems

Although the threat data basically conform to the sort of distribution described in Chapter Three, the threat of cyber attack requires a slightly different interpretation: Rather than seeking to prepare for events of a given magnitude, the aim instead is to keep the consequences below a specific threshold.

Preferential attention and resources should be given to mission-critical systems that support power projection and the employment of military forces to conduct assigned missions.[28] As in other areas of emerging threat, the GAO has advocated the use of threat and risk assessment and risk management and cost-effectiveness to guide DoD responses to the cyber threat.

> In addition, since absolute protection is not feasible, developing effective information systems security involves an often-complicated set of trade-offs. Organizations have to consider the (1) type and sensitivity of the information to be protected, (2) vulnerabilities of the computers and networks, (3) various threats, including hackers, thieves, disgruntled employees, competitors, and in Defense's case, foreign adversaries and spies, (4) countermeasures available to combat the problem, and (5) costs.
>
> In managing security risks, organizations must decide how great the risk is to their systems and information, what they are going to do to defend themselves, and what risks they are willing to accept. In most cases, a prudent approach involves selecting an appropriate level of protection and then ensuring that any security breaches that do occur can be effectively detected and countered. (GAO, 1996a, pp. 1–2.)

---

[28]The GAO indicated that, DoD-wide, resources for Y2K remediation efforts were being spent on nonmission-critical systems even though most mission-critical systems had not been corrected (GAO, 1998a, p. 2). An illustrative list of potential mission-critical systems can be found in Appendix I of this report.

The GAO further recommends a range of actions that can be taken to reduce threats and risks, with decisions ultimately to be based on the analytic or business case that results from risk assessments.

> This generally means that controls be established in a number of areas, including, but not limited to: a comprehensive security program with top management commitment, sufficient resources, and clearly assigned roles and responsibilities for those responsible for the program's implementation; clear, consistent, and up-to-date information on security policies and procedures; vulnerability assessments to identify security weaknesses; awareness training to ensure that computer users understand the security risks associated with networked computers; assurance that systems administrators and information security officials have sufficient time and training to do their jobs properly; cost-effective use of technical and automated security solutions; and a robust incident response capability to detect and react to attacks and to aggressively track and prosecute attackers. (GAO, 1996a, pp. 1–2.)

In the area of cyber threats, prevention, preparedness, and response activities should focus on mission-critical systems, i.e., those systems essential to undertaking or supporting military operations and other key missions.

Unfortunately, the absence of reliable data makes it impossible to establish where the greatest payoffs might be. Consider the following instructive example: Most of the discussion in the broader policy environment is focused on "cyber attack" by state and nonstate actors, and great interest lies in developing advanced technologies to detect and mitigate these threats. However, it generally has been established in the private sector that insider misuse is a more frequent problem than "cyber attacks" from outside organizations.[29] If

---

[29]In the 1999 Computer Security Institute/FBI survey of computer crime, 24 percent of the organizations reported system penetration by an outsider, while 76 percent reported insider abuse of net access and 43 percent reported unauthorized insider access to information. Seventy-nine percent of these organizations judged as unlikely the possibility of foreign government involvement, and 70 percent judged as unlikely the possibility of foreign corporation involvement. Nevertheless, the number of reports of system penetration by outsiders, unauthorized access by insiders, and theft of proprietary information rose from 1998 to 1999. See CSI/FBI (1999) and Department of Defense (1999c).

A study of the threat of insider misuse in the DoD has recently been published.

DoD experience is at all comparable, it would suggest that, rather than emphasizing external attacks, the greatest emphasis should be placed on ensuring that routine administrative and security controls are being effectively implemented to guard against this sort of misuse.[30]

The Department of Defense has taken some actions already on the threat of computer attack, including removing potentially sensitive information from web-accessible locations (Hamre, 1998b), reducing to six the number of "portals" through which Internet users can access DoD computers (Bender, 1999), and standing up a computer network defense center, a Joint Task Force-Computer Network Defense (JTF-CND), and a DoD Computer Emergency Response Team (DoD CERT) (Keeter, 1999, p. 7; Wolfe, 1999, p. 1).[31]

Within the Army, in addition to the consolidation of Information Assurance activities in LIWA and the Army Computer Emergency Response Team (ACERT), an active-duty/reserve component initiative to strengthen the Total Army's information operations posture is under way. The plan is to expand LIWA's ability to respond to emergencies using reserve component CERT/Vulnerability Teams as well as providing tactical commanders with trained reserve component information operations (IO) sections to plan, coordinate, and execute "full spectrum information operations" (DAMO-SSW, 1999).

---

[30]As reported by the National Research Council: "Troops in the field did not appear to take the protection of their C4I systems nearly as seriously as they do other aspects of defense." See National Research Council, *Realizing the Potential of C4I: Fundamental Challenges*, reported in Saldarini, undated. Saldarini reported the following:

> [r]eviewers observed instances of insufficient security such as sticky notes with important systems data attached to computers. In other instances, computers holding sensitive information were found to be vulnerable to hostile applets from the World Wide Web. The report attributed slack computer security to a DoD organizational culture accustomed to mounting offensive attacks. Cyber-terrorist threats instead must be countered with defensive action.

For example, it may well be that 95 percent of the attacks can be prevented by simply making sure that system administrators disable accounts when users leave an organization, that system-level passwords are changed routinely, and that other, similar low-tech measures are taken.

[31]The DoD CERT reportedly consolidated the functions of two earlier teams: ASSIST, which monitored intrusions and provided responses to the attacks, and DIAMOND, a group that surveyed past attack data to enhance future network security.

The ARNG has launched a 15-state Information Operations pilot program that includes nine CERTs with six at the state level, two in direct support of LIWA, and one CERT located at the National Guard Bureau (NGB). Additionally, nine Tactical IO Sections (four division level and five for enhanced brigades); four Vulnerability Assessment Teams (VATs), two of which will be in direct support of LIWA and two supporting National Guard networks and tactical units; and five Field Support Teams have been established. The ARNG's goal in FY 2000 was to establish ARNG CERTs at the NGB and in each state; create five field support teams and four VATs in support of the JTF/theater commanders and warfighting exercises; and establish IO sections in all eight combat divisions and in all 15 enhanced brigades by December 2000 (DAMO-SSW, 1999). The USAR's aim for FY 2000 was to establish three fully mission-capable IO Centers and a LIWA Enhancement Center (DAMO-SSW, 1999).

A number of serious efforts have gone into providing detailed recommendations on reducing the exposure of systems and networks to threats.[32] Although choices should be guided by formal threat and risk assessments, and cost-effectiveness and tradeoff analyses, the following examples will provide a sense of the range of possible actions:

- Improving data on incidents of cyber attack, including capabilities to log suspect activity and analyze these data to discern emerging patterns of activity that need to be addressed.[33] In such a case, there might be tradeoffs between monitoring capabilities and computer performance for legitimate users.

- Prioritizing information assurance efforts to invest preferentially in efforts to protect mission-critical systems at highest risk.

---

[32]For example, the Defense Science Board (1996) provided 13 overarching categories of recommended actions and 50 specific actions to improve the defensive information warfare capabilities of the DoD. See Appendix J of this report. The President's Commission on Critical Infrastructure Protection (1997a, pp. 60–62) provided the outlines of a strategy that included activities in policy formulation; prevention and mitigation; information sharing and operational warning; counteraction (incident management); and response, restoration, and reconstitution (consequence management). See Appendix K for a listing of these activities. Also see Ware's (1998) recommendations and the recommendations in Department of Defense (1999c).

[33]According to press reporting, this is one of the functions being performed by the DoD CERT and possibly Army CERT.

- Performing risk assessments and developing realistic contingency plans for critical systems and activities in the event that service is disrupted.

- Removing mission-critical systems from Internet-accessible servers or placing them on less vulnerable platforms.[34] In this case, the tradeoff would include the costs of having to create or have users rely on secure systems for unclassified computing on mission-critical systems.

- Routine efforts by system administrators to remove old accounts, to change all system-level passwords, and other administrator functions that can reduce vulnerabilities.

- R&D in furtherance of better capabilities to detect and track intrusions and insider misuse, to locate the intruders, and to terminate these sessions. Cyber-counterattacks and FBI action are also being used.[35]

In particular, the Army should continue to develop a more comprehensive and reliable incident data collection effort to assist in understanding the nature of the threats and risks it faces.[36] Such an effort would seek to develop taxonomies to facilitate threat and risk assessments and make possible a "divide-and-conquer" approach to target the highest-priority threats and risks with cost-effective solutions. We believe the best strategy would be the one that

- defines Army-wide, given the potential for inconsistent execution in information assurance activities, which systems are mission-critical and which are to have some sort of centralized execution of information assurance activities;[37]

---

[34]The Army reportedly has switched from Windows NT to Mac OS-based servers for its home page ("Tired of Hacks," 1999).

[35]Pentagon computers reportedly responded to an attack in the form of a flood of requests by "flooding the browsers used to launch the attack with graphics and messages, causing them to crash" (Schwartau, 1999). The FBI also has begun raiding hackers' homes (CNN, 1999c).

[36]ACERT and LIWA have the beginnings of such an effort.

[37]Efforts to ensure system security could be centrally executed, for example, by a security manager associated with each mission-critical system, who would assure its security by validating the dispersed base of user sites.

- establishes the necessary training and procedures to ensure that routine administrative actions (e.g., disabling of old accounts, changing system passwords, installing patches for newly discovered vulnerabilities, installing upgraded security software) are taken;

- on the basis of cost-effectiveness and tradeoff analyses, enables decisions on which systems also should benefit from other actions, e.g., moving the system from an unsecured network (telephone or web-accessible) to a more secure (e.g., NIPRNET or SIPRNET) network, installing additional detection and monitoring software; and

- continues to invest in long-term software RDT&E efforts to develop code that can substantially reduce the risk to mission-critical systems.

Threat Campaigns

As described above, an extended threat campaign that attacked dispersed targets could exhaust capabilities and erode readiness to prevent or respond to still other attacks. Accordingly, an important capacity issue is the rotation base that might be required. In fact, the possible future need for a rotation base might be one of the most important arguments in favor of conversion of the Guard to homeland security functions.

BUDGETING ISSUES

Federal Spending

Because federal funding is reported in governmentwide aggregates, it is exceedingly difficult to establish the funding levels associated with DoD and Army continuity of operations programs.

It is known, for example, that the President's FY 2000 budget included $206 million to protect federal government facilities (White House, 1999a); and $1.464 billion to address critical federal infrastructure protection (White House, 1999a), including

- $500 million for a Critical Infrastructure Applied Research Initiative;

- $2 million for intrusion and detection systems;

- $8 million for Information Sharing and Analysis Centers (ISACs); and

- funding for a "Cyber Corps" to respond to attacks on computer networks (White House, 1999a).

In the area of threats to computer systems and networks, the General Services Administration, the Critical Infrastructure Assurance Office, the National Security Agency, and the FBI's National Infrastructure Protection Center are developing a Federal Intrusion Detection Network that will provide a common center for response to cyber attacks on federal departments and agencies. The system reportedly is based on the DoD's incident-reporting network, which is said to be further along than civilian agencies' efforts (Frank, 1999). More recently, the Clinton Administration offered a revised plan that, it was hoped, would raise fewer fears about on-line privacy (White House, 1999c; O'Harrow, 1999, p. A31).

The Senate Armed Services Committee has reported that DoD-wide information assurance activities are underfunded:

> The committee notes the important steps taken by the administration and the Department to secure critical information infrastructures. In particular, DOD has established a Task Force for Computer Network Defense, a Defense-wide Information Assurance Program, and an integrated working relationship with the National Infrastructure Protection Center at the Federal Bureau of Investigation. Notwithstanding these positive steps, significant funding deficiencies remain in the Department's fiscal year 2000 budget request and the FYDP for information assurance and related matters.
>
> During a hearing on March 16, 1999, the Assistant Secretary of Defense for Command, Control, Communications, and Intelligence (C3I) stated that a $420.0 million increase to the fiscal year 2000 budget request and a $1.9 billion increase to the FYDP would be required for information assurance programs. These funding shortfalls are of great concern to the committee. Therefore, the committee recommends additional funding in this area and provision that

would strengthen the Department's information assurance program and provide for improved congressional oversight. (U.S. Senate, 1999, pp. 7–8.)

In large part, this funding shortfall appears to have been because the Critical Asset Assurance Program (CAAP), which was slated to address the security of facilities and systems, essentially was an unfunded mandate ("DoD: Infrastructure," 1999, p. 1).[38]

As of late summer 1999, the DoD planned to create a new program to replace CAAP, and was weighing additional funding for infrastructure protection;[39] including increased funding for R&D aimed at improving detection and reducing the vulnerability of defense computer systems.[40] The Senate Armed Services Committee approvingly cited the ASD (C3I)'s claim that a $420.0 million increase to the FY 2000 budget request and a $1.9 billion increase to the FYDP were required to address information assurance problems (U.S. House of Representatives, 1999b, pp. 7–8).

This suggests to us that DoD (and the Army) may be faced not so much with the question of how it will pay for information assurance but rather what the priorities and allocation of resources should be to protect its computer systems and networks. As described earlier, it seems that justifications for programs to mitigate threats increasingly will need to rely on formal threat and risk assessments and cost-effectiveness analysis.

Army Spending

The Army also tends to deal in budgetary aggregates when spending on the security of systems and facilities is concerned. These data suggest that Army-wide spending on security programs will increase

---

[38]The CAAP ultimately was canceled in August 1999.

[39]The report suggested that one option under consideration was to put $149 million in additional funding into the FYDP for information assurance activities.

[40]This may include a spending increase for a DARPA demonstration project on a computer system concept that employs random network paths and computer redundancy techniques to reduce the vulnerability of military information technology systems (U.S. Senate, 1999, p. 227).

through FY 2001, while spending on information security is hovering around $40 million annually.[41]

CONCLUSIONS

The analysis provided in this chapter has suggested that the continuity of operations task area consists of three principal activities: force protection for deploying forces, the protection of mission-critical facilities and systems, and the continuity of higher headquarters operations.

Our analyses suggest that, although the threats seem remote, it is prudent to begin planning now to ensure the continued security of Army forces, facilities, systems, and higher headquarters and, in the case of computer systems and networks, actually make investments. In other words, planning should begin for additional force protection capabilities, although acquisition of additional capability in other than cyber areas should be delayed until formal threat and risk assessments and cost-effectiveness and tradeoff analyses reveal where the greatest leverage is to be found. In the case of computer security, investments also should have an analytic basis.

In the area of force protection, it may be desirable to plan for more robust monitoring and surveillance capabilities near key forts, ports, and airfields, as well as capabilities for assuring the safety of fly-out zones and air corridors. It is easy for us to imagine hundreds of deaths resulting from a missile attack on a departing airlifter, as well as the cessation of deployments until security is established.

Multiple attacks within CONUS against civilian and military targets during a wartime mobilization also could stress low-density assets that have dual missions of warfighting and homeland security (e.g., the TEU, but also chemical units). In such a circumstance, military commanders could be confronted with the need to leave behind certain low-density units for homeland security activities that also

---

[41]Security Programs (BA 4) constituted $372 million in 1998, $402 million in 1999, $427 million in FY 2000, and $439 million in FY 2001, while spending on Information Security in the Other Procurement, Army, category, was $26 million in FY 1998, $44 million in FY 1999, $40 million in FY 2000, and $42 million in FY 2001 (Assistant Secretary of the Army, 1999a, pp. 40–41; 1999b, p. 19).

their capacity to capture, neutralize, destroy, or otherwise eliminate the threat of WMD and other potentially mass casualty–producing weapons:

- The probability of detecting WMD before it enters the United States, whether on land, sea, or in the air.

- The time until smugglers can be located and targeted.

- The time until WMD can be secured, rendered safe, and safely transported to a secure location.

- Both measures of actual preventions (e.g., preventions or arrests for smuggling such weapons, planned attempts that were disrupted) and measures of the apparent base level of threat activity (e.g., suspected smuggling attempts).

Preparedness activities for border and coastal defense thus need to be measured by the national capability to detect weapons and agents of interest before they can be introduced into the United States and the ability to secure them, render them safe, and transport them to a secure location.

Notional Performance Levels

For border and coastal defense activities involving the potential smuggling of WMD, notional performance levels might be an ability to reliably detect and prevent a very high percentage (e.g., 99-plus percent) of efforts to smuggle WMD or other potential mass casualty–producing technologies into the United States.[5] To achieve such a capability, however, might require a substantial amount of RDT&E or units dedicated to surveillance and reconnaissance of the threat at borders and coastlines.[6]

---

[5] Of course, as with the other task areas, the performance level chosen by policymakers could turn out to be lower or higher than the illustrative one provided here. Further, a fixed performance level should be used as a guide for planning and program development only after cost-effectiveness and tradeoff analyses have identified the most cost-effective means of providing the needed level of performance, and as it becomes clear where "the knee of the curve" is, i.e., where additional resources are unlikely to much improve performance.

[6] Exercises and tests could be used to establish the sensitivity and specificity of detection capabilities to various radiological and nuclear threats.

Program Design Issues

The Federal Context. The principal program design issue involves the current arrangements and respective roles of the civilian departments and agencies charged with border and coastal defense and, in the case of radiological and nuclear weapons, managing specific types of WMD, as well as the military services' contributions to these activities (see Table 7.1). The case of radiological and nuclear threats will be used to illustrate the responsibilities.[7]

Table 7.1

Capacity for Border and Coastal Defense:
WMD Smuggling

Department of Justice
    FBI (LFA in domestic incidents)
    FBI Critical Incident Negotiating Team
Department of State (LFA in foreign incidents)
Department of Energy
    Office of Military Applications
    National Laboratories
    DOE Communicated Threat Credibility Center (at Lawrence
        Livermore National Laboratory)
    Nuclear Emergency Search Team (NEST)
    Federal Radiological Monitoring & Assessment Center
        (FRMAC)
    Accident Response Group
Department of Defense
    Joint Special Operations Command (JSOC)
    U.S. Army
        SOF (Army Special Mission Units (SMUs))
        TEU
        52d EOD
    U.S. Navy
        SOF
        Defense Technical Response Group (DTRG)
        Navy EOD units
    U.S. Air Force
        SOF
    U.S. Marine Corps

---

[7]We address the nuclear threat here because RDT&E and operational capabilities for chemical and biological threats were addressed in some detail in Chapter Four.

Table 7.1—continued

SOF
U.S. Coast Guard (DOT/DoD)
Other Agencies
U.S. Customs Service
U.S. Secret Service
U.S. Marshals Service
U.S. Border Patrol
Immigration and Naturalization Service (INS)
Federal Aviation Administration (FAA)

Detection Capabilities. The long-term R&D of surveillance capabilities for smuggled nuclear weapons and materials appear primarily to be the purview of the Department of Energy:[8]

> DOE's efforts to prevent and detect smuggling . . . are focused on securing nuclear material at its source, detecting stolen material in transit, responding to threatened and actual events, and determining the origin of intercepted material. . . . To deal with materials in transit, DOE works closely with DoD, U.S. Intelligence, and others in the interagency community providing technology support for detection and interdiction of stolen nuclear materials. . . . Planned funding for these activities in FY 1998 is $43.5 million, up from $31.0 million in FY 1997. (CPRC, 1997, Section Six, "DOE Nonproliferation Programs.")

The DOE program includes development of a wide variety of detection capabilities, including the following:[9]

- The Surveillance Accident Nuclear Detection System includes various nuclear radiation detection systems developed for the DOE Office of Military Application for use in surveying an area for lost or diverted nuclear weapons and special nuclear material (DOE, 1999).

- The Wide-Area Tracking System (WATS) was developed to detect and track ground-delivered nuclear weapons and cue interdic-

---

[8]For an overview of DOE's RDT&E nonproliferation program, see CPRC (1997), Section Six, "DOE Nonproliferation Programs."

[9]RDT&E is guided by the Technical Support Working Group, which includes DoD, DOE, U.S. Intelligence, Secret Service, U.S. Marshals Service, Federal Aviation Administration, U.S. Customs Service, and the Centers for Disease Control and Prevention.

tion forces. WATS is an expandable array of low-cost unattended sensors (radiation and vehicle detectors) strategically deployed within the area to be protected. The sensors relay their information via standard communications protocols to a central computer at a control station. WATS can detect the entry of a nuclear device or radioactive material into the protected area, track its movement, and coordinate interception by security forces (Lawrence Livermore National Laboratory, 1999).

Operational Responses. The Atomic Energy Act directs the FBI to investigate all alleged or suspected criminal violations of the Act in the United States and, under the Federal Radiological Emergency Response Plan (FRERP), the FBI is legally responsible for locating any nuclear weapon, device, or material and for restoring nuclear facilities to their rightful custodians (NRC, 1996).

The FBI has concluded formal agreements with the Lead Federal Agencies under various circumstances that provide for interface, coordination, and technical assistance in support of the FBI's mission. Accordingly, memoranda among FBI, DoD, and Department of Energy (for domestic incidents) have been signed, as have memoranda among DoD and the Departments of State and Energy (for foreign incidents), each of which provides additional clarification of roles and missions ("Joint Federal Bureau of Investigation," 1980; "Joint Department of State," 1982).

The FBI coordinates and manages the technical portion of the response and activates or requests assistance under the FRERP for measures to protect the public health and safety and relies on the DOE for radiological monitoring and assessment assistance and on the Nuclear Emergency Search Team (NEST) for additional support:

> Made up of several components, NEST capabilities include search and identification of nuclear materials, diagnostics and assessment of suspected devices, and disablement and containment programs. NEST personnel and equipment are deployable at all times. They can be quickly transported by military or commercial aircraft to any location worldwide. NEST possesses the capability to render a rogue device safe and package it for transport to a secure location for follow-on disassembly operations. This program consists of an all-volunteer community composed of scientists, engineers, and technicians from the nuclear weapons design laboratories. The

operational capability deployed in response to an incident of nuclear terrorism varies in size from a five-person advisory team that supports specialized classified programs, to a NEST deployment with as many as 800 searchers and scientists, complemented by their technical and logistical equipment. (Gordon-Hagerty, 1997.)

DOE maintains several emergency assets postured to respond to events that may occur should proliferation efforts fail. DOE conducts analyses and provides operational and technical support in response to nuclear emergency and terrorism events worldwide. This includes the Nuclear Emergency Search Team (NEST), which has primary responsibility for responding to acts of nuclear terrorism or other incidents involving nuclear weapons or devices. It can be deployed under the authority of the FBI for domestic incidents and the Department of State for foreign incidents. Requested funding for DOE emergency management and response programs in FY 1998 is $41.1 million up from $35.3 million in FY 1997. (CPRC, 1997, Section Six, "Nonproliferation Programs.")

Department of Defense Roles. According to DoDD 3150.5 (1987), "DoD Response to Improvised Nuclear Device (IND) Incidents":

It is DoD policy to assist the lead Federal Agency during an IND incident. The Federal Bureau of Investigation is the lead Federal Agency for IND incidents in U.S. territories and possessions. The Department of State . . . is the lead agency for acts not under FBI responsibility. When the Department of Defense responds to an IND incident, operational control over DoD assets is exercised by the DoD senior representative.

The 1997 Counterproliferation Program Review Committee report provided an elaboration on DoD and other agency roles:

DoD responsibilities include designating military personnel and equipment to perform emergency technical response missions, such as NBC sample collection, analysis, and identification of on-site contaminants; decontamination; air monitoring; medical treatment; and securing, transporting, and disposing of NBC devices "when beyond the capability of an otherwise cognizant agency" (i.e., the FBI, Environmental Protection Agency (EPA) for CW/BW, or DOE or EPA for nuclear and radiological materials).

DOE responsibilities include "analyzing threat messages . . . for technical content, nuclear design feasibility, and general credibility, and for providing such analyses to the FBI"; designating personnel and equipment to provide technical and scientific advice and recommendations, including risk/consequence assessments, to the on-scene commander; and designating Nuclear Emergency Search Team (NEST) units to assist in locating and identifying nuclear materials and assessing and disabling suspected nuclear devices. Both DoD and DOE counterterrorism responsibilities directly assist the FBI in its role as on-scene commander for NBC terrorist incidents in the U.S. (CPRC, 1997, Section Eight, "DoD, DOE, and U.S. Intelligence Programs for Countering Paramilitary and Terrorist NBC Threats.")

More specifically, DoD activities and programs to counter paramilitary and terrorist NBC threats are described as follows:

In coordination with the FBI and other U.S. Government counterterrorism components, DoD is continuing to pursue several activities to counter paramilitary and terrorist NBC threats. These efforts include supporting, training, and equipping DoD teams to detect, neutralize, and render safe NBC weapons and devices in permissive and nonpermissive environments both in the U.S. and overseas. These DoD teams include the Army's Technical Escort Unit (TEU) and the 52d Ordnance Group, the Navy's Defense Technical Response Group (DTRG), Navy Explosive Ordnance Disposal units, and SOF units. (CPRC, 1997, Section Eight, "DoD, DOE, and U.S. Intelligence Programs for Countering Paramilitary and Terrorist NBC Threats.")

The basic procedures that are expected to prevail in IND incidents are outlined in DoDD 3050.5:[10]

1. When the National Military Command Center (NMCC) is notified of an IND incident, the Operations Team shall notify the lead federal agency, the appropriate service or CINC, and other appropriate agencies.

---

[10]The two DoD mission documents that guide DoD counterterrorism responses are the CJCS's Counterproliferation 0400 CONPLAN and the Counterterrorism 0300 CONPLAN. Each CINC reportedly is developing such documents for his Area of Responsibility (CPRC, 1997, Section Eight, "DoD, DOE, and U.S. Intelligence Programs for Countering Paramilitary and Terrorist NBC Threats").

2. The Operations Team within the NMCC shall interface with non-DoD organizations and shall facilitate interservice support required for such operations. When the U.S. government responds to an IND incident in a foreign country, the U.S. ambassador shall coordinate U.S. response operations with the host government.

3. In U.S. territories and possessions, the FBI Senior Agent in Charge shall be the senior U.S. government official and shall coordinate and communicate with local authorities.

4. The DoD response team shall be prepared for deploying within four hours of notification of an IND incident. The DoD response team shall be under the command and control of the DoD senior representative, provided by the lead federal agency. In accordance with the joint agreement, the lead federal agency shall be responsible for establishing coordination with non-DoD response agencies. The DoD response team shall establish secure communications, when possible, with the NMCC or the respective CINC and Service Command Center. The DTRG shall deploy at the discretion of the DoD senior representative or the NMCC.

The Army Role. We do not see a substantial future role for the Army in surveillance and reconnaissance of U.S. borders and coastlines.

Nevertheless, DoDD 3050.5 directs the Secretaries of the Army, Navy, and Air Force to provide resources to address responsibilities in accordance with the memoranda of understanding and implement the directive. The Secretary of the Army is further instructed to take the following actions:

> Provide a trained response team of EOD personnel and other required support for responding to IND incidents on Army installations in the CONUS, the CONUS land mass (except for those installations specifically assigned as a responsibility of the Navy, Air Force, or Marine Corps), and other areas as directed by the . . . NCA through the Joint Chiefs of Staff;

> Submit IND countermeasures technology and training requirements to the Executive Manager for DoD Explosive Ordnance Disposal Technology and Training . . . in accordance with DoDD 5160.62;

Fund Army IND response team training, exercises, and operations; and

Participate in joint working groups, NEST technical working groups, and interdepartmental exercises.[11]

Finally, the services and CINCs are made generally responsible for funding the incurred costs of operational and joint deployments under the directive.

It is easy to envision an Army role in at least three types of operations, although in each case, other civilian or military organizations also may be able to take that role:

- Using force to secure WMD is a task that probably would be given to elements of the JSOC. We would anticipate that Army SOF SMUs in JSOC would be used for land-based threats, and Navy SMUs in JSOC would be used for seaborne efforts to smuggle WMD.[12]

- "Render safe" WMD on the ground is a task that probably would be performed by the Army's TEU or an EOD team, although the DOE's NEST also has such a capability; sea-based "render safe" activities probably would be performed by properly configured Navy EOD teams.

- "Technical transport" also would probably be performed by an Army TEU or an EOD team, but it also could be performed by the DOE NEST or EPA or, in the case of seaborne threats, by a comparable Navy team.[13]

---

[11]DoDD 3050.5. DoDD 5160.62, titled "Single Manager Assignment for Military Explosive Ordnance Disposal Technology and Training (EODT&T)," and dated November 24, 1971, assigns the Secretary of the Navy to be the Single Manager.

[12]The 1997 CPRC Report indicates an "access phase," i.e., physically gaining access to the weapon or device before such specialized mission units as the TEU or NEST arrive to begin disabling the device, and indicates that EOD teams have the capabilities for these activities (CPRC, 1997, Section Eight, "DoD, DOE, and U.S. Intelligence Programs for Countering Paramilitary and Terrorist NBC Threats").

[13]Table II-1, "Identification of Lead Federal Agency for Radiological Functions," of the FRERP identifies the EPA as the lead federal agency for transportation of radioactive materials in cases involving "shipment of materials not licensed or owned by a Federal Agency or an Agreement State." See NRC (1996).

Budgeting Issues

Detection, Prevention, and Response Capabilities. Beyond some of the specific unit costs described in this chapter and Chapter Four, budgeting for these capabilities is rolled up in various budgetary aggregates associated with combating terrorism and WMD and counterproliferation.[14]

R&D. The R&D activities for operations that aim to prevent the smuggling of WMD into the United States are part of the broader range of counterproliferation-related RDT&E activities—undertaken predominantly within the Army, DoD, and DOE—to detect and respond to potential WMD incidents.[15]

LARGE-SCALE REFUGEE FLOWS

Threat and Risk Analyses

According to presidential statements, large-scale refugee flows can create threats to national security. Consider President Clinton's justification for the U.S. intervention in Haiti in September 1994:

> Now the United States must protect our interests—to stop the brutal atrocities that threaten tens of thousands of Haitians, to secure our borders and to preserve stability and promote democracy in our hemisphere and to uphold the reliability of the commitments we make, and the commitments others make to us.
>
> . . . But when brutality occurs close to our shore, it affects our national interests. And we have a responsibility to act. Thousands of Haitians have already fled toward the United States, risking their lives to escape the reign of terror. As long as [Haitian General Raul] Cedras rules, Haitians will continue to seek sanctuary in our nation. This year, in less than two months, more than 21,000 Haitians were rescued at sea by our Coast Guard and Navy. Today, more than 14,000 refugees are living at our naval base in Guantanamo [Cuba].

---

[14]For a functional breakdown of federal and DoD spending, see the data in the tables in Appendix L.

[15]See Appendix L, Tables L.4 through L.6 for a summary of the resources allocated to counterproliferation activities and CPRC (1997), Appendix C, for program element–level detail on RDT&E.

The American people have already expended almost $200 million to support them, to maintain the economic embargo, and the prospect of millions and millions more being spent every month for an indefinite period of time loom[s] ahead unless we act. Three hundred thousand more Haitians, five percent of their entire population, are in hiding in their own country. If we don't act, they could be the next wave of refugees at our door. We will continue to face the threat of a mass exodus of refugees and its constant threat to stability in our region and control of our borders. (White House, 1994a.)

The scale of refugee flows can be overwhelming, particularly when they are the consequence of war and civil strife:

- The number of Indochinese refugees who left Vietnam after the fall of Saigon in the spring of 1975, for example, is estimated at 1.2 million, and spending on their resettlement by the United Nations High Commissioner for Refugees alone was an estimated $1.5 billion (Ogata, 1995).

- And the number of Afghan refugees was estimated by the UNHCR at 5.5 million, with another 2 million to 3 million internally displaced (Rubin, 1996).

And in the Western Hemisphere:

- The number of Cubans in the Mariel exodus beginning in April 1980 was estimated at over 125,000 (Unzueta, 1981), approximately 2,500 of whom were criminals who were held for subsequent return to Cuba.[16]

- The number of Haitian refugees in 1994 appears to have been in the tens of thousands,[17] and the number of refugees fleeing Cuba at the same time reportedly was nearly 30,000, 12,000 of whom were processed at Guantanamo (Close Up Foundation, 1999).

---

[16]The total number of such "excludable" aliens appears to have been around 2,500, most of whom were returned to Cuba in the late 1980s.

[17]For example, the number of Haitian immigrants admitted in 1994 reported by the INS was 13,200, the number of Haitian refugee arrivals was 3,766, and the number of Haitians offered asylum was 1,060. The State Department's Bureau of Population, Refugees, and Migration, reports that between July 5 and September 19, 1994, 21,000 Haitians were granted safe haven (U.S. Department of State, 1997).

- Most recently, during Operation Allied Force, Kosovar refugees were airlifted to the United States and temporarily received shelter in the United States.

One easily can envision future such large-scale refugee flows, for example, from Haiti or Cuba again,[18] and even Mexico, which occasionally has experienced political unrest (e.g., in Chiapas). In such large-scale flows of refugees, refugee processing operations could be required.

The U.S. Army and the other services—particularly the U.S. Marine Corps—frequently have been called on to help manage large-scale refugee flows and resettlement operations:[19]

- After the fall of Saigon, the Army assisted in Indochinese resettlement to Guam, Fort Chaffee, Arkansas, and Fort Indiantown Gap, Pennsylvania, from April to November 1975. More than 100,000 refugees from Indochina passed through the refugee center at Point Orote, Guam, which, at its peak on May 14, 1975, held more than 50,000 refugees.

- In the wake of the Mariel boatlift, from May to September 1980, the Army assisted in the resettlement of over 54,000 Cubans to Fort Chaffee, Fort Indiantown Gap, and Fort McCoy, Wisconsin.

- Navy and Marines reportedly cared for 50,000 Haitian and Cuban asylum-seekers over the 18 months from September 1994 (Federation of American Scientists, 1999b).

Not only did these operations process substantial numbers of refugees, but they also involved significant Army resources:

- The Indochinese refugee resettlement operations in Guam involved a total of 2,103 active-duty Army personnel, devoting a

---

[18]In the former case, if the high (70 percent) unemployment, grinding poverty, and modest economic growth continue, and in the latter case, if the departure of Fidel Castro is not followed by a "soft landing."

[19]The data that follow are from U.S. Army Concepts Analysis Agency (1991, pp. 2-2, 2-3, 3-21, and pp. 3-49 through 3-54). In addition to Army and Marine Corps involvement, the Navy and Coast Guard are involved in interdiction and seaborne processing activities. Additionally, the U.S. Merchant Marine assisted in the repatriation of Vietnamese after the fall of Saigon.

total of nearly 386,965 man-days, and 32 Army Reserve personnel spent a total of 6,175 man-days on the operation, and those in Fort Indiantown Gap, involved 1,705 active-duty Army personnel for 381,915 man-days and 185 Army Reserve personnel for 9,315 man-days.

- Fort Chaffee processed more than 50,000 Indochinese refugees and involved 1,804 active-duty Army personnel for a total of nearly 444,000 man-days and 57 Army Reserve personnel for a total of 14,022 man-days.

- Fort Indiantown Gap processed more than 22,000 refugees and involved 1,705 active-duty Army personnel and nearly 382,000 man-days and 185 Army Reserve personnel for a total of 9,315 man-days.

- An estimated total of 1,200 personnel (including 300 Marines, more than 700 Army, 150 Air Force, and local personnel from the Navy base and Marine barracks) reportedly participated in the 1994 Haiti and Cuban refugee processing operations (Federation of American Scientists, 1999c),[20] while an unidentified number of Navy and Marine Corps personnel cared for the refugees thereafter.

The Mariel refugee resettlement operations also involved substantial Army involvement:

- Operations at Fort Chaffee processed more than 21,000 Cuban refugees and involved 3,889 active-duty Army personnel for 117,797 man-days, 672 Army Reserve personnel for a total of 8,923 man-days, and 2,140 Army National Guard personnel for a total of 37,482 man-days.

- Operations at Fort McCoy processed 14,360 refugees, and involved 1,618 active-duty Army personnel for 217,560 man-days, 135 Army Reserve personnel for 20,100 man-days, and 732 Army National Guard personnel for 10,248 man-days.

---

[20]At its peak, the temporary camp at Guantanamo reportedly held over 12,500 Haitians.

- Operations at Fort Indiantown Gap processed 19,094 refugees and involved 3,587 active-duty Army personnel for 92,832 man-days, 1,235 Army Reserve personnel for 17,142 man-days, and 1,647 Army National Guard personnel for 45,146 man-days.

In fact, of the 49 combat and noncombat operations studied, refugee resettlement operations accounted for a total of six of the 49 operations and more than 19 percent of the total man-days in Army deployments from 1975 to 1990.[21]

Measures of Performance

The key measures of performance for refugee management operations are capacity measures, both in terms of the total number of refugees that can be processed and in terms of the rate at which they can be processed. Table 7.2 provides several different measures of processing capacity for six past Army resettlement operations.

Table 7.2

Army Performance in Indochina and Cuban Refugee Resettlement Operations

Case	Refugees per Troop	Refugees per Man-Day	Refugees per Day
Indochina (1975)			
Point Orote, Guam	46.8	0.25	518.1
Fort Chaffee	26.9	0.11	203.3
Fort Indiantown Gap	11.6	0.06	106.3
Cuba (1980)			
Fort Chaffee	3.2	0.13	97.9
Fort Indiantown Gap	3.0	0.12	139.4
Fort McCoy	5.8	0.06	108.8
Average	11.2	0.14	195.6

SOURCE: U.S. Army Concepts Analysis Agency (1991).

---

[21]In the Concept Analysis Agency's computations, each local refugee resettlement operation constituted a separate operation, resulting in three operations for Indochinese resettlement (Guam, Fort Chaffee, and Fort Indiantown Gap) and three for Cuba (Fort Chaffee, Fort Indiantown Gap, and Fort McCoy).

Notional Performance Levels

An illustrative performance level for this area would be a capability to manage a refugee processing situation of approximately 125,000 refugees and be able to process them at the historically observed rate for processing refugees, which, as shown in Figure 7.1, suggests a capability for processing more than 500 refugees per day.[22]

Program Design Issues

The Federal Setting. The principal program design issues involve the respective roles of the civilian departments and agencies charged with border and coastal defense and the service contributions to these activities (see Table 7.3).

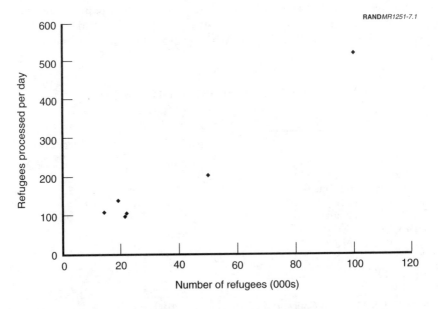

Figure 7.1—Rate of Refugee Processing Versus Number of Refugees

---

[22]Policy deliberations might lead to establishing a lower or higher stated performance level.

Table 7.3

**Capacity for Border and Coastal Defense:
Large-Scale Refugee Flows**

Department of State (LFA)
    Bureau of Population, Refugees, and Migration
Department of Justice
    FBI (LFA in domestic incidents)
    FBI Critical Incident Negotiating Team
Department of Defense
    Assistant Secretary of Defense for Strategy and Resources
    U.S. Army
    U.S. Navy
    U.S. Air Force
    U.S. Marine Corps
    U.S. Coast Guard (DOT/DoD)
Other Agencies
    U.S. Merchant Marine
    U.S. Customs Service
    U.S. Secret Service
    U.S. Marshals Service
    U.S. Border Patrol
    INS
    FAA

The State Department is the lead federal agency for refugee affairs and large-scale refugee incidents. The Department of Defense is a supporting agency to the State Department for refugee operations, with Assistant Secretary of Defense for Strategy and Requirements having primary DoD responsibility for policy on DoD disaster relief assistance.

The Army Contribution. The sorts of Army capabilities that have been associated with performance in refugee settlement activities relies both on considerations or scale (or mass), and specific capability mixes.

Scale (mass) issues. Figure 7.2 plots the manpower requirements in terms of man-days of activity against the rate at which refugees were processed. Unlike Figure 7.1, the figure does not suggest a clear linear relationship. Instead, it either suggests a curvilinear relationship or the possibility that the operations varied in their effectiveness or the efficiency with which they processed refugees.

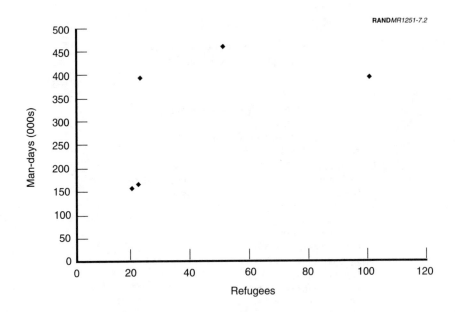

Figure 7.2—Number of Man-Days Versus Refugee Processing Rate

Capability mix considerations. The outlying case—the Guam reset-tlement operations—can be used to identify the sort of capability mix required to achieve the more than 500 per day processing rate observed in that operation (see Table 7.4).[23]

In the Indochinese resettlement operations in Guam, about one-third of the man-days were attributable either to the infantry (IN) battalions or the Medical Service (MS) units (34.8 and 32.5 percent, respectively), while almost one-quarter (24.9 percent) of the total level of effort was contributed by Combat Support (CS) units (U.S. Army Concepts Analysis Agency, 1991, p. 3-21). One interpretation is that the most effective force mix is one consisting of IN, MS, and CS units in the proportions just described.[24]

---

[23]More detailed analysis of the other operations could reveal additional insights into key capabilities responsible for performance.

[24]Of course, other variables, such as the size and nature of the facilities available, also would be important. No information on this is available, however.

Table 7.4

Army Units in Guam Indochinese Resettlement Operations

Unit	Type	Strength	Component
96 CA CO, Fort Bragg, N.C.	CA	14	AA
45 SUP GRP HQ, Hawaii	CS	655	AA
CO D, 411 ENGR BN, Guam	EN	32	AR
1st BN, 5 INF, 25 ID, Hawaii	IN	500	AA
1st BN, 27 INF, 25 ID, Hawaii	IN	419	AA
155th MS DET, Fort Bragg, N.C.	MS	9	AA
172d MS DET, Fort Ord, Calif.	MS	9	AA
1st MS GRP HHD, Fort Sam Houston, Tex.	MS	50	AA
702d MS CO, Fort Meade, Md.	MS	104	AA
423d MS CO, Fort Lewis, Wash.	MS	138	AA
714th MS DET, Fort Bragg, N.C.	MS	9	AA
Tripler Army Medical Center, Hawaii	MS	34	AA
73d MS DET, Fort Jackson, S.C.	MS	6	AA
515th OD CO, Guam	OD	130	AA
8th PSYOP BN, Fort Bragg, N.C.	PSYOP	26	AA

SOURCE: U.S. Army Concepts Analysis Agency (1991), p. D-23.

Budgeting Issues

Between 1997 and 1999, the State Department's Migration and Refugee assistance program spent approximately $700 million on Migration and Refugee Assistance and Emergency Refugee and Migration Assistance, with the latter accounting for between $20 million and $50 million over the same period; the State Department Migration and Refugee Assistance account funds 105 positions in the State Department.

Army refugee resettlement operations are contingency operations, i.e., they typically are not funded prior to the operation.[25] We have

---

[25]Rather, efforts to recover the costs of contingencies typically are made through requests for emergency supplemental appropriations or, failing that, in the next year's President's budget submission. For example, the FY 1996 President's budget request included the costs of Haiti contingency operations, the deployment to Kuwait, operations in Bosnia, and Cuban refugee relief operations (Deutch, 1994).

seen few specific budget or cost numbers associated with funding Army refugee resettlement activities.[26]

CONCLUSIONS

This chapter has provided an overview of two illustrative activities that constitute the homeland security task area of border and coastal defense.

The analysis has suggested that the border and coastal defense task area overlaps both nonproliferation and counterproliferation activities, along with humanitarian assistance operations or, more specifically, refugee resettlement activities. The analysis also showed that, as in most of the other task areas of homeland security, border and coastal defense activities are undertaken in a broader federal context in which DoD capabilities support civilian authorities—in this case, the State Department. Additionally, in the case of refugee resettlement, the analysis was made somewhat more tangible through the use of actual data, enabling an exploration of historical performance levels and the Army capabilities associated with a high performance level. Finally, as a general observation, it appears that border and coastal defense is an area of homeland security in which the Army does *not* have the lead military role, although large numbers of Army personnel and equipment can be used for certain operations.

The next chapter provides a number of illustrative planning vignettes to assist in identifying key Army roles and responsibilities, and key areas where additional Army efforts are needed.

---

[26]The FY 1997 request included a total of about $1.1 billion for *total* contingency funds, with $590 million set aside for Southwest Asia and $541.7 million set aside for Bosnia. These funds were for contingencies already under way because Congress is generally loath to set aside such funds in advance, since it would compromise their "power of the purse" (Garamone, 1996).

Chapter Eight

ILLUSTRATIVE PLANNING VIGNETTES

This chapter provides illustrative planning vignettes to assist in thinking through the key consequences, key tasks, key Army tasks, and current and needed Army capabilities, as well as key issues for Army doctrine, organization, training, leadership, materiel, and soldier systems (DOTLMS). In all, a total of nine vignettes address

- domestic preparedness, including three vignettes (high explosives, chemical, biological, and radiological or nuclear attacks);

- continuity of government;

- continuity of operations, including three vignettes (force protection, critical infrastructure protection, and continuity of headquarters operations); and

- border and coastal defense.

A more detailed analysis of Army DOTLMS for each homeland security task area is provided in Chapter Nine.

DOMESTIC PREPAREDNESS

High-Explosives Event

Illustrative Vignette. Attackers construct a fertilizer–diesel fuel bomb in a truck stolen from a sports arena concessionaire. On the evening of a collegiate basketball game at the sports arena, the attackers drive their truck to the 17,000-seat arena and gain access by posing as concession workers. They park the truck in one of the access tunnels underneath the main seating, leave, and detonate the bomb.

Key Consequences. The bomb's blast destroys several load-bearing pillars and causes several tiers of seating to collapse. The blast also ignites a number of small fires in adjacent concession booths, which produce acrid smoke. The lighting is affected as well, and the sections of the arena nearest the blast fall dark when the backup lighting fails. The bomb produces an abundance of rubble, and many victims of the explosion are trapped in it. The explosion, smoke, and fire causes panic throughout the arena, and the crowd surges toward the exits. Many people are injured in the stampede to safety. All told, the blast kills 250, injures 450 severely enough to require hospitalization, and injures an additional 300 who seek care on an outpatient basis. Eighty people are simply missing after the blast.

As radio reports of the bombing alert the community, doctors, nurses, and other health care providers from all shifts report voluntarily to their hospitals and clinics to assist in treating the injured. Hospitals from adjacent states call to inquire whether additional surgeons and other medical staff are needed. Passers-by begin bringing the injured to the hospital in private cars.[1]

Key Tasks. The immediate tasks are fire-fighting and evacuation. Once it is safe for rescue workers to enter the arena, search-and-rescue personnel can begin locating and aiding victims trapped in the rubble. Emergency first aid will be needed to treat the injured spectators. The seriously injured will require transportation to hospitals and more extensive medical treatment. Rubble removal is necessary to rescue some of the victims. In addition, the fire department and law enforcement will want to conduct an investigation into the cause of the blast. Security will be necessary to preserve evidence at the blast site and to prevent the curious from wandering onto the site. Eventually, clean up and repairs will be necessary to restore the arena to its original condition.

To begin work on these tasks, FEMA establishes a command post on the scene. The ATF dispatches 25 laboratory experts and technicians

---

[1]This behavior is consistent with that at the Oklahoma City bombing of the Murrah federal building.

to the site, and the FBI ultimately provides 65 agents to investigate the bombing. The Secret Service details two explosives experts to the investigation. The U.S. Air Force sends two ambulances, a fire and rescue squad, a security police canine unit, and an 11-man engineering team to aid with excavation of the site. The nearest Army post, some 120 miles away, sends two medevac helicopters and a detail from the post's ordnance detachment consisting of bomb technicians and bomb-detecting dogs. The post hospital sends a medical detachment including a physician, four nurses, and 20 medics to assist with emergency medical support. The Army National Guard sends a battalion of infantry to perform security duties and to assist with evacuation.

Key Army Tasks. The National Guard establishes a security cordon around the blast site. They work in shifts, detailing one company at a time to help with rubble removal in support of the ordnance experts and search and rescue teams. The medics and ambulance section of the headquarters company assist with patient evacuation. The medevac helicopters fly some victims to outlying hospitals to avoid overloading local facilities.

Current and Needed Army Capabilities. Most battalion-size units have medics organic to their headquarters companies. Depending on the individual modified table of organization and equipment of the unit, it might have four to six medics and perhaps a warrant officer physician's assistant assigned. Combat units may have combat lifesavers among the rank and file. If circumstances required additional medical support, the DCO might call for an Army field hospital or other medical unit as appropriate. Units might detail the remainder of their personnel to search and rescue or rubble removal, as required.

Key Issues for Army DOTLMS. *Doctrine.* Many of the doctrinal needs of domestic preparedness have been identified by TRADOC, and development is under way.

Organization. Questions remain, however, regarding organizations. Is there a need to assign specific, domestic preparedness missions to select units? Are RTFs and JTFs likely to remain the optimal means for responding to an event? Is there any value in involving non-governmental organizations (NGOs) beyond the American Red Cross and private volunteer organizations in consequence management (they play often critical roles overseas)?

Training. Where training is concerned, should training for some units address specifically domestic events? If so, what size event? Is there potential value in specialty courses for medical, engineer, or other personnel aimed at specific consequence management tasks?

Leadership. Does institutional leadership training prepare commissioned and noncommissioned leaders appropriately for the challenges that confront them in a domestic preparedness event? Are there incentives to provide these leaders with specific domestic preparedness instruction, either in resident professional military education or via distance learning?

Materiel. Are organic equipment and expendables appropriate to the domestic preparedness support mission? Are stock levels and storage sites appropriate, given a unit's potential taskings? Are medical supplies, for example, also appropriate for the treatment of children? Should specialty stocks be considered for issue to units likely to undertake a domestic preparedness task?

Soldier systems. Are soldiers properly prepared and indoctrinated for likely missions? Are the dimensions to a domestic response different enough from combat operations to justify special preparation and training? Does a code of conduct for domestic preparedness have potential value?

Chemical Attack

Illustrative Vignette. A domestic millenarian group plans to attack an enclosed sports arena with sarin, choosing sarin because of its inherent volatility and tendency to vaporize at room temperature. After bribing several security guards, the attackers secret a number of small canisters into the arena, fasten them under seats where they would remain unnoticed by the janitorial and security staffs, and open the containers by remote control or a simple mechanical timer once the arena is full of spectators.

Key Consequences. Well distributed, the canisters produce symptoms throughout the crowd, causing a wave of panic to sweep through the arena. Running and movement within the crowd helps disseminate the sarin vapors, prompting more casualties. The stampede resulting from the panic kills and injures as many people as fall victim to the sarin. Sarin poisoning claims 2,500 lives. Another 400 require hospitalization for nerve gas–related injuries, and another 600 suffer injuries sustained in the panic to get out of the arena.[2]

The attack produces both contaminated victims and facilities. Paramedics first to arrive on the scene and initially unaware of the danger enter the danger zone and begin experiencing symptoms themselves. Subsequently, other rescue workers await hazmat teams to help ascertain what the toxic material is. In the meantime, more people fall victim to the sarin.

As news of the attack spreads, medical personnel volunteer to return to their hospitals and treatment facilities. Once local hospitals discover how many of the victims require assistance breathing, they issue a call for ventilator pumps and Mark 1 antidote injectors to hospitals from adjacent areas. Federal Express, the commercial parcel carrier, volunteers its services to move 350 ventilator pumps from 180 different hospitals to the stricken town.

Key Tasks. Among the first tasks confronting officials would be to establish what was causing the symptoms. Once they discovered that it was a chemical agent, the next tasks would involve controlling access to the arena to prevent further injuries, conducting an NBC survey to establish the exact type and extent of the contamination, and rescuing and treating the victims. Rescue and treatment would further require emergency crews to don protective equipment, a patient decontamination process to assure the safety of medical personnel attempting treatment, and provision of appropriate medical care. Law enforcement would need to investigate the attack and attempt to determine who perpetrated it. Finally, the arena would have to be decontaminated or destroyed.[3]

FEMA and the FBI would arrive at the scene early and establish contact with local officials. The FBI would ultimately detail 30–50 agents

---

[2]Casualty figures postulated are consistent with the FEMA scenarios explored in FEMA (1997a).

[3]Destruction and disposition of the rubble as hazmat may be the only way to ensure public safety, especially if persistent agents are used.

to the investigation. ATF laboratory experts and technicians would work with Army experts to establish the forensic trail and origins of the sarin. The Air National Guard sends four patient decontamination teams (these units, because of their arrival times, are used for technical and corpse decontamination). The Army National Guard sends an infantry battalion to provide site security and a chemical company to assist with survey, monitoring, and decontamination. The 310th Chemical Company sends a five-man team of experts to provide additional advice. The Army also dispatches a mortuary services company to the site. Finally, facility decontamination and cleanup may be required or, if the insurers of the facility are unwilling to accept the risk that future attendees might be exposed to residue, the demolition of the facility and decontamination of the site.

Key Army Tasks. The Army National Guard battalion establishes a perimeter around the arena. The battalion, in cooperation with the local authorities, creates a holding area, a decontamination area, and a first aid area, facilitating triage, patient decontamination, and emergency medical treatment before moving victims to local hospitals and clinics. The NBC staff officer and company-level NBC NCOs play key roles in these activities.

A key task is dealing with the contaminated remains of victims. Since sarin is a nonpersistent agent, the decontamination and removal problem is somewhat simplified. Sarin decomposes if sprayed with a water and ammonia mixture. Nevertheless, the danger remains that the sarin has not yet completely evaporated from some stairwells, under seats, or from victims' clothing, leaving pockets of dangerous contamination. Local hazmat teams, assisted by members of the chemical company, recover the dead, and move them to a temporary morgue. The mortuary services company operates the temporary facility and coordinates with the local medical examiner.

Current and Needed Army Capabilities. There are 170-some NBC platoons and companies in the ARNG. By the end of FY 2000, the Army and Air National Guard and the Army and Air Force Reserve collectively will have 43 chemical-biological reconnaissance units and 127 decontamination elements trained for domestic preparedness missions (U.S. House of Representatives, 1999a). In addition, most battalion-size units have an NBC staff officer assigned, and most company-size units have NBC NCOs. The NBC equipment at company level typically includes agent-sensitive paper and sensor/alarms. Many units maintain stocks for decontamination of their own equipment. Army NBC protective equipment is not designed, however, for sustained operations in a contaminated environment and does not meet Occupational Safety and Health Administration (OSHA) standards. Army protective equipment is intended to afford initial protection until personnel can move out of the danger zone and decontaminate. Thus, even though unit personnel may have NBC training, their equipment is not intended to support long-duration activities in a dirty environment.

Key Issues for Army DOTLMS. The first Army elements (WMD CSTs) on the scene are intended to respond within four hours. In four hours, most of the chemical victims will have died or received other care. Therefore, in addition to the fundamental issue of the WMD CST's relevance, the DOTLMS issues arising specifically from a domestic preparedness event involving chemical weapons emphasize the longer-term aftermath of the attack rather than the immediate and specifically medical issues.

Doctrine. Doctrine should establish guidelines for operating on a sustained basis in a contaminated area to recover casualties and to decontaminate the area. Doctrine should determine the amount of risk that Army personnel should accept in rescuing chemical casualties or recovering the contaminated remains of chemical agent victims. Doctrine should also provide guidance on mortuary services/graves registration support to equip Army personnel to deal effectively with civilian expectations on the handling of the dead, especially under mass casualty conditions. Doctrine should guide cooperation with the local medical examiner and establish under what circumstances mass treatment, preparation, and interment of the deceased are warranted.

Current doctrine seems premised on the belief that the WMD CST will provide a rapid assessment and initial detection capability that can be used to identify the follow-on capabilities the RTF will provide. The Army should scrutinize the plausibility of this premise and the associated doctrine because in a chemical incident the WMD CST is likely to arrive too late and with too little capability to make much of a difference in the outcome. Within four hours, local hazmat and other first responders seem likely to have identified (e.g., by conferring with reachback capabilities, such as SBCCOM) the agent and the proper response. In attacks using nerve agents, in four hours most of the deaths already will have occurred.

Organization. The key organizational issue—after the question of the utility of the WMD CST—is whether further specialized chemical units may be desirable. If current training programs will prepare local emergency units to perform the necessary tasks in accordance with reasonable standards under the conditions likely to result from the near-term threat, the need for further Army specialty chemical units is probably minimal. If, however, current plans and training are thought not to be adequate, given the threat, perhaps the Army should consider creating stopgap units until local capabilities mature fully.[4]

Training. Although training programs and essential tasks for chemical preparedness are well established within the Army, training issues that involve supporting domestic preparedness incidents remain to be addressed fully. Training programs should be developed that equip individuals and units with techniques and procedures specifically for supporting rescue and wide-area cleanup operations. For example, field decontamination training pays little attention to the runoff after decontaminating equipment. Tactical units often look for streams or rivers as a water source, but runoff is toxic and must be dealt with carefully, especially at the scene of an incident.

Leadership. Leadership issues devolve from the doctrinal questions raised above. The Army should consider at what ranks its commissioned and noncommissioned leaders require training in chemical situations other than today's battlefield cases.

Materiel. Materiel issues should address the differences between the requirements to operate in a tactical NBC environment and the requirements to support search, rescue, and recovery operations in a contaminated environment. Some important distinctions between the two cases involve the frequency and extent of exposure. Encountering battlefield attacks, Army units have alarms to alert them to the

---

[4]See GAO (1999b) for suggestions that current capabilities are not fully mature.

danger, protective equipment to shield their personnel from it, and means to move out of the contaminated area. The Army has yet to encounter battlefield conditions where it must stay in an area contaminated by chemical agents for an extended period. The equipment the Army has may be adequate for the conditions likely on the battlefield, but it is not up to the task of protecting personnel operating in response to a domestic preparedness event. Here, soldiers face the likelihood of repeated, prolonged exposure and may have to recover contaminated corpses. The Army should consider acquisition of equipment appropriate for the task, especially for units with domestic preparedness among their contingencies.

Biological Attack

Illustrative Vignette. A foreign terrorist organization smuggles anthrax bacillus into the United States and places it in the heating, ventilating, and air conditioning (HVAC) ducting at an indoor sports arena, exposing some 17,000 in attendance at a hockey game. The game concludes without incident and the spectators return to their homes.

Key Consequences. Within three days, many experience flu-like symptoms and seek treatment. Six days after exposure, some 3,200 have died and another 4,250 are seriously ill. As news of the illness circulates through the population, hundreds of people begin flooding emergency rooms complaining of flu-like symptoms. Most of those seeking treatment are completely healthy and complicate the work of health care providers.

Key Tasks. The medical community must diagnose the illness correctly. Public health officials, law enforcement and the FBI must ascertain whether the disease results from a deliberate attack or is a natural occurrence and, in either case, whether or not longer-term epidemiological consequences are associated with the outbreak. Public health officials must also consider the possible value of immunizations for locales thought to be in danger and must plan to assist local medical examiners, whose mortuary facilities will quickly be filled. Facility cleanup also may be required.

Key Army Tasks. The Army can provide "reach back" to expertise in U.S. Army Medical Research Institute for Infectious Diseases

(USAMRIID). It can also make vaccines available in at least limited quantities if directed to do so. Perhaps most important in a mass casualty crisis, the Army can provide mortuary support services to help local officials operate temporary mortuaries and make appropriate disposition of the dead. Casualty tracking and reporting teams and casualty assistance personnel can assist in maintaining accurate records of the victims and notifying next of kin, respectively.

Current and Needed Army Capabilities. USAMRIID does leading-edge, primary research in infectious disease and epidemiology. It maintains habitual associations with other elements of the national public health infrastructure, including the Public Health Service.

Graves registration, mortuary support, and casualty tracking and reporting are all capabilities resident within the general-purpose force. Division Support Commands, Corps Support Commands, and Theater Army Area Commands all have appropriate units.

Key Issues for Army DOTLMS. None.

Radiological or Nuclear Attack

Illustrative Vignette. Attackers detonate a truck bomb at the loading dock of the reactor building at a major metropolitan university. The explosion was intended to attack the physics department's nuclear research reactor and succeeds in rupturing the containment vessel, disabling the control rod mechanism, and cracking the reactor pool, which starts leaking badly. When the damaged reactor's carbon-graphite insulation catches fire, radioactive contaminants escape into the atmosphere in the smoke. Because the university is in the heart of a major city, the attack has potential consequences for the entire downtown area, including the business and financial quarters.

Key Consequences. Radioactive steam and particles escape through the rubble. Some of the radioactive material is born aloft in the smoke resulting from secondary fires, spreading contamination further. Although the actual extent of the contamination and the danger it poses has yet to be assessed, the news media cover the story as if it were Chernobyl, spreading panic throughout the region. Although university officials try to head off panic, students and business people in the vicinity of the attack react as if they are in immediate danger of being contaminated. Traffic jams and accidents fueled by panic make some of the surface streets impassable for emergency vehicles. Subways and surface trains are overwhelmed by the crush of people seeking to escape the stricken region.

Officials face two daunting tasks immediately: to evacuate the population downwind from the reactor and to ascertain the extent of the contamination and begin containment operations. Television and radio stations broadcast warnings to evacuate the neighborhoods directly in the path of radiological contamination.

FEMA deploys to the scene to coordinate federal efforts with local officials. The Department of Energy and Nuclear Regulatory Commission dispatches 20 experts to help estimate the extent of the contamination. Forty FBI and ATF agents rush to the area to work with local law enforcement in identifying and arresting the attackers. The President declares the county a federal disaster area. Twenty elderly residents suffer heart attacks from the news, and dozens crowd local emergency rooms with symptoms ranging from vomiting and diarrhea to shortness of breath and chest pains. Population evacuation is complicated by the need for the FBI and ATF to establish roadblocks as part of their search for the attackers.

Key Tasks. For officials attempting to manage the crisis, the immediate task is to contain the radiation to the damaged physics building. Emergency crews will have to work in proximity to the damaged reactor to stanch the leakage of contamination. A fleet of 100 medium- and heavy-lift helicopters from the Air National Guard and Army National Guard is assembled to assist. They first dump boron into the remains of the reactor building to smother any residual critical reactions, then fly large tarpaulins—perhaps tentage—over the damaged building to provide a base. Next they drop loads of closed-cell, fire retardant foam onto the tentage. Two local construction companies begin moving mobile cranes to the site to assist in covering the tentage with gunite. They attach concrete hoses to their cranes and pump gunite over the entire site to encase it. Aircrews and crane operators must wear protective clothing and dosimeters and carefully monitor their cumulative exposure to radiation.

In addition to containment, tracking and monitoring the spread of contamination will be essential to warn the population. Surveying and predicting the path of contamination become key tasks, complicated by the valleys between tall buildings in the area that concentrate the winds and smoke and allow them to carry further before dissipating. Protecting the population requires immediate evacuation and relocation of 5,000 residents, with a subsequent 10,000 at risk, depending on how the radiation spreads. Some of the evacuees, those who reside in the area, will require temporary shelter, food, and clothing. Where evacuations occur, there is also a need to protect the homes and property left behind from looters.

Key Army Tasks. Army National Guard and active-duty Army units provide 12 CH-54, 24 CH-47, 36 UH-60, and eight UH-1 helicopters. Walter Reed Army Medical Center details two experts in radiological exposure to advise on managing flight crew exposure.

While the Air Force monitors and tracks airborne radiation with its specialized aircraft, the Army units conduct ground reconnaissance. Five National Guard NBC companies help monitor the edge of the hot zone. These units are augmented with six *Fuchs* NBC reconnaissance vehicles airlifted to the scene from two different Army posts. The *Fuchs* vehicles' on-board sensors measure and report ground contamination.

The National Guard orders a brigade equivalent into the area to provide security, help maintain public order, and assist in evacuating contaminated neighborhoods. A battalion of infantry augments local police and highway patrol at maintaining a perimeter just outside the hot zone. A transportation battalion supplements local school district and commercial buses to provide transportation for evacuees. Three forward support battalions from the DISCOM work with the local Red Cross and emergency services to provide food, shelter, bath support, and clothing to the displaced. A psychological operations detachment helps warn those neighborhoods likely to be ordered to evacuate and instructs residents on what to bring and where to assemble. A veterinary detachment examines area pets for signs of contamination.

Current and Needed Army Capabilities. Divisional NBC companies could perform radiological survey and monitoring. Virtually any unit would contribute to the operation of a cordon or perimeter or assist with house-to-house warning. Psychological operations units would supplement local broadcast media in issuing evacuation instructions. Transportation units and others with significant numbers of trucks could help with evacuation.

Key Issues for Army DOTLMS. *Doctrine.* Doctrine, tactics, techniques, and procedures already exist for many of the tasks described above. At a policy level, the question is the degree to which Army elements, especially engineers and aviation, ought to be directly involved in attempts to contain a radiological event. The answer to the policy issue would clearly have implications for subsequent DOTLMS, since a decision favoring a more limited role would require less of DOTLMS, and a decision favoring an extensive role might require more.

Organizations. Organizationally, the Army has no units designed, trained, or equipped to cap or contain a damaged reactor. The training, leadership, and materiel are not in place to carry out such a task.

CONTINUITY OF GOVERNMENT

Illustrative Vignette. Four days ago, the President held a working lunch with his cabinet. The Vice President did not attend because of a fund-raising commitment. Within 24 hours, all those in attendance complained of aching joints and fevers. In all instances, the fever rose despite medical intervention. The President and several cabinet officials ultimately succumbed, while the others fell into comas. Investigators concluded that the president and his cabinet had been victims of a biological attack of unknown origin.

Key Consequences. The Vice President and successor cabinet members had to reconstitute the Executive Branch of government. Security considerations led to their evacuation from Washington and movement to a secure facility elsewhere until the enemy campaign could be uncovered and defeated. Other key elements of the Executive Branch were also relocated for security reasons.

Key Tasks. Immediate tasks include moving elements of the Executive Branch to secure locations, providing full facilities and capabilities to support officials' continued execution of their duties in office, and providing accommodations for officials' family members. While essential elements of the Executive Branch relocate, other tasks involve investigating to discover the source of the attack, the nature of the campaign in which it was conducted, and the enemy's ultimate objectives. The attackers must be identified, located, and destroyed. If the enemy campaign threatens other elements of the government, appropriate security measures must be instituted.

Key Army Tasks. The Army could provide secure facilities and logistics support for the relocated Executive Branch elements. The Army could also support the Secret Service and other law enforcement agencies in providing security. It may also provide transportation and aviation support. The service's intelligence arm would cooperate with other intelligence agencies in attempting to identify the enemy, his plans, and his objectives.

Current and Needed Army Capabilities. Providing COG requires secure facilities—both office space and living quarters for a substantial number of people. The Executive Branch also requires full communications support so it can conduct business with other branches of government and foreign capitals. Ground and air transportation is also essential, given the Executive Branch's need to move around the country and send representatives abroad. The capabilities must be robust enough to sustain Executive Branch operations indefinitely.

The Army has long contributed to these capabilities, along with other agencies. The concern is not whether the Army can satisfy all of these requirements if they were levied against the service but rather how coordination with other actors that also play a role in COG can be optimized.

Key Issues for Army DOTLMS. The current DOTLMS generally support COG. At issue is whether the contingency plans currently in place anticipate the challenges of an enemy campaign plan aimed at decapitating the U.S. government.

CONTINUITY OF OPERATIONS

Force Protection

Although it also can include base security, in the homeland security context, Force Protection (FP) primarily focuses on ensuring the security of forces during fort-to-port deployments, i.e., providing a high probability that mobilization and deployment will not be disrupted by attacks.

Illustrative Vignette. Terrorists from the Osama bin Laden organization purchase nine Stinger missiles from an Afghan arms broker and, for assistance in training, download from the U.S. Army doctrine website both U.S. Army FM 44-18, *Air Defense Artillery Employment: Stinger,* and U.S. Army FM 44-18-1, *Stinger Team Operations,* for training with six of the Stingers.[5]

At the onset of a U.S. crisis response to Iraqi troop movements in Southwest Asia, the terrorists contract with South American narcotics traffickers to smuggle three Stingers into the United States via aircraft and, on receipt of the cargo, disperse to Altus AFB, Oklahoma, Pope AFB, North Carolina, and Dallas–Fort Worth. The terrorists then undertake nearly simultaneous attacks on two USAF airlifters and a commercial passenger plane and down all three aircraft.

Key Consequences. The aircraft crash, killing all on board. The USAF, FBI, National Transportation Safety Board (NTSB), Federal Aviation Administration, and local officials move to the crash sites, along with fire-fighters and paramedics. The FBI, and subsequently, ATF, deploy some 80–90 technicians, laboratory experts, and special agents to investigate each incident.

Key Tasks. The immediate tasks include fire-fighting and search and rescue. Subsequently, incident investigation and analysis and notification of next of kin must take place. Mortuary service support would be required. Once officials determine that a missile struck the aircraft, a general aviation warning would have to be passed to all other airfields—commercial and military. In addition, all "fly out" zones at and around the end of runways would have to be searched and secured before air deployments to Southwest Asia could continue.

Key Army Tasks. Army units could assist law enforcement with search and security of fly out zones. At least one company would be needed to search and secure each fly out zone—perhaps many more if the zone includes urban or otherwise dense terrain. Army intelli-

---

[5]The URL for Army ADTDL is http://www.adtdl.army.mil/

gence would assist in tracking the air defense missiles used in the attacks and help to establish an estimate of the size of the enemy's total holdings. Army casualty notification teams would notify next of kin for military personnel. Unit family support teams would assist the families of Army victims.

Army casualty teams would also assist with casualty tracking and reporting for all victims. Graves registration teams from a DISCOM or COSCOM would support the local medical examiner. DISCOM or similar units could provide housing for federal personnel. A transportation center would be established to provide transportation coordination and vehicles to move investigators and officials from the crash site to their local base of operations. If the crash site is in difficult terrain or the investigation encounters bad weather, the Army would provide field clothing appropriate to the conditions.

Current and Needed Army Capabilities. Holding, controlling, and observing ground is a core attribute of Army forces. Combat and combat support units should be able to assist with search and security of the fly out zones. The Army has well-established processes for casualty notification and family support. Mortuary support services can be found at corps and echelons above corps. Army units have a well-established history of providing housing and other logistics support to other officials in such circumstances.

Key Issues for Army DOTLMS. *Doctrine.* Doctrine exists to support search and surveillance of fly out zones; the task is a basic infantry operation. Doctrine on military support to law enforcement also exists but should be augmented to address cases suggested in this vignette, where military personnel may have to perform security duties for an extended period or where specifically military surveillance is essential (for example, where terrain, buildings, and other circumstances make the use of electronic security systems and commercial security services impractical).

Leadership. Leadership, especially for the noncommissioned leaders who would supervise the tasks outlined above at a practical level, should be strengthened. Low-level leaders must be properly prepared to coordinate the handoff of surveillance information to law enforcement when intruders are discovered.

Soldier systems. Likewise, soldiers must be properly indoctrinated and prepared for support to law enforcement. Every soldier must be prepared and instructed to understand the limits of his or her role in the security operation.

Critical Infrastructure Protection

Illustrative Vignette. Guessing that U.S. power projection forces are heavily dependent on computer-based systems, many of which run on commercial software, the enemy, a determined U.S. adversary with a mature information warfare program, undertakes a campaign of attacks on an unclassified system considered mission-critical for Army deployment. Overworked systems administrators respond to the detection of an intrusion by following procedures to isolate the penetration, but not before a Trojan Horse program is inserted, which steals processing cycles and grinds the infected operating systems to a halt. In addition, the inserted code leads to the corruption of load planning and other databases. As a result, planning tools indicate aircraft loads are too large or heavy when in fact they are not, slowing the deployment process.

Key Consequences. Military planners from Joint Staff to unit level experience difficulties. Major subelements of the Joint Operational Planning and Execution System (JOPES) run slowly, delaying deployment orders and similar instructions. Unit identity codes go missing from the databases. At the local level, units at departure airfields discover their automated load-planning tools do not operate properly. Most resort to manual planning, which requires more time and does not fill space aboard each aircraft as efficiently, which ultimately increases the airlift requirement to accomplish the deployment.

Key Tasks. For the Joint Staff, the immediate task is to find a reliable way to disseminate deployment orders, especially for those elements tasked to deploy independently of their parent organizations. Other elements of the Global Command and Control System must take over for the stricken planning and alert tools. Air movement planners and air movement NCOs at unit level must revert to manual planning techniques. Airlift squadrons, too, must revert to earlier, slower practices.

Key Army Tasks. Army unit deployment sequences have been disrupted because JOPES has notified some units late that they have been alerted for movement. For the ARFOR commander, this introduces a new, potentially dangerous degree of uncertainty into his deployment plans. He and his staff and his major subordinate units must revise their estimates as to when the ARFOR will have enough strength in the theater of operations to respond to the crisis.

Unit commanders must now devote more time to ensuring that their personnel can deploy aboard the allotted aircraft and must compromise the rest of their predeployment troop leading and rehearsal time to do so.

Current and Needed Army Capabilities. Army units need reliable, free-standing (perhaps laptop) tools that can be used to plan unit movement and configure equipment loads. More broadly, the Global Command and Control System and JOPES should be insulated both procedurally and technically from the possibility of corruption or compromise.

Key Issues for Army DOTLMS. The nature of the problem in this vignette calls more for a contingency plan than for adjustments to DOTLMS. The Army should identify its essential computer and communications systems and perform a vulnerability assessment. For critical and vulnerable facilities and systems, the Army should devise a protective plan and a fallback plan in the event that attack is successful. Part of the protective considerations should be evaluating Army personnel with access to key systems to ensure that these people are reliable and pose no threat themselves. The Army might review its very successful nuclear surety program in this regard, with special attention to the personnel reliability program.

Continuity of Headquarters Operations

Illustrative Vignette. It is winter, and the Washington, D.C., area is experiencing periodic snowstorms. In anticipation of another snowstorm, the enemy contaminates with plutonium oxide the Pentagon's supply of salt and sand used for clearing walkways. When the next storm occurs, the regular maintenance personnel salt and sand the sidewalks. Pentagon workers subsequently track the contamination throughout the building. The contamination spreads to individual cars and homes as workers leave at the end of the day. Some employees inadvertently inhale small amounts of plutonium oxide while others ingest contamination after handling their shoes. The conspirators announce their attack to CNN. Subsequent investigation confirms their allegations.

Key Consequences. Once the attack is confirmed, the consequences are profound. Although the attack forces the Army and all other resident agencies in the Pentagon to activate alternative sites to carry out their essential functions, the attack also has wider-reaching consequences. It is not only a military attack, it is also an area crisis. All facilities—automobiles, the Metro (subway and bus) system, homes, convenience stores, dry cleaners—that Pentagon employees may have visited after becoming contaminated must be screened for plutonium. Contaminated areas must be cleaned up. Everyone who entered the building after the contamination must be decontaminated and medically examined to ascertain the level of plutonium exposure they have experienced. Key personnel, therefore, may not be immediately available to man an alternative site. Other officials at other headquarters would have to perform the Headquarters, Department of the Army, role, at least on an interim basis. Moreover, reestablishing DoD functionality would be one of many competing priorities. FEMA, local governments, and other agencies could have requirements that would interfere with reestablishing headquarters' capabilities. For example, quarantine of the Pentagon could prevent vehicles from coming and going. Those employees remaining on-site might not be allowed to leave until they were decontaminated. Safes and file cabinets containing essential records might not be immediately removable until they have been examined for contamination.

Key Tasks. The broadest task is area emergency response to ascertain the scope and extent of contamination, begin cleanup of contaminated areas and medical treatment for the population exposed to the plutonium. Survey and monitoring would be a massive undertaking because Pentagon employees commute to their homes in two states and the District of Columbia. Many officials routinely make day trips to other headquarters and agencies elsewhere and thus could spread the contamination widely. The Metro would have to be shut down so its cars and stations could be inspected and decontaminated. Businesses, supermarkets—every place that might have been patronized by a contaminated person—would have to be surveyed. Buildings found to be heavily contaminated might have to be sealed off permanently or demolished and their residue treated as hazardous material.

Plutonium exposure is potentially very dangerous, requiring everyone who might have had contact with it to be examined. Because symptoms of radiation damage might not manifest themselves immediately, public health officials would have to monitor a relatively large population for the effects of plutonium.

Finding the attackers would be a high-priority task for law enforcement.

Key Army Tasks. The Army would face multiple responsibilities. It would have to provide additional medical personnel, NBC specialists, and units to assist with the aftermath of the attack. The job of determining the extent of the contamination would require large numbers of radiological monitors. The Army might also reinforce local hospital staffs with its medical personnel. Army units might be required to help secure contaminated facilities until they can be dealt with.

The Army would also have to provide medical assessment and care to its civilian and uniformed personnel and their families that were exposed to the plutonium. The Army might provide some of this care through its established network of hospitals and clinics. Primus and Tricare facilities would also contribute.

At the same time, the Army would have to reestablish its headquarters functions somewhere else. Other officials would have to stand in for those members of the senior leadership incapacitated by the attack or detained as part of the initial response. While reestablishing its headquarters, the Army must expect other key installations to come under attack and respond accordingly with heightened security postures.

Key Issues for Army DOTLMS. The Army has long practiced moving headquarters and handing off missions between headquarters and has doctrine to inform the task. Organizationally, the Army has other headquarters—Training and Doctrine Command and Forces Command, for example—that could take on the mission of Headquarters,

Department of the Army, in an emergency. The problem comes from the complexity of the circumstances represented in the vignette, which would generate competing priorities for the Army. The service would simultaneously face reestablishing its headquarters, caring for its contaminated personnel and their families, fulfilling its responsibilities to assist DoD, cooperating with emergency officials in managing the contamination in the Pentagon, and supporting the clean-up.

The training and materiel challenges are less about skills and more about the scope of the problem. Army NBC personnel are trained and equipped to monitor for radiation and other forms of contamination. But if plutonium were distributed as envisioned in the scenario, the scale of the monitoring and cleanup problem could be huge.

BORDER AND COASTAL DEFENSE

Illustrative Vignette. A credible threat is received that enemy agents will attempt to cross the Mexico-U.S. border bringing a nuclear device into the United States. They select a remote site in the desert far from towns or legal border crossings.

Key Consequences. The enemy agents also create a base of operations, including safe houses, communications, bank accounts, and other support systems necessary to sustain his operations in the United States. The FBI asks DoD for assistance in identifying the infiltration route into the United States and tracking those who use it.

The DOD creates JTF Border Protect. The task force includes Air National Guard, Army National Guard and active-duty Army elements. The National Guard elements provide surveillance and communications capabilities. The Air National Guard operates four AC-130 gunships equipped with low-light-level television for detailed, local area surveillance. The Army National Guard flies four OV-1D Mohawk surveillance aircraft equipped with side-looking airborne radar for deeper surveillance along the border. A corps-level signal battalion provides the communications. The Army National Guard also provides imagery support for wide-area surveillance of the frontier. A military intelligence battalion installs and monitors unattended ground sensors in those areas where enemy agents are likely to or suspected of crossing the border as a means to alert law enforcement officials of an intrusion. The active component forces include 10 personnel for the JTF headquarters and a six-man liaison party located with the FBI.

Key Tasks. The first task is to conduct border surveillance and begin intelligence collection that will lead to identification and arrest of the actors involved. Law enforcement deploys its military surveillance assets in accordance with its best intelligence. The surveillance platforms provide capabilities to detect nuclear weapons at a great distance and "cue" NEST and FBI responses on the ground. Law enforcement officers then move to intercept the enemy agents.

The coordination involved between surveillance systems and law enforcement is critical. The military elements of the equation must provide real-time alerts and warnings so that the law enforcement elements can respond in a timely fashion. The coordination involved demands a robust communications suite linking the military to the civilian elements. The surveillance platforms must be able to steer the ground elements to a successful interception of the enemy.

Key Army Tasks. Other Army units in addition to military intelligence could support border surveillance and reconnaissance by making their organic battlefield surveillance systems (e.g., ground surveillance radar, night vision equipment) available to law enforcement efforts. Once it becomes clear that the enemy threatens military installations and operations, Army counterintelligence can assist.

Current and Needed Army Capabilities. There is no shortage of useful capabilities. Reconnaissance units, target acquisition batteries, and aviation units with side-looking airborne radar, among others, could offer support to law enforcement officials for border surveillance. The Army's Intelligence and Security Command could cooperate with the FBI on domestic intelligence matters.

Key Issues for Army DOTLMS. JTF-6 and military support to counterdrug operations have resolved some but not all of the issues associated with border surveillance. The shooting of a teenage goatherd along the Mexico-Texas border last year by a U.S. Marine has reopened the policy question of whether military personnel should be deployed for direct observation and protection of the border.

An initiative that might prove less controversial would limit Army units to performing wartime reconnaissance, surveillance, and target acquisition missions in support of law enforcement. Such a policy, designed in part to keep the Army at arms-length from the intruders, would maximize wartime DOTLMS and require fewer other preparations.

Chapter Nine

ANALYSIS OF ARMY DOTLMS

Chapter Eight described a number of illustrative planning vignettes that illuminated the sorts of capabilities that the Army might need to provide under different circumstances. This chapter analyzes Army DOTLMS and addresses the Army's preparedness to undertake the missions identified in the vignettes. The chapter also addresses the question of adequacy of forces—whether the Army has enough of the right types of units for the likely homeland security contingencies.

The analysis began with an assessment of the DOTLMS in each of the four homeland security task areas that are the focus of this report:

- Domestic preparedness for WMD terrorism.

- COG.

- Continuity of operations, including force protection, critical asset assurance, critical infrastructure protection, and the continuity of headquarters operations.

- Border and coastal defense.

This analysis suggested that the Army's DOTLMS have not been fully optimized for the challenges of homeland security, although areas of high capability exist. Figure 9.1 depicts our assessment of the current state of Army DOTLMS, with dark gray indicating a "high" level of capability, light gray a "medium" level, and black a "low" level.

The figure suggests that the greatest shortfalls are found in the continuity of operations areas of critical asset assurance and critical infra-

RAND*MR1251-9.1*

Task Area	D	O	T	L	M	S
Domestic preparedness						
COO						
Force protection						
CAA						
CIP						
HQDA CO						
COG						
Border and coastal defense						

Figure 9.1—Summary of Homeland Security DOTLMS Status

structure protection and, for these two areas, in the realm of training. Where DOTLMS were assessed as less than high we then performed a screening analysis to try to identify cost-effective (i.e., high-payoff, low-cost) options for improving the relevant DOTLMS.

Next is the detailed evaluation of the DOTLMS for each homeland security task area. Where the assessment leads to a grading that is less than high, we describe the sorts of actions that would be necessary to bring them up to a high level, and their cost-effectiveness.

DOCTRINE

Domestic Preparedness

Overall, doctrine for domestic preparedness is rated high because, although the entire body of doctrine necessary for this task area has yet been developed, TRADOC is well on the way. Task lists are under study and other progress is evident. Of particular importance will be the work already underway to develop the doctrinal underpinnings for the Response Task Forces (RTFs) and, if it is actually fielded, doctrine for Joint Task Force–Civil Support (JTF-CS).

The Army conception of WMD CSTs is in part based on the premise that the service must have a reconnaissance element establish requirements before attempting to dispatch substantial response elements to the scene of an incident. This notion, while sound in many circumstances, may be unfounded, given the need for prompt response to chemical events, the fact that other authorities—local and state—with appropriate training will most likely already be on-scene and able to provide credible assessments of initial requirements, and that biological events are most likely to be initially detected by health care providers.

COG

Army doctrine for federal COG activities is rated high. This doctrine should be reviewed periodically to ensure that it is relevant to emergent threats, however. Doctrine also should be reviewed to ensure the adequacy of local and state COG operations, at the very least, doctrine to ensure the speedy reestablishment of civilian governmental functions.

Continuity of Operations

Evaluation. *Force protection.* Doctrine for force protection is rated medium because additional doctrinal development is necessary to treat the critical issues of self-defense practices and cooperation with civilian security forces during movement to ports of embarkation.

Critical Asset Assurance/Critical Infrastructure Protection (CAAP/CIP). Critical asset assurance and critical infrastructure protection doctrine are assessed as medium because, although progress has been made in this area (e.g., creation of the ACERT), much remains to be done. Although the DoD instructions make clear the areas included in CAAP and CIP, funding has been tight, and the Army has not evolved doctrine for either of them.

For example, no clear doctrinal basis exists for identifying which facilities and systems are mission-critical, for performing the necessary threat and risk assessments that would help in targeting mitigation efforts, or cost-effectiveness or tradeoff analyses to determine the most attractive of the available options. Neither is there clear guidance on how best to hedge against the possibility of interruptions that might arise from the failure of supporting civilian infrastructures (e.g., through the establishment of stockpiles or inventories of needed materiel) or how best to speed the post-incident reconstitution of supporting civilian services. Finally, it is unclear what if any role the Army should have in protecting civilian information infrastructure. Our view is that such a role will be the exception rather than the rule.

Continuity of Headquarters Operations. Army Headquarters continuity of operations doctrine is evaluated as high because doctrine and decades of Army field practices have established the basis for reconstituting the functions of any key headquarters. Nevertheless, the unique functions of Army Headquarters (e.g., its Title 10 functions raising, training, and equipping forces) and the size and scope of any reconstitution effort place a premium on exercising plans for continuity of operations. Furthermore, because most of the doctrine and planning for this area were aimed at addressing continuity of operations in the context of a nuclear exchange, doctrine and planning should be reviewed to ensure that they remain salient with regard to emerging threats.

Cost-Effectiveness Considerations. *Force protection.* Force protection doctrine currently emphasizes those actions necessary to protect U.S. forces overseas while very little attention is paid to force protection requirements for the fort-to-port deployment sequence.

To overcome this shortfall, doctrine should generate more guidance on self-defense appropriate for CONUS. The practices outlined in the guidance must be both legal (not overstepping the bounds between self-defense and police activities) and useful. Doctrine should adapt those tactical practices that could improve force protection at home station when confronting an enemy campaign plan.

In some instances, a need will arise for additional guidance. For example, normal tactical convoy security practices—rules of deadly force—would have to be modified to fit behind the primary security offered by civilian law enforcement. In other instances, local commanders must be made more aware of their options. For example, doctrine might stress the potential desirability of taking precautionary measures when alerted to the possibility of attack. Units in their predeployment load-out areas might deploy their NBC detection equipment or increase their overall protective posture in accordance with the best current information. Or, if the concern runs toward food tampering, unit veterinarians might be detailed to inspect food service at the deployment airfield or port. Alternatively, packaged rations might be issued. Finally, there is almost sure to be a need to jointly develop procedures and doctrine with the Air Force and Navy regarding CONUS-based force protection roles and missions, particularly at points of embarkation.

Fundamentally, doctrine must provide a basis for prudent military actions for safeguarding Army forces in the United States, in conformity with peacetime law, while confronting a concerted enemy campaign aimed at attacking those forces.

The principal costs in upgrading doctrine fall in three areas: arriving at agreement with civil and police authorities on an appropriate role for deploying units; developing new doctrine, as required, to fulfill that role; and screening and selecting current tactical practices and modifying them to make them suitable for the new force protection tasks.

Any agreement with civil authorities must address the difference between today's understanding of the use of deadly force in direct self-defense and the potential requirements that arise from facing down an enemy campaign carried out in the United States. For example, will units awaiting deployment be allowed to conduct patrols to increase their own security? If so, must they wait until they are fired on before they can use deadly force? New doctrine and rules of engagement may need to contemplate other means of providing force protection—use of less-than-lethal-force weapons, for example. The principal task confronting the adaptation of common tactical practices for CONUS must deal with the reasonable public expectation that recourse to the use of force will be reserved for civilian law enforcement organizations. That is, the public is completely unaccustomed to war on its doorstep. Doctrine should therefore consider what steps make sense for coordinating with law enforcement officials and informing the public under circumstances where the Army must combat enemy special operations forces and similar hostile military elements on U.S. soil.

CAAP/CIP. The whole approach to critical infrastructure protection makes crafting appropriate doctrine very difficult. At its heart, the problem is a lack of DOD-wide consensus on what constitutes critical infrastructure, no standardized procedures for threat and risk assessments or cost-effectiveness and tradeoff analyses in the area, and decentralized interpretation and execution of guidance.

In fairness to the Army, the problems in this area arise at least in part because CAAP/CIP has been somewhat of an unfunded mandate. They also arise from a rather unrealistic perception that appears to be widely held in DoD, that commercial organizations will make investments to improve the security of critical infrastructure on some basis other than the business case that arises from risk assessments. Although the Army (or DoD) may have influence in cases where it is a large customer, in other—perhaps most—cases, neither mandates nor sufficiently compelling incentives may be possible.

Because OSD is currently reevaluating CAAP/CIP and Executive Branch responsibilities in this area, however, and because it appears that funding may be forthcoming for protecting mission-critical systems, the Army needs to address these issues to ensure that continuity activities are analytically justified and well-coordinated, so that available resources are well spent

Army doctrine should, to a greater extent than the CAAP program did, emphasize centralized direction, coordination, and monitoring to ensure that vulnerabilities to Army-wide mission-critical facilities and systems are treated consistently across the Department of the Army and that a realistic appraisal of the options available to enhance the security of supporting civilian infrastructures is made.

Discussions with DOMS officials indicate that installation commanders tend to be fairly parochial and short-sighted in their appreciation of what is critical. Within DoD, the process of nominating various assets as "critical" has produced an uneven collection of assets that the executive agency is responsible for surveying and, potentially, safeguarding.

To be assessed as high, doctrine for CAAP/CIP must somehow describe an Army role appropriate to safeguarding all the various types of infrastructure that potentially could be identified as "critical," as well as the nature of any supporting infrastructure (e.g., civilian public utilities). The appropriate doctrine would have to address both the Army's peacetime role, in which it is more or less a consultant to the infrastructure owners, and the wartime role, in which the Army is expected to take active measures to safeguard critical infrastructure in the face of an enemy campaign intended to attack, disrupt, and destroy it.

Sound doctrine also must establish the practices Army units follow. Some types of infrastructure will prove more straightforward to deal with than others. For example, it is not at all clear that the Army has leading-edge expertise in safeguarding computer and communications systems. Its ACERT notwithstanding, given the rapid changes in software and processing systems—and the constant evolution and adaptation of computer threats—the Army should not view itself as a consultant or protector for commercial systems. Therefore, doctrine must establish for the Army a reasonable role, consistent with DoD directives and mindful of its ability to influence civilian actors. That is, the Army's doctrine should play to the service's strengths and steer clear of those areas in which its expertise may be highly circumscribed (e.g., in caring for its own computer and communications systems).

The principal costs associated with appropriate improvements in doctrine will arise from two areas.

First, the governmental and civil sectors must reach a consensus about what constitutes critical infrastructure. Although the Army can embark on some missions without a clear consensus, without one in this case, the danger is that some asset that ought to be included might be omitted. Despite the current emphasis in the critical infrastructure debate on computers and networked electronic systems, other infrastructure may also be critical. Doctrine must anticipate the need to provide a wide variety of safeguards, perhaps including guarding physical facilities but also extending to providing other sorts of security—perhaps encryption, for example. The Army will probably face a major educational challenge in the effort necessary to acquaint the rest of the governmental and civil sectors with its capabilities and limitations for critical infrastructure protection. The danger of unwanted outcomes also exists. For example, in the early days of World War II, many industrial officials argued for Army units to secure their plants. The point is, in undertaking the educational mission necessary to build a consensus for the Army role, the Army must be prepared to deal with bad ideas that might impinge on its primary warfighting role.

Second, as just noted, critical infrastructure responsibilities must somehow be reconciled with deployment and other warfighting tasks. Doctrine should address the critical infrastructure protection responsibilities of the table of organization and equipment (TO&E) and the table of distribution and allowances parts of the Army in such a way that the TO&E forces are not distracted by infrastructure protection tasks when they should be preparing to fight.

The use of reserve component forces may be particularly appropriate in protecting such mission-critical facilities as power projection platforms, and options to involve the Guard and Reserve should be actively explored.

Border and Coastal Defense

Evaluation. Border and coastal defense doctrine is rated medium. Although doctrine already establishes a basis for cooperation and joint operations with other services, doctrine should also specifically treat the Army role in support of the U.S. Customs Service, ATF, Coast Guard, and other agencies involved in border and coastal defense. For example, doctrine should indicate the level of involvement appropriate for troops from the general-purpose force (e.g., directly confronting intruders or merely supporting law enforcement officers) and procedures for resolving any friction that might arise.

Cost-Effectiveness Considerations. The doctrinal shortcoming attending border and coastal defense reflects the policy-level ambiguities surrounding the question. Doctrine can only mature when the Army receives appropriate policy guidance to indicate what specific role the service will have, its level of interaction with the civilian populace, and the specific types of support it will provide to other federal and local agencies. Put another way, the Army could play any number of roles in border and coastal defense, depending on the charter worked out with the FBI, the Customs Service, and others. The Army might support at arms-length, by providing surveillance and communications, or play a more direct role, depending on the latitude available in the law and the preference of other agencies, such as the Department of Justice. The doctrinal challenge is to develop appropriate practices, tactics, techniques, and procedures for whatever role emerges.

ORGANIZATIONS

Organizations deserve careful scrutiny for several of the task areas.

Domestic Preparedness

Evaluation. Domestic preparedness organizations currently rated medium in part because of the ambiguity surrounding the utility of the WMD CSTs. A broader problem arises because the actual capacity of civilian organizations to deliver services is unmeasured, so the need for Army organizations is difficult to ascertain. The question of "missioned" forces for domestic preparedness can only be answered when the size of specific gaps in civilian capabilities is understood. Continued reliance on RTFs and JTFs—organizational approaches that have proven their worth responding to individual events— should be reviewed to determine whether these organizational forms are optimal for combating a protracted enemy campaign.

There also are some reasons for concern about the WMD CST. Although the WMD CST can perhaps be justified on the basis of providing force protection to the follow-on incident response capabilities of the RTFs, it appears to be of questionable value to localities and states. In large part, this is because it effectively lacks the key sort of capacity (i.e., decontamination) that would make the greatest contribution. It is also because it is unclear that the WMD CST can be on-scene in the four hours claimed. We have seen little evidence that the WMD CSTs can provide the claimed 24-hour-a-day, seven-days-a week quick response capability; that sufficient Air National Guard or other mobility assets will be maintained at the necessary state of readiness and alert to move the WMD CST to the incident site in the four-hour window; or that the WMD CST will be maintained at a sufficiently high state of readiness to be on-scene in four hours.

Accordingly, the Army should examine closely the WMD CST concept; its personnel, readiness, and mobility requirements; and the full costs associated with a responsive WMD CST. The Army also should explore the possibility of a different sort of WMD CST, providing a rapid assessment and initial *decontamination* element that would exercise with state and local first responders for incidents ranging from standard hazmat incidents to WMD incidents. The Army also should examine more closely how the integration of the Pennsylvania WMD CST into "all hazards" responses, ranging from hazmat to WMD, may offer a good model for integrating WMD CSTs into state and local response systems, which might serve as a better model in terms of ensuring the WMD CST's involvement in incident responses.

Cost-Effectiveness Considerations. The trouble with the organizations for domestic preparedness results from uncertainties about the type, frequency, and magnitude of events; shortfalls in civilian capacity to respond to them; and the resulting net requirement for support to domestic preparedness that devolves to the Army and other military forces. For the Army, the problem extends to options for providing supporting capabilities.

To achieve a high assessment, the Army must be able to base its decisions about further organizational requirements on sound threat and risk assessments and cost-effectiveness and trade-off analyses. These must be calculated at a level of detail that will allow the Army to understand whether it, among all possible providers, is capable of providing the most cost-effective capabilities in an area and, ultimately, "how much is enough." For example, the Army needs to understand better whether WMD CSTs or some other organization (perhaps chemical companies optimized for civilian support requirements) are better situated to enhance first providers' capabilities.

The second issue the Army must deal with to achieve a high assessment is maintaining the RTF/JTF framework as the primary basis for facing an enemy campaign plan. Although the approach makes sense as a means for dealing with individual consequence management missions, these organizations appear inadequate for confronting an enemy campaign in the United States. To garner a high assessment in organizing for domestic preparedness, the Army must consider a total organization, complete with planning and budgeting arms as well as action arms so that, collectively, the various functions of a U.S. countercampaign can be planned, resourced, executed, and controlled. These organizations must also be adequate in number and capability to handle a threat campaign of multiple incidents, spread over time and space.

The price of attaining a high rating for organizations is fairly steep because it involves a level of problem-solving and local-federal, civil-military cooperation rarely encountered. To ascertain which organizations are necessary for domestic preparedness, the Army and its interlocutors must come to a common understanding of the total requirement to respond to an enemy domestic campaign. That task in hand, the next requirement is to establish how much response capacity exists in the civilian sector and the requirement for military capacity to round it out. Finally, it requires the Army to develop simple, industrial measures of capacity for decontamination, patient treatment, victim housing, and similar services so that civilian communities that consume Army domestic preparedness support have a common basis for ordering help.

COG

Organization for COG rates a high assessment because the program is long-standing and sized to the perceived threat. The program has undergone a number of adjustments since 1989 and could expand if future threats warranted doing so. Army COG organizations should be reviewed to ensure that they are relevant to emerging threats.

Continuity of Operations

Evaluation. *Force protection.* Organizations for force protection currently are rated high, but, if the immediacy of the threat grows, installations should consider the value of installation reaction forces to protect the fort-to-port sequence and potential for reserve component forces to enhance security at mission-critical facilities, such as power-projection platforms.

Critical Asset Assurance. Critical asset assurance organizations are judged medium because of the high degree of uncertainty surrounding what is critical. Until the Army garners further intelligence that enables it to discern the priorities enemy campaign plans place on attacking various assets and relies on threat and risk assessments to assist in prioritizing mitigation efforts, the service will be unprepared to create organizations to protect its own critical assets and to exercise its responsibilities as the executive agent for the CAA program in DoD.

Critical Infrastructure Protection. Organizations for critical infrastructure protection are assessed as medium for basically the same reasons. Consideration of likely enemy campaign plans is essential to understanding the value of additional specialized organizations for critical infrastructure protection (e.g., CERTs).

Continuity of Headquarters Operations. Organization for Department of the Army Headquarters continuity of operations earns a high rating because an abundance of four-star headquarters could assume Department of the Army Headquarters functions on an interim basis. Both TRADOC and FORSCOM are reasonably available. Officer assignment practices make it highly likely that a significant percentage of officers at these headquarters would have Army Headquarters experience, making them suitable temporary substitutes or staff augmentees.

Cost-Effectiveness Considerations. *CAAP/CIP.* CAAP and CIP, although distinct from each other, share common problems insofar as organizations go. In order to be rated high, they both need a clear definition of what "critical" means. Until a common picture of critical infrastructure and assets emerges, both task areas will find it difficult to determine how many and what types of organizations are necessary to fulfill the Army's responsibilities. Both programs will remain medium until a better idea of vulnerabilities and enemy interest in various facilities emerges. Only when the dimensions of the threat are better understood will it be possible to ascertain whether the current organizations (e.g., JTF-CND) are sufficient or not.

The costs of addressing the current uncertainties about critical assets and infrastructure are considerable. In the military sector, for example, it will be necessary to assess power projection installations and facilities to determine which are mission-critical and what additional force protection capabilities are necessary. Doing so means understanding the role of civilian utilities and infrastructure as well as on-post assets. Understanding must also be comprehensive. It cannot be overly focused on computer resources to the exclusion of potentially important hardware and facilities. In the civilian sector, a similar survey is essential to understanding those resources central to the functioning of society.

Intelligence must evolve to provide a clearer sense of the threat and potential enemy capabilities for attack. This task could be especially demanding for computer and network security because the attackers themselves could be insular and difficult to identify, much less collect against.

Finally, the Army may have to build a consensus with the civilian sector about what the service can and cannot help to protect. By understanding with greater specificity what the civilian sector will demand of it, the Army will then be in a position to determine the size, type, characteristics, and number of organizations it will need to fulfill its responsibilities for CAAP and CIP.

Border and Coastal Defense

Organization for border and coastal defense is assessed as high because the tasks involved suit mainstream Army tactical units. Most maneuver units are designed to occupy or control terrain and so are well designed for this task area.

TRAINING

Training contains the most shortcomings across the homeland security task areas.

Domestic Preparedness

Evaluation. In domestic preparedness training, the Army is rated medium. Civilian authorities expect Army units to be prepared to handle tasks that local emergency workers are not: large numbers of contaminated corpses, for example. No evidence exists that mainstream Army units are trained for this task. Neither is it clear that civilian authorities and the Army are generally in agreement on the conditions and standards for accomplishing the job. Put another way, civil authorities and the Army might have different notions about how some tasks would be carried out. Civilians may expect individual treatment for the dead, while the Army may expect to treat them en masse.

Our concerns about the WMD CST suggest that it will be quite important for the WMD CSTs to exercise with local and state first responders to establish whether they are as responsive and capable as they need to be. This training and exercising should be an "all hazards" curriculum and include training across the full spectrum of potential operations, from standard hazmat incidents to chemical and biological WMD incidents.

Also of concern in the domestic preparedness area is the possibility of confusion regarding the scope and applicability of the Posse Comitatus Act and the exceptions that have been specified in congressional or executive action. There were indications of confusion regarding the applicability and constraints imposed by the Posse Comitatus Act in Joint Task Force–Los Angeles (JTF-LA) in 1992 that suggest to us that additional attention should be given to curriculum development, education, and training regarding the circumstances under which specific restrictions apply when National Guard forces are acting in their state and federal capacity and when other Army forces are acting in a federal capacity. See Appendix D, "Overview of the Posse Comitatus Act," for a more detailed discussion.

Cost-Effectiveness Considerations. The concern leading to a medium assessment of domestic preparedness arises from some of the scenarios about WMD. There appears to be a gap between civilian expectations and Army capabilities for dealing with WMD contingencies. For example, in questioning participants in local exercises, a commonly held expectation is that the Army will be able to handle large numbers of contaminated human remains. Few units train for this task. Moreover, in mass casualty conditions, disposition may involve earth-moving equipment and mass burial rather than individual recovery, preparation, and burial. The concern is that communities expect a different standard of treatment and a certain level of specialized capability that does not exist in large amounts. Earning a high rating involves training together and discussing the specific requirements of various scenarios in enough detail to square civilian expectations with Army capabilities. Earning a high assessment also requires that psychological aid and bereavement programs become part of the training so the Army can assist survivors in accepting the kind of treatment their deceased relatives receive.

The costs of addressing the issue could be moderate. The Army could produce training support packages that deal with mass casualty events and its doctrine for handling them. These packages could be a resource issued independently to localities to support their training, whether or not a military unit is participating in the training event. Nevertheless, if an agreed-on set of practices is to be developed, the Army must send participants to more local training events. Through such interaction, the tasks, conditions, and standards can be discussed and if necessary, modified.

COG

Training for COG rates high. The program has operated for years at different levels of intensity, and its current posture seems appropriate for today's environment, where the threat is probably small but may be growing. If the threat becomes more immediate, it would be relatively simple to increase the training and exercises involved in this task area.

Training programs for federal COG nevertheless should be reviewed to ensure that they are relevant to the emerging threats. Training for local and state continuity of government activities also should be reviewed.

Continuity of Operations

Evaluation. *Force protection.* Training for force protection is evaluated as medium because it still emphasizes protection in the theater of operations to the exclusion of defensive measures during deployment. The Army should emphasize potential force protection tasks for units during crisis deployment, including NBC preparedness during movement and security (e.g., in the load area control center, the passenger terminal, and similar places where troops may be highly concentrated and vulnerable).

Critical Asset Assurance. Critical asset assurance is rated low because so little has been done to prepare for the relatively large number of training tasks associated with this area. Despite the existence of detailed plans at highly classified levels, critical asset dependencies are not completely understood at the installation (or Army) level and are not reflected in unit mission-essential task lists. Most installations have very limited conceptions of critical assets: the ammunition storage area, load-out rail head, and similar facilities.

Critical Infrastructure Protection. Critical infrastructure protection also rates low. This task area potentially includes many training challenges for the Army, because the service could find itself responsible for securing transportation nodes and networks off post as well as on. The Army should create a specific set of JMETLs/UJTLs as a basis for understanding all of the tasks they may have to be trained for.

Continuity of Headquarters Operations. Army Headquarters continuity of operations is rated high for the present. However, if threats become more immediate, the headquarters would benefit from a more deliberate training program that exercises the transfer of functions to another major headquarters. At present, however, the experiential base in officers who have served in the headquarters and who are also experienced in transferring control between tactical headquarters (e.g., division main and forward command posts) seems adequate.

Cost-Effectiveness Considerations. *Force protection.* Force protection training rates medium because it overemphasizes the overseas theater and pays insufficient attention to the potential requirements for force protection in the United States. To achieve a high assessment, a set of force protection practices suitable for CONUS should be developed and units indoctrinated in them.

Some force protection practices could be transplanted directly from current training. For example, training a unit to deploy its chemical agent alarms would be no different in the United States than overseas. That said, the unit commanders must be trained to think about CONUS as a part of the theater of war and to place their units in protective postures commensurate to the threat. Other costs would be slight and would involve recasting today's force protection practices for application in the United States, with special emphasis on protecting units during deployment. The training tasks would emphasize force protection at home station on alert, force protection in the railyard, force protection at the departure airfield, and force protection at the port of embarkation.

CAAP/CIP. The conceptual problems mentioned above (e.g., what is "critical") manifest themselves in training, to earn low ratings. Although some basic training tasks will transfer to CAA and CIP (i.e., those that call for Army strong-suit skills in observing, occupying, guarding, controlling, denying access), others may not. The low assessment reflects the high levels of uncertainty about training requirements and the dangers associated with that lack of knowledge. To train effectively and earn a high assessment, the Army must know what assets and infrastructure it must protect and safeguard so it can develop the appropriate set of tasks, conditions, and standards. It can then get the asset and infrastructure protection missions on the mission-essential task lists of appropriate units.

The costs in correcting the CAAP/CIP training shortcomings are minimal. Once the difficult intellectual work of identifying critical resources is done, involved parties agree on what the critical resources are that must be assured, and the Army's role is agreed on (e.g., will the Army really play a direct role in securing the money and banking system? If so, what role?), then the Army can develop the requisite tasks, conditions, and standards for accomplishing the mission.

Border and Coastal Defense

Evaluation. Training for border and coastal defense is rated medium because the ambiguities surrounding the policy issue of the specific role that military forces should have raise questions about the adequacy of the Army's training. Although the tasks involved in border and coastal defense are mainstream Army business, it is difficult to imagine effective training to appropriate conditions and standards until the policy question surrounding the exact Army role is resolved.

Cost-Effectiveness Considerations. As noted in the earlier chapters treating border and coastal defense, the military could play any number of roles, from direct support to law enforcement to more removed roles. These ambiguities must be resolved before training can be assessed as high.

Once the role of the Army and other military forces is agreed on, the costs of addressing the associated training issues should be modest. Most of the tasks involved in border and coastal defense fall in the mainstream of Army and other service skills. If a more direct form of involvement with security emerges, training might have to expand somewhat to include use of less-than-lethal weapons. Otherwise, much of the mission-essential task list for peace support, stability, and humanitarian assistance operations can be repackaged for border and coastal defense.

LEADERSHIP

As the threats to homeland security grow or become more imminent, leadership preparation must keep pace. The professional military education system for officers and NCOs should consider which homeland security task areas should be dealt with in leadership training and how they should be addressed—in institutional training, unit schools, distance learning, or some other mode of instruction.

Domestic Preparedness

Leadership for domestic preparedness is currently assessed as high because the basic leadership skills in the officer and NCO corps have served well in the domestic preparedness and disaster relief events that served as case studies.

COG

Evaluation. Leadership for COG is rated medium because, although the COG program has a record of sound training, few officers are exposed to the notion until they serve in the Pentagon. The subject might be treated at the War College and as part of the curriculum in the Army Management College. Curricula should be reviewed to ensure that leadership programs address the sorts of issues that could arise in the emerging threat environment, as well as issues related to local and state level continuity of government.

Cost-Effectiveness Considerations. Few officers are familiar with COG before assignment to the National Capital region. The overall program is not as robust as it was prior to 1991. To overcome this rating, COG requires a basic introduction among more senior field grade officers so that an adequate pool of leaders is available as a hedge against surprise.

The cost of hedging would seem to be slight. The War College might provide a special instructional module to familiarize those for whom the next assignment will be Washington. Civilian leaders could be likewise prepared at the Army Management Staff College.

Continuity of Operations

Evaluation. *Force protection.* Leadership in force protection is rated medium for an easily correctable reason. The current mind set of most leaders emphasizes the overseas, deployed nature of force protection. The Army could quickly correct this by teaching force protection at officer advanced courses and the basic NCO course, where the curriculum could treat explicitly the homeland security and overseas dimensions of the question.

Critical Asset Assurance. Leadership in critical asset assurance is medium because midlevel Army leaders receive so little preparation for understanding these issues. Most conceive of critical assets as their motor pools and the major items of equipment in them or the post ammunition dump. Few members of the service in tactical units have been exposed to the CAAP. This condition could easily be remedied with professional military education. Indeed, it might be a suitable topic for the precommand course and Sergeants Major Academy.

Critical Infrastructure Protection. Critical infrastructure protection leadership is assessed as medium for the same reasons. Few officers and NCOs encounter the issue unless they work at installation headquarters or in major command headquarters that must confront the matter. Education again is the remedy, perhaps as part of the initial orientation for newly assigned personnel in jobs where CIP figures prominently. The Army should consider leaders' needs for specific types of civilian technical expertise, especially for such areas as information assurance.

Continuity of Headquarters Operations. Leadership for headquarters continuity of operations is rated high. Training, problem-solving skills, and other attributes of Army leaders seem well suited to this task area.

Cost-Effectiveness Considerations. *Force protection.* Concerns about leadership in force protection, reflected in its medium rating, involve the mental orientation that surrounds this task area. Force protection in the United States tends to address two programs: operations security (OPSEC) and subversion and espionage directed against the U.S. Army. Otherwise, most officers and NCOs conceive of force protection issues as matter for deployed forces. To earn a high rating, leadership must expand the current conception of force protection and cause Army leaders to consider the impact of an enemy campaign in CONUS on their force protection requirements.

If and when the threat becomes acute, leadership can address it by adjusting professional military education courses and the distance learning curriculum appropriately. The basic NCO course and the officer advanced courses may be appropriate venues for in-residence instruction. Leaders at all levels may eventually need instruction, however, so distance learning programs should also be contemplated.

CAAP/CIP. The medium rating reflects the lack of common understanding of critical assets and infrastructure. To overcome this rating, leadership must prepare officers and NCOs with an appropriate appreciation of the dependencies their units have on installation and civilian utilities, networks, computers, and facilities for operational success.

The costs involved in addressing CAAP are probably minimal. Curriculum adjustments in the precommand course for officers and the Sergeants Major Academy for NCOs could in short order provide a common perception of the issue and an appropriate appreciation of critical local dependencies. CIP will require a somewhat different approach. In addition to curriculum adjustments, for officials in positions involving critical infrastructure, they may need more specialized preparation. Special coursework could be designed to meet the needs of officers in CIP-related positions.

Border and Coastal Defense

Border and coastal defense are rated high because the vast majority of Army officers and NCOs are well-prepared for mainstream Army work like this.

MATERIEL

Human performance in most missions can be enhanced or undermined by the quality and readiness of the materiel supporting it. Materiel considerations appear in several task areas.

Domestic Preparedness

Evaluation. Materiel for domestic preparedness earns a medium rating because of four critical uncertainties.

The first uncertainty involves the amount of actual decontamination capability that the WMD CST brings to an incident. With a potentially modest expenditure, at least in terms of equipment, the WMD could be transformed from a rapid assessment and initial *detection* element to a rapid assessment and initial *decontamination* unit, retaining its assessment and detection capabilities, while enhancing its decontamination capabilities.

The second uncertainty involves the availability of mobility assets to move the WMD CST (and other Army response elements) to the scene of the incident. Mobility assets, predominantly Air National Guard or other Air Force airlifters probably will need to be maintained on a reasonably high state of alert, and quick, short-haul transportation will be needed to move the WMD CSTs to these mobility assets.

The third uncertainty involves the stockpiling and movement of emergency stocks of consumables that will be needed in incident responses. The uncertainty reflects the paucity of information about local stockpiles and the need for additional capabilities, provided by the Army. Site surveys to establish requirements and provisioning needs are essential to understand where, what, and how much in terms of Army stocks—if any—should be positioned to support domestic preparedness.

The fourth uncertainty is related to the first—as RDT&E yields much less costly chemical and biological detection equipment, it will be possible to distribute the equipment widely to first responders. This is likely to further blur the distinction between the WMD CST's assessment and detection capabilities and those of first responders and increasingly call into question the value of a WMD CST that has no decontamination capabilities.

Cost-Effectiveness Considerations. Because a clear picture of the cost-effectiveness of the overall (local, state, and federal) response system is lacking, it is difficult to establish whether the costs that would be incurred to address each of these areas would be worth the benefits.

While the costs of transforming the WMD CST to give it decontamination capabilities could be relatively modest, the costs associated with giving the WMD CST a high enough state of readiness for 24-hour-a-day, seven-days-a-week response capabilities, and providing it with the necessary mobility assets could be quite substantial. The Army should look more closely at the missions and materiel requirements of the WMD CST.

COG

COG is rated high.

Continuity of Operations

Evaluation. *Force protection.* Force protection materiel is rated high.

Critical Asset Assurance. CAAP materiel is assessed as medium. The rating reflects uncertainty about the appropriateness of Army equipment for defending the full suite of critical assets. The uncertainty results in part from the lack of thorough understanding about the Army's dependencies.

Critical Infrastructure Protection. Critical infrastructure protection materiel rates medium according to the same logic. On one hand, JTF Computer Network Defense, a DoD asset, exercises defensive and offensive responsibility over all Defense Department networks, including the Army's. At the same time, however, great uncertainty exists about attacker ways and means, making it very difficult to be confident that materiel for CIP is entirely adequate to the challenge. Particularly important in this arena will be RDT&E that enhances the ability to detect intrusions and execute the necessary counter-measures.

Continuity of Headquarters Operations. Materiel sufficiency in support of headquarters continuity of operations is evaluated as high.

Cost-Effectiveness Considerations. *CAAP/CIP.* Earlier reservations about the lack of full appreciation of Army dependencies manifest themselves here in a medium rating for materiel. This rating is reinforced by the lack of concrete intelligence about potential enemies and their campaign plans. The Army cannot say where it needs materiel solutions to assist in safeguarding its critical assets and infrastructure because it lacks intelligence about who might attack or what means the attackers might employ. To overcome this medium assessment, the Army must more fully understand what constitutes its critical assets and infrastructure. The Army also needs better intelligence on enemy campaign plans that target critical assets. Finally, it should consider the sorts of hedging options that can be taken in advance of an attack on critical infrastructure to weaken its consequence (e.g., enhancing stockpiles or inventories of needed consumables).

Costs in addressing the shortcomings could be relatively high. Many of the nonstate actors posited by the Defense Science Board and similar studies as future adversaries are shadowy and elusive and do not necessarily lend themselves to traditional intelligence collection techniques. In some instances, because their means of attack may be so nontraditional, knowing such basic military intelligence information as order of battle is not very helpful in understanding their campaign plans and objectives. The essential elements of information for protecting against critical asset and infrastructure attack could be quite different. For example, knowing the specific assets that are attractive targets to an enemy could demand tactical intelligence specificity at the strategic intelligence level. Only when intelligence develops in such detail can the Army understand with high confidence what the materiel requirements for safeguarding its infrastructure and other assets might be.

Border and Coastal Defense

Evaluation. Border and coastal defense materiel is rated medium. As discussed in the earlier analysis of DOTLMS for this task area, the basis for the assessment lies in the ambiguity surrounding the Army's ultimate responsibilities. For example, if policy decisions lead to a larger and more direct role in border and coastal defense, less-than-lethal weapons and specialized communications suites able to network with key civilian agencies should be explored.

Cost-Effectiveness. This task area rates a medium because of the ambiguity about the Army's role and responsibilities. To overcome the rating, the Army must have a clearer notion of exactly what type of role it will play and what specific responsibilities it might have. For example, if the Army is to play a more direct role in border and coastal defense, then materiel solutions to provide less-than-lethal weapons might be appropriate. The interagency process must first settle on a clear set of responsibilities for the Army.

The associated materiel could be substantial and could involve the sort of scale of materiel needs associated with the military involvement in the war on drugs. Nevertheless, it is not clear that the Army would incur these costs. For example, while materiel needs could include capabilities to provide long-range detection of chemical, biological, radiological, or nuclear materials before they cross U.S. borders, it seems more likely that the U.S. Customs Service, the Coast Guard, the INS, the FAA, or even the Navy or Air Force, might have a more substantial role in the employment of these technologies. In our view, the answer to this is more of a policy question that will probably reflect the preferences of the Executive Branch and Legislative Branch more than anything else.

SOLDIER SYSTEMS

Soldier systems generally appear well prepared for homeland security, with two exceptions.

Domestic Preparedness

Evaluation. Domestic preparedness soldier systems are assessed as medium. The rating results from concerns that, while most demands on soldiers in domestic preparedness events will be similar to those they prepare for, certain events, especially those involving mass killings, may find soldiers less than fully prepared. Needs include medical readiness, psychological preparedness for operations at home, and indoctrination in a code of conduct appropriate for operations among the nation's citizens.

Cost-Effectiveness Considerations. Little has been done to equip soldiers for the stresses and special conditions of supporting a mass casualties event. Soldiers are prepared for overseas deployment in part by a code of conduct that indoctrinates them in the proper treatment of combatants and noncombatants. No such code of conduct exists to guide soldiers' actions at home in dealing with civilians, police and rescue officials, and others they may encounter at the scene. In a similar way, soldiers are conditioned to the sights and sounds of the battlefield through, among other things, combined arms live fire exercises. Although these exercises have their limitations, they provide soldiers with some basic notion of what to expect in terms of noise and confusion in combat. No similar institutional preparation exists to support domestic preparedness response forces.

Overcoming today's shortfalls would be relatively inexpensive. A domestic code of conduct could be fashioned to parallel the points in today's code of conduct.

COG

COG is also assessed as high for soldier systems because current soldier systems seem well-suited to the individual soldier responsibilities in this task area.

Continuity of Operations

Evaluation. *Force protection.* Soldier systems for force protection are assessed as high. At an individual soldier level, countering subversion and espionage directed against the U.S. Army, OPSEC, situational awareness training, and medical readiness appear to be adequate.

Critical Asset Assurance. CAA earns a high rating for soldier systems. There appears to be no new demands on soldier systems from CAA responsibilities.

Critical Infrastructure Protection. CIP also earns a high rating for the same reasons CAA did.

Continuity of Headquarters Operations. Headquarters continuity of operations likewise earns a high rating.

Border and Coastal Defense

Evaluation. Border and coastal defense rates medium for soldier systems because of the uncertainty about the ultimate Army role in this task area and the demands it may or may not levy on soldier systems.

Cost-Effectiveness Considerations. This area reflects the uncertainties and ambiguities about what the Army's ultimate role and responsibilities will be for border and coastal defense. Whether the Army plays any substantial role and whether that role involves direct or standoff involvement will determine the need for additional soldier systems. The medium rating reflects the current uncertainty about future Army involvement and is not an evaluation of soldier systems used in ongoing operations in support of the Customs Service, ATF, or any other federal agency.

The costs associated with reducing the uncertainties surrounding the ultimate Army role are small. The question of the type and degree of Army involvement is a policy issue, to be decided within the parameters of the law.

ASSESSING THE ADEQUACY OF ARMY CAPABILITIES

Table 9.1 summarizes the homeland security task areas and the types of Army units most likely to be useful in responding to contingencies in each task area.

Given our understanding of the current threat (low), the ambiguity surrounding the requirements for support, and the limited amount

Table 9.1

Units Useful for Homeland Security Contingencies

Task Area	High-Value Units	Other Supporting Units
Domestic Preparedness	NBC Engineer Medical Infantry	Explosive ordnance disposal Mortuary services Casualty reporting
Continuity of Operations	Similar units to those damaged or destroyed	
Force Protection	Intelligence Air defense NBC Medical Military police Infantry	Other units on the same installation
Critical Asset Assurance	LIWA	Signal Engineer
Critical Infrastructure Protection	Military police Engineer Infantry	Other units adjacent to critical infrastructure
Department of the Army Headquarters Continuity of Operations	Major Command Headquarters	
Continuity of Government	Individual staff officers Signal Intelligence	Any secure facility
Border and Coastal Defense	Intelligence Aviation Air defense	Infantry Cavalry

of information on the cost-effectiveness of alternatives, it is difficult to provide a highly detailed assessment of the adequacy of capabilities in the current Army force structure.

That said, Table 9.2 summarizes the main units available in the active-duty and reserve component Army force structure of interest for the repertoire of homeland security tasks. We believe that, given these resources, there is no reason at present for the Army to assign or earmark additional units for homeland security task area contingencies. Nevertheless, as discussed earlier, since many of these units may be low-density and dual-missioned to homeland security and warfighting, additional planning may be required to deconflict competing claims for the same resources.

Table 9.2

Available Units in Army Force Structure

Type of Unit	Number in the Army
Medical brigade	13
Medical group	11
Hospital	78
Chemical battalion	12
Air defense battalion	46
Military police battalion	36
Military intelligence battalion	49
Signal battalion	94
Engineer battalion (combat)	91
U.S.-based maneuver divisions	14

SOURCE: Association of the U.S. Army, 1999.

Chapter Ten

OPTIONS, RECOMMENDATIONS, CONCLUSIONS

This report has analyzed four of the homeland security task areas: domestic preparedness, continuity of operations, continuity of government, and border and coastal defense; the fifth homeland security area—national missile defense—was not addressed. For each of the four, we used the following approach.

First, we described an illustrative notional planning magnitude for each threat based on a stylized threat and risk assessment, while noting that a more comprehensive threat and risk assessments could reveal that these illustrative magnitudes were either too high or too low. Our illustrative threat assessments relied on historical data revealing observed frequencies and consequences of each threat type, trend analyses of threat data, and intelligence assessments presented in congressional testimony and other open sources.

Second, for each task area, we identified notional measures of performance and performance levels for judging the responsiveness and capacity of the total local, state, and federal response.

Third, to better differentiate the Army's role in homeland security from those of other actors, we analyzed the current array of local, state, and federal players, including the Army, the other services, and other elements of DoD, as well as the threats—high explosives, chemical, biological, radiological, nuclear, or cyber—they could address. Chapter Eight provided vignettes describing the probable consequences of incidents of specified magnitude and the local, state, and federal (including Army) response. Chapter Nine examined the adequacy of Army DOTLMS for addressing each of the four homeland security task areas. This resulted in a number of suggested Army actions whose benefits were seen to be commensurate with costs and with the current level of threat.

Fourth and finally, this report explored some of the issues associated with resourcing homeland security. It argued that a long-term adaptive strategy is needed that ties additional investments in homeland security more closely to threat assessments and a better understanding of the cost-effectiveness of available options. Although the threat does not appear at present to warrant further large-scale investments, the report argued, an increased threat could dictate increased investments in homeland security, assuming they passed simple cost-effectiveness criteria. It also argued that, although the Army is making progress in tracking homeland security–related TOA, the DoD would benefit from a new homeland security major force program and appropriate program elements for categorizing line-item expenditures. Although OMB has made similar strides in clarifying federal spending on combating terrorism and WMD, and critical infrastructure protection, the federal government would similarly benefit from a new budget subfunction to account for these activities.

THE KEY QUESTIONS REMAIN UNANSWERED

Chapters Four through Seven addressed the four key analytic tasks associated with assessing homeland security capabilities in each of the four task areas.

For each task area we addressed, in turn, the key issues associated with threat and risk assessments, measures of performance and performance levels, cost-effective programs, and budgeting. These four pieces of a comprehensive assessment can now be integrated into a single nomogram that captures the analytic flow of homeland security analyses (see Figure 10.1).

The nomogram shows how decisions taken in each panel contribute to the larger analysis. A decision about planning magnitude (m*) taken in Panel I is refined when a decision is taken in Panel II that establishes performance criteria (c*) for assessing alternatives. The planning magnitude and performance criteria then set the stage in

RAND*MR1251-S.1 & 10.1*

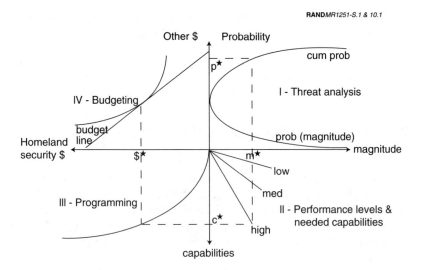

Figure 10.1—Nomogram for Assessing Homeland Security Options

Panel III for designing cost-effective programs, and the total cost of these programs ($*) is traded off against other budgetary claimants in Panel IV. To be sure, behind each panel there is a great deal of policy discussion, as well as analytic effort in the way of studies and analyses, and modeling.

Despite a great deal of important work done to redress shortfalls in local, state, and federal capabilities to address emerging threats to the homeland, the four key questions—the questions associated with each panel of the nomogram—remain substantially unresolved:

- What magnitudes of events should the United States plan against for high-explosive, chemical, biological, radiological, nuclear, and cyber threats? (Panel I, threat analysis)

- What levels of performance will the nation demand in the national (local, state, and federal) responses to these events? (Panel II, performance levels and needed capabilities)

- What are the most cost-effective options for providing the capabilities that will address these events at the desired performance levels? (Panel III, programming)

- What resources will be made available, and will they be sufficient to provide the necessary capabilities? (Panel IV, budgeting)

We now provide suggested or illustrative answers to these questions, although we conclude that they will only be answered satisfactorily— if at all—if they are the subject of larger policy discussions.

What Magnitudes of Events Should the United States Plan Against?

Throughout, this report has suggested that planning magnitudes for various types of incidents are needed that are larger than historically observed incidents (and therefore likely to provide reasonably good hedges against future incidents, at least in the near term) while not being large enough to pose an insurmountable barrier to developing effective counters.

To illustrate, the analysis suggested that local, state, and federal planners could aim to mitigate the consequences of chemical incidents in which 2,500 could die, biological incidents in which 5,000 people could die, and radiological incidents in which 25,000 people require evacuation, testing for exposure, and treatment. To emphasize, each of these magnitudes appeared to be well above the historical experience with terrorism, but policymakers need to engage with intelligence analysts and others to establish specific planning magnitudes. The report also noted that nuclear incidents would likely result in catastrophic losses whose magnitude would overwhelm national response capabilities—on the order of tens to hundreds of thousands of dead and injured. The report also suggested that the response to cyber threats might be sized on the basis of time until detection and isolation.

The notional planning magnitudes offered in this report to illustrate the analytic process are not meant to substitute for the set of planning magnitudes that would result from a thorough, reasoned effort by federal, state, and local actors to establish planning norms. Accordingly, this report urges that Army leaders engage with other relevant policymakers and intelligence and law enforcement specialists in serious discussions to establish the necessary planning norms. Such an effort would need to establish a current baseline using historical data on terrorist incidents and preventions and then reconcile these data with intelligence estimates of current trends and future prospects for attacks. It also would need to explicitly address any additional hedging that may be desirable for each type of threat—i.e., to err, if at all, on the side of overpreparedness—tackling the question of whether the benefits of this hedging are worth their costs.

Finally, constant monitoring of key threat indicators will be required in each of the task areas, so that any indications of a change in the threat would necessarily lead to consideration of the need for new planning magnitudes and additional hedging efforts.

What Levels of Performance Will the Nation Demand?

The second question that needs to be answered is also a normative one and arises from the need to establish performance levels against which total local, state, and federal response capabilities can be gauged.

Aggregate measures of performance need to be developed for each task area so that resource allocation decisions can be based on objective performance criteria. Available measures of performance would enable various options to be scored in terms of the levels of threat or consequence mitigation they provide—the reduction in the probability of terrorist attack, for example, or the number of deaths prevented.

With agreement on a modest but meaningful list of performance measures, norms could be established in terms of various performance levels. For example, a desirable performance level might be the ability to reduce by 50 (or 75 or 90) percent the probability of attack or the number of fatalities that would otherwise result in a chemical weapons attack. Designing capabilities to agreed-on performance levels and examining the technology and other requirements to achieve those levels—as well as their cost implications—can provide a long-term framework for improving responsiveness and capacity that focuses on reducing the length of the "long poles."

What Are the Most Cost-Effective Program Options?

The third question, addressed in Chapter Four, is not so much a normative one as an analytic one and requires assessing the contributions of alternative mixes of local, state, and federal capabilities in terms of their cost-effectiveness to craft a cost-effective program mix.

As described in Chapter Four, many local, state, and federal actors, particularly in the domestic preparedness arena, are in the "layer cake" that constitutes the nation's prevention and response capabilities. Further, a great deal of money is spent at each level, on training and equipping first responders, for example, and on fielding new operational units of various types (e.g., MMSTs, WMD CSTs).

It is almost certain that the nation's response capabilities have improved since the authoring of Nunn-Lugar-Domenici. Nevertheless, we have no basis for establishing what performance improvements might have resulted or whether even greater improvements might have occurred had resources been allocated differently among federal, state, and local programs. In large part, this uncertainty springs from the volume of newly established programs and organizations and because data on cost and effectiveness (responsiveness and capacity) are, at best, notional.

What is needed is more systematic production and compilation of relevant effectiveness and cost data and broader-gauge systems and policy analyses that explore the performance and cost of alternative architectures of federal, state, and local actors.

Viewed from the Army's (and DoD's) perspective, homeland security lacks the analytical basis taken for granted for defining needed warfighting capabilities. Although admirable progress has been made in modeling the effects of WMD, no authoritative cost or effectiveness data are available for homeland security analysis, and no simulation or other models have been crafted that might assist in understanding programmatic trade-offs. Further, there appear to be no standard studies (or processes) that provide a basis for DoD decisionmaking on resource allocations for homeland security.

Because so little effort has been made to encourage the development of such an infrastructure and because the Army has the greatest interest in improving this situation, the Army should press for more serious analytic treatment of this issue, within the Army, DoD, and the larger federal, state, and local setting. More specifically, the Army should seize the initiative and take a leadership role in creating the necessary framework and supporting capabilities (databases, models, etc.) for homeland security studies and analyses.

The probability that threats are increasing suggests that additional Army preparations for homeland security are warranted.

In Chapter Nine we evaluated the adequacy of current Army DOTLMS for the four homeland security task areas and suggested areas where short-term improvements can be realized at modest cost.

Additionally, given the poor understanding of the cost-effectiveness of alternative homeland security units or organizations, we recommend that the Army aggressively explore alternative future operational concepts for homeland security that may be more cost-effective than the current ones (e.g., WMD CSTs). A combination of experiments and exercises to generate lessons learned and efforts to design new future operational concepts that can be tested in these exercises and experiments clearly seem warranted.

To accomplish this, the Army might promote the use of joint warfighting experiments to test the likely responsiveness and capacity of the current DoD capabilities to perform homeland security missions. The Army can use the lessons from these experiments to refine its understanding of existing Army capabilities and limitations.

The Army also should consider creating a Homeland Security Battle Lab to design and test alternative future Army operational concepts and organizations whose responsiveness and capacity are greater than the present ones. When experimentation and testing have confirmed the cost-effectiveness of these concepts, the Army can begin developing the doctrine, organizational templates, training, and equipment packages needed and, when the threat level warrants, the number of units that need to be fielded. Such an approach will improve the Army's ability to provide the necessary capabilities as the threat changes.

What Resources Will Be Available?

Although the federal government is spending more than $11 billion to combat terrorism and WMD, to address critical infrastructure protection, and other homeland security–related areas, there is at present no clear way of answering the question, "How much is enough?"

Just as there are trade-offs in resource allocation decisions for warfighting in MTWs and smaller-scale contingencies (SSCs), so too there are trade-offs between homeland security and warfighting. Nevertheless, DoD presently lacks the capacity to address these trade-offs.

As noted in Chapter Four, current defense planning appears to treat threats to the homeland as modestly complicating factors, rather than in terms of their potential to seriously disrupt mobilization and deployment activities. In cases where combat, combat support, or combat service support capabilities have dual missions—i.e., are identified both for warfighting abroad and for homeland security activities—attacks on the homeland during a deployment easily could lead to difficult decisions regarding which set of missions had precedence. Given the attendant constitutional and political issues, it is not at all clear that warfighting abroad would be given the highest priority.

At present, the Defense Planning Guidance (DPG) and Quadrennial Defense Review (QDR) seem likely to address the homeland security mission only tangentially—as little more than a nuisance in this larger warfighting setting. Neither do homeland security activities receive serious treatment in the Future Years Defense Program (FYDP). They are treated, if at all, as separate line items buried deep within the budget.

As a result, we conclude that the Army should press for more explicit and serious treatment of homeland security in the DPG, QDR, and FYDP. In the DPG and QDR, homeland security requirements should be reconciled with warfighting needs to ensure that sufficient capabilities exist to accomplish both types of operations. And a new homeland security major force program (MFP) should be created to assure that homeland security is treated comprehensively.

The situation is not much better in the larger setting. At the federal level, OMB provides cost data on federal department and agency spending on antiterrorism, counterterrorism, and defense against WMD. While the numerous federal programs created and the allocation of money appears at first glance to be sensible, the data are at too high a level of aggregation to determine where undesirable redundancies might exist and whether an alternative funding mix might not be more effective. In short, while some cost data are available, no effectiveness data are readily available to determine whether federal dollars might be better allocated. The situations at the state and local levels are even more difficult to assess.

The Army should accordingly also press for governmentwide effort—federal, state, and local—to go beyond simply documenting shortfalls in responsiveness and capacity and to begin development of data on the cost and effectiveness of first, second, and later responders at the federal, state, and local level. These data can then be used to inform spending decisions to ensure that the highest-payoff actions are the first claimants.

EXPLAINING THE ARMY ROLE IN HOMELAND SECURITY

In light of the desire of national political leaders to alert the public to gain support for programs and prevent complacency without overstating the threat, the Army should studiously avoid hyping threats in these areas. Public opinion on the matter already suggests widespread awareness of the threats and a desire for the U.S. government to take action. Instead, the Army should focus its statements on finding the best ways to meet the threat, given the resources it receives.

The Army furthermore needs to establish a consensus for its role in homeland security and an ability to reassure the population and articulate the Army's role in a way that diminishes the risks of endangering the public's current positive perception of the Army.

The definition and the taxonomy of threats described earlier leads both to the identification of homeland security task areas and "bumper stickers" the Army can use to explain its role in homeland security (the "bumper stickers" are in quotations):

- "Protecting Americans at Home" (WMD domestic preparedness and civil support).

- "Ensuring Constitutional Authority" (COG, i.e., operations to ensure or restore civil authority).

- "Securing the Borders" (border and coastal defense, including the prevention of WMD smuggling into the United States and managing large-scale refugee flows that can create threats to the national security).

- "Assuring Military Capability" (continuity of military operations, including force protection—primarily for deploying units—protection of mission-critical facilities and systems, and protection of higher headquarters operations).

- National missile defense (not considered in this report).

CLOSING OBSERVATIONS

The work presented here suggests that the Army has a reasonable basis for arguing that, of the services, it has the leading role in many homeland security task areas. Nevertheless, the Army can improve its capacity to undertake the homeland security missions it is being assigned in a number of important ways.

While arguing that the Army has a leading military role in homeland security, the opportunities for Army leadership in the broader civilian arena are quite circumscribed.

First, leadership opportunities are circumscribed by the characteristics of response scenarios. The adequacy of responses to chemical attacks will hinge on the capabilities of civilian first responders; it is uncertain whether Army capabilities (e.g., WMD CSTs) can arrive soon enough to make any difference. And in the case of biological attacks, the outcome of these incidents is far more likely to depend on the performance of public health systems than on Army responders.

Additionally, leadership opportunities are circumscribed by the larger federal setting. The current efforts to enhance DoD and Army response capabilities seem premised on the expectation that civilian response capabilities will be inadequate, and these efforts envision a role well beyond that envisioned by the lead federal agencies for crisis management (the FBI) and consequence management (FEMA). Furthermore, increasing attention is given to the question of how well the DoD program is integrated into the larger federal effort.

If it offers few real opportunities, homeland security does offer some potential risks to the Army. First, the Army's role in domestic preparedness activities seems likely to lead to criticism from both the left and the right as a result of concerns about the possible militarization of domestic preparedness and law enforcement. This criticism seems inevitable despite apparent agreement at all levels of the Army that the Army's role is to provide military support to civilian authorities and in spite of the fact, as argued here, that one of the highest priorities of homeland security will necessarily be the swift restoration of civilian governmental functions following a catastrophic event.

Risks are also inherent in the ability of the current "layer cake" of local, state, and federal participants to respond effectively. The current system seems to have been constructed with little attention to cost and effectiveness and may have resulted in a system that has critical gaps (in responsiveness, for example, or capacity), effectiveness shortfalls, or unnecessary redundancies that only become apparent in an actual incident, and with potentially grave consequences. Far better to begin exercising this system and to undertake the necessary analyses to understand where, at the margin, investments and divestments should be made at the local, state, and federal levels.

Its substantial investments in homeland security dictate that the Army, as the nation's servant, continue to perform to the best of its ability the missions it is assigned, given the resources at its disposal. The Army accordingly must seek to use its portion of homeland security funding to greatest effect. It also must recognize the risks of over- or underfunding and should press for a comparable degree of rationalization in the allocation and use of resources in DoD and in the larger federal setting.

Finally, although the threat is still somewhat remote, the Army should begin planning to resolve a looming, future conundrum it may face. In the event of an asymmetric campaign of attacks on civilian and military targets in the CONUS during a wartime mobilization, not only could mobilization be disrupted, but fierce competition could flare for low-density units that have dual missions of warfighting abroad and homeland security. Actions taken now can greatly reduce the possibility and consequences of such trade-offs.

CONSIDERING THREAT CAMPAIGNS

A thread that has run through most of the preceding chapters is the possibility of prolonged threat campaigns. This appendix provides a detailed summary of our thinking on the matter of threat campaigns. As we see it, two types of enemy campaigns need to be considered:

- Those conducted independently of international events to punish the United States for imagined wrongs and injustices.

- Those carried out as a component of an adversary's plan to prevent the United States from deploying its forces in response to a crisis in a distant theater.

THE INDEPENDENT CAMPAIGN

The Threat

In the case of independent campaigns, the threat could come from any number of quarters:

- One or two persons sharing a profound antigovernment animus (e.g., the Oklahoma City and Atlanta bombers).

- A small cell of amateur terrorists manipulated by professionals (e.g., World Trade Center bombing).

- Members of a transnational terrorist movement numbering in the thousands, with a salient religious imperative (e.g., Aum Shinrikyo in Japan, religious groups in Russia and elsewhere, bin Laden and al-Qaeda).

- State-sponsored terrorists with superior capabilities and support. (Hoffman, 1999.)

Campaign Objectives

An independent campaign would seek to inflict pain, suffering, and damage—punishment for the "evil ways" of the United States.

Illustrative Campaign Targets

A punitive campaign may simply seek opportunities for mass killing and massive damage. Historical examples include the following:

- Using a biological agent or toxin, e.g., salmonella, to cripple an entire town (Rajneeshee group in The Dalles, Oregon, in 1984).

- Poisoning municipal water supplies (white supremacists in Chicago and Washington, D.C., in 1984).

- Blacking-out an entire state (Fuqra and Colorado).

- Toppling one skyscraper into another (World Trade Center).

- Simultaneous bombings in urban areas causing mass casualties (Bombay in 1993; Kenya and Tanzania in 1998) (Hoffman, 1999).

Campaign Weapons

In terms of the likely weaponry:

- Conventional bombs and arson remain the favorites.

- Specialty weapons, e.g., man-portable air defense missiles to attack troop transport aircraft could be used when available.

- State-sponsored or otherwise well-resourced actors (e.g., Aum Shinrikyo, bin Laden) may turn to WMD.

Campaign Concept

The operational concept for the independent campaign could be as follows:

- Avoid high-security targets and attack targets of opportunity.

- Make liberal use of hoaxes, risk real attacks less frequently.

- Take a leisurely pace since time pressure is probably minimal and results more from need to keep the conspirators motivated than from any requirement to accomplish specific levels of damage by a certain point in time.

A CAMPAIGN AS PART OF A BROADER CRISIS

Threat

The sources of threat probably are drawn from the same pool of actors as the independent campaigners, but state-sponsored actors and agents in the employ of the enemy (e.g., intelligence officers, professional saboteurs, special operations troops) are more likely suspects.

Campaign Objectives

Notional campaign objectives might include the following:

- Disrupting U.S. attempts to deploy its forces to the scene of a crisis overseas.

- Dissuading the United States from further involvement in the crisis by inflicting unacceptable levels of damage on U.S. territory.

Illustrative Campaign Targets

Campaign targets in this sort of campaign would tend to focus on military targets that could impede mobilization and deployment, and could include

- U.S. forces attempting to deploy from CONUS;

- departure airfields and ports of embarkation for U.S. forces;

- transport aircraft and ships;

- related power projection infrastructure; and

- to complicate the allocation of military forces, and to create widespread fear in the U.S. population, possibly attacks against "soft" civilian targets.

Campaign Weapons

The likely weapons include the following:

- Small arms, bombs, and arson, which probably will remain a mainstay.

- For state-sponsored and other well-resourced actors, such specialty weapons such as mortars, rocket-propelled grenades, and man-portable air defense missiles.

- For state-sponsored and other well-resourced agents, possibly WMD.

Campaign Concept

The campaign must give the impression that it is formidable both in breadth and depth and can continue its actions indefinitely, ultimately inflicting massive destruction on both military forces and civilian targets:

- The campaign requires prompt, effective attacks before U.S. forces can deploy significant numbers of units.

- Multiple (e.g., two to four) attacks will inflict severe damage on U.S. forces and prompt commanders to call a halt to the deployments until the security of the deploying forces can be ensured.[1]

- Extensive use of hoaxes—particularly after an actual incident has established the credibility of the threat—will magnify the overall campaign's effectiveness in waging psychological warfare.

---

[1]This is consistent with the estimates in the Defense Science Board's 1997 Summer Study Task Force report.

THREATS AND RISKS

Because the bars to successful acquisition and employment are relatively high, one incident of a specific type (e.g., the use of WMD), increases the risk of other such uses.[2]

Nevertheless, threats may aim at breadth rather than depth. In part, this is because targets of a given type can offer an attacker a finite number of approaches. Attacks in depth, therefore, run the risk of becoming stereotyped, leading to their perpetrators' death or capture. Attacks in breadth, seeking different types of targets and different conditions under which the attacks take place, are likely to be greater challenges to U.S. security because they offer more and varied options for approach and attack. They also will convey the impression of a large, well-organized assault on the homeland and feed greater levels of concern. They will therefore be more attractive to would-be assailants.

Attacks in Breadth

Attacks in breadth may be widely distributed and involve a variety of targets. The enemy may attempt to exploit the "it can't happen here" psychology by striking in very different parts of the country or striking only those targets that have not been hardened. As noted above, the targets themselves will probably be of different types.

Attacks in Depth

Attacks in depth are somewhat more likely to be part of a campaign supporting an ongoing foreign crisis. This is so because the enemy must accomplish specific objectives to disrupt the deployment of U.S. forces and dissuade the government from further involvement in the overseas issue. Therefore, the attackers must concentrate their efforts against U.S. forces and their supporting facilities. Even under these circumstances, however, the enemy may seek to limit his vulnerability by selecting different types of targets.

---

[2]In the language of Bayesian statistics, new evidence will force us to adjust the prior probability.

If this line of thinking is correct, the enemy might attack troops at ports and airfields, because a successful attack would not only kill deploying forces but might destroy important facilities, preventing them from being used again during the crisis.

MEASURES OF PERFORMANCE

To effectively counter an enemy campaign, the United States will need the ability to manage multiple, large-scale incidents. Fighting an enemy embarked on a campaign involves gathering intelligence about the campaign plan and taking actions to preempt and disrupt it, while also taking steps to defend against the attacks it plans.

To succeed in a countercampaign, the United States must have sufficient JTFs, RTFs, and other assets to respond to the individual attacks, but the country will also need intelligence and planning capabilities for the preemptive, disruptive, and protective measures that are also part of the countercampaign. Finally, recognizing that most JTFs are intended for specific missions and disbanded once those missions have been accomplished, the United States also may need a headquarters superior to the JTFs and RTFs that can command and control the overall effort.

NOTIONAL PERFORMANCE LEVELS

Notional performance levels for the performance measures described above include

- an ability to field two to four JTFs/RTFs over a prolonged campaign; and
- a headquarters capability for managing two to four separate JTFs/RTFs allocating resources amongst them, and synchronizing their activities.

PROGRAM DESIGN ISSUES

Two of the CONUS Armies, one on each coast, have dedicated RTFs, one called RTF-E and the other RTF-W. Because of the possible need for multiple responses, the other CONUS Armies should develop plans for fielding additional RTFs based on the doctrinal and organizational developments in the two extant RTFs and based on whatever lessons are learned in exercises or actual employment.

While such key units as the TEU have multiple deployable assets, others, such as the USMC Chemical Biological Incident Response Force (CBIRF), are unique, and that could cause problems if multiple incidents occurred.

The responsiveness and capacity of the JTF/RTF and its components are also of concern, particularly in the context of a threat campaign that occurs during a mobilization and deployment, when mobility assets will be at a premium. Threat campaigns, we believe, could severely tax military response capabilities.

A NOTIONAL WMD CST TRADE-OFF ANALYSIS

The key issues in designing a layered defense are determining how many units of what sort of capability to procure, where to locate them, and how best to deploy them from their duty stations to the location where they will be employed. Using the WMD CST as an illustration, this appendix provides several examples of how trade analyses can be used to illuminate the merits of alternatives for consequence management activities.

Although the focus is on the trade-off space for WMD CSTs and improved city-based hazmat teams, such analyses could be useful in comparing a wider range of alternatives (e.g., Army TEU CBRTs, Marine CBIRFs, FBI HMRUs, and HHS MMSTs), assessing the cost-effectiveness of alternative mixes of these units, or even assessing alternative mixes of funding for prevention (e.g., intelligence, law enforcement, SOF) versus response activities.

THE ANALYSIS

Next is a very narrow sort of notional trade analysis of a choice between WMD CSTs and other alternatives, including city-based hazmat teams, where the trade space includes two types of effectiveness; to assure that these investments make sense, broader trade-off analyses are desirable, including assessments of various mixes of preventive, preparedness, and response activities as described in this report.

The first type of effectiveness we consider is the capacity of each unit, with two basic dimensions: its capability for assessment and detection and its capability for decontamination. The second type of effectiveness is the responsiveness of the unit, i.e., how quickly it can be at the scene and ready to begin operations. Importantly, the needed responsiveness depends greatly on the type of WMD incident. For example, incidents involving many chemical weapons (e.g., sarin or VX) require a very quick response. The consequence of delays is the greater likelihood that many of the victims will already be dead by the time responders arrive. To highlight the importance of responsiveness, the following examples focus on response capabilities for chemical attacks where there is a premium on time.

GAO has provided estimated costs for WMD CSTs,[1] and notional costs for city-based hazmat units at several levels of capability.[2] The 10-year total costs of each type of unit is described in Table B.1.

Public statements suggest that present DoD planning envisions a total of 27 WMD CST teams and enhanced training and equipping for

Table B.1

WMD CST Costs and Possible Costs to Equip a City of 500,000 to Respond to a WMD Event

Equipment Level	Initial Procurement[a]	10-Year Sustainment[a]	10-Year Total Cost[a]
WMD CST	$3.9	$27.25	$31.2
Basic hazmat	$1.3	$3.30	$4.6
Modest	$5.2	$13.10	$18.3
Moderate	$8.3	$20.90	$29.2
High	$12.2	$30.70	$42.9

[a]In dollar millions.

SOURCES: WMD CST costs are from GAO, 1999b, p. 5, and DoD, 1998a. City hazmat costs are from GAO, 1999e, p. 3.

---

[1]WMD CST costs assume $1.99 million in startup costs for each RAID team, $1.92 million in equipment costs, and $2.725 million in annual sustainment costs. RAID costs are from GAO (1999b, p. 5).

[2]GAO costed out a basic hazmat capability, a modest increase over basic equipment that included additional detection and decontamination equipment, a moderate increase that included a greater array of detection equipment than the modest level, and a high level of increased equipment that included additional and more expensive detection equipment (GAO, 1999e, p. 3).

first responders in 120 of the nation's cities.[3] Table B.2 compares the 10-year costs of the planned 27 and a possible total of 54 WMD CST teams with the costs for 120 basic, modestly capable, moderately capable, and highly capable city-based hazmat teams.

Illustrative Trade Analyses

Now, consider the following five stylized cost-effectiveness analyses, the purpose of which is to illustrate how one can explore the trade space for such homeland security capabilities as WMD CSTs. In many cases, the numbers used are illustrative only and not at all definitive.

Example One: On-Scene WMD CSTs. Assume that we have identified (per panel one of the nomogram used in Figure 10.5) a planning magnitude for chemical and biological threats, have decided that we want a minimum performance capability comparable to the Basic Hazmat unit, and have determined that the WMD CST has this level

Table B.2

Total 10-Year Costs for Program Alternatives

Option	10-Year Total Cost[a]
27 WMD CSTs	$842.5
54 WMD CSTs	$1,685.0
120 Basic Hazmat	$552.0
120 Modest Capability	$2,196.0
120 Moderate Capability	$3,504.0
120 High Capability	$5,148.0

[a]In dollar millions, based on unit costs in Table C.1.

---

[3]In 1999, speculation arose that a total of 54 WMD CSTs would be stood up. In a DoD news briefing on January 13, 2000, however, Charles Cragin, principal deputy assistant secretary of Defense for Reserve Affairs, stated that the DoD had no plans to create 54 teams but instead planned to implement the 27 teams authorized by Congress (Bacon, 2000; Berkowsky and Cragin, 2000). We have included estimated costs for both a total of 27 and 54 WMD CSTs.

of capability.[4] Assume further that WMD CST teams can be at the scene of a WMD incident prior to any actual incident (as a result, for example, of predeployment for Special Events or timely threat warning information). In such a case, the choice would be made solely on the basis of effectiveness and cost. In this case, we would prefer 120 Basic Hazmat units to 27 (or 54) WMD CSTs because they provide the desired level of capability at a smaller cost.

Example Two: Predeployed WMD CSTs with Additional Decontamination Capabilities. Assume now that we have decided we want a minimum performance level comparable to that of the moderately capable hazmat unit, both in terms of detection capabilities and in terms of decontamination capabilities. Because WMD CSTs lack any decontamination capabilities to speak of, assume that deployable mass decontamination units comparable to those in the moderately capable hazmat unit could be created for deployment with WMD CSTs for a total of $1 million per unit per year, bringing the total 10-year cost of 27 WMD CSTs to $1,382.5 million.[5] In such a case, we would prefer buying 27 (or even 54) WMD CST units to 120 local hazmat units because the cost is less than the estimated $3,504 million it would cost to field 120 moderately capable hazmat teams.

Example Three: WMD CSTs with Additional Decontamination Capability and Mobility. Next, assume we have decided that we want a minimum performance level compared to that of the highly capable hazmat unit, that the highly capable hazmat unit has no more decontamination capabilities than the moderately capable hazmat unit, and that we should add decontamination capabilities to the WMD CST, as described in the previous example. Also assume the more realistic situation that the WMD CSTs will not be pre-deployed in most instances but will require mobility assets to transport them to the scene of the incident. In this case, the trade space includes both capacity (in terms of assessment, detection, and

---

[4]In this example, we ignore the RAID's lack of decontamination capabilities beyond those for its own team.

[5]We estimated costs of $2,765 million for 54 WMD CSTs, which derive from the initial cost of $2,225 million for the WMD CSTs, plus $540 million for 54 decontamination units at $1 million a year for 10 years. The 27 WMD CSTs would cost half of that, or $1,382.5 million.

decontamination) and responsiveness (in terms of the speed with which the unit can be deployed to the scene).

In this case, the highly capable hazmat unit and the WMD CST are basically identical in capacity for assessment and decontamination. Thus, the main issue of interest is the mobility costs that would need to be incurred to put the WMD CST on the scene rapidly enough to be as responsive as the local hazmat unit. It is clear that we would be willing to spend up to $3,765.5 million—the difference between the $5,148 million for the highly capable hazmat units and the $1,382.5 million cost of 27 WMD CSTs, enhanced with decontamination units—to provide mobility assets that could place a WMD CST at the scene of the incident. If this could be accomplished for less than $3,765.5 million, we would prefer the WMD CST.

Assume that each WMD CST will be at a high state (24 hours a day, seven days a week) of readiness and have available a ready C-130 that would make its responsiveness comparable to the city hazmat team.[6]

If we assume that the annual sustainment costs of a C-130 airlifter are about $3.1 million and that each of the 27 WMD CSTs would require four C-130s to maintain one C-130 at the required readiness level, the total 10-year cost would be about $3,348 million for the 108 airlifters required for 27 WMD CST elements.[7] Because this is cheaper than the city-based alternative, we prefer the WMD CST option with mobility assets.[8]

Example Four: WMD CSTs on Regional Airborne Alert. We might, however, posit an entirely different solution. Assume that plans for WMD CSTs expand to a total of 54 units, that we desire round-the-clock airborne alert status for one WMD CST team in each of the 10

---

[6]At present, the 22-man WMD CSTs appear to have insufficient rotational personnel to assure a high state of readiness 24 hours a day, seven days a week.

[7]Total 10-year costs for 54 WMD CSTs would be twice that, or $6,690 million. This is computed as follows: 54 RAIDs x 4 C-130s is 216 C-130s, and 216 x $3.1 million per C-130 x 10 years is $6,696 million.

[8]A real analysis of the options would need to consider the fact that the city hazmat team also would be used for standard hazmat incidents. If a WMD CST were chosen over city hazmat teams, this capability would be foregone unless the WMD CST also could respond to these incidents. The focus should probably be on a comparison of the total costs of a WMD CST with the marginal costs of improving the city hazmat capability.

FEMA regions, and that we can use as a rotation base the 54 WMD CSTs in these regions. Assume that the regional program would maintain the same level of responsiveness as the previous example, comparable to the city-based hazmat team. In such a case, the cost for airlifters would fall to $1,240 million,[9] bringing the total cost of the package to $4,005 million, $1,143 million cheaper than the city-based alternative. If the responsiveness were somewhat less than then city-based team, we would be willing to use a large portion of the remaining $1,143 million to improve responsiveness, so long as the total 10-year cost was lower.

Example Five: Trade-Off Between Deployable Units. Now assume that the units under consideration for trade-off include three U.S. Army units (a single TEU, 54 WMD CSTs, and 76 reserve component chemical companies), and one Marine unit (the CBIRF), with costs, responsiveness, decontamination capability, and mobility needs as described in Table B.3.

On a simple cost and effectiveness basis, the single TEU is the least expensive unit, but it has only a moderate decontamination capability. The single USMC CBIRF has a high capability for decontamination and is only slightly more expensive than the TEU. Finally, most expensive are the 54 WMD CSTs, each having a low decontamination capability. Because all three require mobility assets, the CBIRF is probably the preferred option of the three, while the WMD CST is the least preferred. Nevertheless, the responsiveness of each of these three options for chemical attacks may be too low.

Assuming that the option of 76 U.S. Army reserve component chemical companies provides a high decontamination capability on scene within two hours and has minimal nonorganic mobility needs, it is an order of magnitude more expensive than the next available options. Nevertheless, if these companies also are to be used in warfighting, only the incremental costs associated with improving its capability for WMD response would be of interest. If we use these incremental costs as a basis for costing, the Army should prefer the

---

[9]The computation is 40 C-130s x $3.1 million each x 10 years, or $1,240 million. This probably understates total costs, which could be somewhat higher given the higher operational tempo, which could affect average operations and maintenance costs, fuel consumption rates, and other factors.

76 U.S. Army reserve component chemical companies with their organic transportation capabilities to the 54 WMD CSTs plus the needed mobility assets.

At this point, the trade space would be narrowed to the most capable of the chemical response alternatives that need mobility (the USMC CBIRF) and the best of the alternatives that do not (the Army chemical companies). Because the mobility costs for the CBIRF are unlikely to make that option as expensive as the Army reserve component chemical companies, the issue would need to be settled on responsiveness (where the reserve component chemical companies are preferred) and capacity (where the two options are comparable). Because the ability to respond within two hours makes the Army alternative reserve component quite attractive, the decision might be taken to fund this option but, because the costs are relatively modest, also to continue funding one or more alternatives (e.g., the USMC CBIRF or the TEU and associated mobility assets) as a hedge.

Table B.3

Illustrative Chem-Bio Response Options to Be Traded

Unit	Start-Up Costs	Sus-tain Costs	Units	Annual	10-Year	Re-sponse	De-con	Mob Need-ed
USA TEU (AA)	None	9.40	1	*9.40*	*94.00*	4/?	Med	C-141
USMC CBIRF	None	6.97	1	*6.97*	*99.69*	4/?	High	2 C-17
USA WMD CST (RC)	3.91	2.73	54	*358.29*	*1,682.64*	?/4	Low	C-130
USA Chemical Company (RC)	2.60	*42.50*	76	*3,427.60*	*32,497.60*	0/2	High	No
Increased costs only	2.60	*1.80*	76	*335.31*	*1,574.74*	0/2	High	No

SOURCES: GAO, 1999b, 1999e; DoD, 1999b; authors' estimates.

NOTES: All costs expressed in dollar millions. Numbers in italics are authors' estimates. Assumes that startup costs for USMC CBIRF ($10 million) and USA TEU (estimated to be $13.5 million) already have been incurred, but costs for others have not. "Response" should be read as time until "wheels up"/time until on-scene. For USA Chemical Company, startup costs are actually conversion costs, i.e., costs to equip and train the companies for WMD response operations.

CONCLUSIONS

As illustrated by these examples, the preferred option depends greatly on cost-effectiveness, where we define effectiveness both in terms of responsiveness (time until the unit arrives on scene) and capacity (in this case, ability to perform assessment and detection and to perform decontamination) and where costs include whatever fixed and incremental equipment, training, and sustainment costs necessary to provide the desired performance level over a specified period, as well as any mobility costs that might be necessary to provide the desired level of responsiveness.

Of course, in addition to the cost and effectiveness measures, we would want to do more detailed modeling and other analyses to establish the robustness of our preferred solution. And as described at the beginning of this appendix, the best response options that emerge from analyses, such as those described here, should be evaluated as part of larger studies that examine trade-offs between prevention, preparedness, and response capabilities and suggest the most desirable mix of these capabilities. In any case, these calculations are illustrative only and are meant to be suggestive of the kind of analyses needed to explore the trade space.

HOMELAND SECURITY DoD DIRECTIVES

This appendix identifies some of the key Department of Defense Directives (DoDDs) for homeland security, including domestic preparedness defense (combating terrorism and WMD), continuity of operations, COG, and border and coastal defense.

DOMESTIC PREPAREDNESS

In the area of domestic preparedness—combating terrorism and WMD—key DoDDs include the following:

- DoDD 3025.1, Military Support to Civil Authorities, 1/15/93.

- DoDD 3025.12, Military Assistance for Civil Disturbances, 2/4/94.

- DoDD 3025.15, Military Assistance to Civil Authorities, 2/18/97.

- DoDD 1330.5, American National Red Cross, 8/16/69.

- DoDD 2000.15, Support to Special Events, 11/21/94.

- DoDD 2060.2, Department of Defense Counterproliferation Implementation, 7/9/96.

- DoDD 3005.7, Emergency Requirements, Allocations, Priorities, and Permits for DoD Use of Domestic Civil Transportation, 5/30/85.

- Assignment of National Security Emergency Preparedness (NSEP) Responsibilities to DoD Components, 11/2/88.

- DoDD 3150.5, DoD Response to Improvised Nuclear Device (IND) Incidents, 3/24/87.

- DoDD 3150.8, DoD Response to Radiological Accidents, 6/13/96.
- DoDD 4270.36, DoD Emergency, Contingency, and Other Unprogrammed Construction Projects, 5/17/97.
- DoDD 4715.1, Environmental Security, 2/24/96.
- DoDD 5030.14, Oil and Hazardous Substances Pollution Prevention and Contingency Program, 6/1/77.
- DoDD 5230.16, Nuclear Accident and Incident Public Affairs (PA) Guidance, 12/20/93.
- DoDD 5505.9, Interception of Wire, Electronic, and Oral Communications for Law Enforcement, 4/20/95.
- DoDD 5525.5, DoD Cooperation with Civilian Law Enforcement Officials, 1/15/86.
- DoDD 5525.7, Implementation of the Memorandum of Understanding Between the Department of Justice and the Department of Defense Relating to the Investigation and Prosecution of Certain Crimes, 1/22/85.

CONTINUITY OF OPERATIONS

Continuity of Headquarters Operations

- DoDD 3020.26, Continuity of Operations (COOP) Policy and Planning, 5/26/95.
- DoDD 1400.31, DoD Civilian Work Force Contingency and Emergency Planning and Execution.
- DoDD 1404.1, Emergency-Essential (E-E) DoD U.S. Citizen Civilian Employees, 4/10/92.

Force Protection

- DoDD 2000.12, DoD Antiterrorism/Force Protection (AT/FP) Program.
- DoDD 5160.5, Responsibilities for Research, Development, and Acquisition of Chemical Weapons and Chemical and Biological Defense, 5/1/85.

- DoDD 6205.3, DoD Immunization Program for Biological Warfare Defense, 11/26/93.
- DoDD 6490.2, Joint Medical Surveillance, 8/30/97.

Critical Asset Assurance/Critical Infrastructure Protection

The following DoDDs apply generally:

- DoDD 5160.54, Critical Asset Assurance Program (CAAP), 1/20/98 (withdrawn).
- DoDD 5200.2, DoD Personnel Security Program, 4/9/99.
- DoDD 5200.26, Defense Investigative Program, 6/12/79.
- DoDD 5205.2, DoD Operations Security Program, 7/7/83.

These DoDDs apply to physical assets:

- DoDD 5100.76, Physical Security Review Board, 2/10/81.
- DoDD 5100.78, United States Port Security Program, 8/25/86.
- DoDD 5126.46, Defense Energy Information System (DEIS), 12/2/87.
- DoDD 5200.8, Security of DoD Installations and Resources, 4/25/91.
- DoDD 5210.46, DoD Building Security for the National Capital Region, 1/28/82.
- DoDD 5210.63, Security of Nuclear Reactors and Special Nuclear Materials, 4/6/90.
- DoDD 5210.64, Alternate Joint Communications Center Protection Program, 11/6/78.
- DoDD 5210.65, Chemical Agent Security Program, 12/8/80.

These DoDDs apply to computers, networks, and communications assets:

- DoDD 5100.41, Executive Agent Responsibilities for the National Communications System (NCS), 5/1/91.

- DoDD 5145.3, Surveillance of DoD Security Programs, 10/19/62.

- DoDD 5200.1, DoD Information Security Program, 12/13/96.

- DoDD 5200.28, Security Requirements for Automated Information Systems (AISS), 3/21/88.

- DoDD 5215.1, Computer Security Evaluation Center, 10/25/82.

COG

- DoDD 3020.4, Order of Succession of Officers to Act as Secretary of Defense, 7/3/96.

- DoDD 3025.13, Employment of Department of Defense Resources in Support of the United States Secret Service, 9/13/85.

- DoDD 4640.5, Defense Metropolitan Area Telephone Systems, 4/5/85.

- DoDD 4640.7, DoD Telecommunications System (DTS) in the National Capital Region (NCR), 10/7/93.

- DoDD 5030.46, Assistance to the District of Columbia Government in Combating Crime, 3/26/71.

- DoDD 5210.55, Department of Defense Presidential Support Program, 12/15/98.

- DoDD 5210.56, Use of Deadly Force and the Carrying of Firearms by DoD Personnel Engaged in Law Enforcement and Security Duties, 2/25/92.

BORDER AND COASTAL DEFENSE

- DoDD 3025.12, Military Assistance for Civil Disturbances, 2/4/94.

- DoDD 3025.15, Military Assistance to Civil Authorities, 2/18/97.

- DoDD 5100.78, United States Port Security Program, 8/25/86.

OVERVIEW OF THE POSSE COMITATUS ACT

This appendix provides a broad overview of the Posse Comitatus Act, which restricts the participation of the military in domestic law enforcement activities under many circumstances.

LANGUAGE

The origins of "posse comitatus" are to be found in domestic law. *Black's Law Dictionary* defines the term "posse comitatus" as:

> the power or force of the county. The entire population of a county above the age of fifteen, which a sheriff may summon to his assistance in certain cases as to aid him in keeping the peace, in pursuing and arresting felons, etc.[1]

The Posse Comitatus Act, 18 U.S. Code, Section 1385, an original intent of which was to end the use of federal troops to police state elections in former Confederate states, proscribes the role of the Army and Air Force in executing civil laws and states:

> Whoever, except in cases and under circumstances expressly authorized by the Constitution or Act of Congress, willfully uses any part of the Army or the Air Force as a posse comitatus or otherwise

---

[1]Lujan (1997) notes that the commander of JTF-LA mistakenly believed his activities were subject to Posse Comitatus restrictions when they were not.

to execute the laws shall be fined not more than $10,000 or imprisoned not more than two years, or both.[2]

According to Lujan (1997), the Air Force was added to the original language in 1956. Although the Navy and Marine Corps are not included in the act, they were made subject to it by DoD Regulation (32 C.F.R. Section 213.2, 1992).

KEY EXCEPTIONS TO THE POSSE COMITATUS ACT

A summary of key exceptions to the Posse Comitatus Act follows:[3]

- National Guard forces operating under the state authority of Title 32 (i.e., under state rather than federal service) are exempt from Posse Comitatus Act restrictions.

- Pursuant to the presidential power to quell domestic violence, federal troops are expressly exempt from the prohibitions of Posse Comitatus Act, and this exemption applies equally to active-duty military and federalized National Guard troops.[4]

- Aerial photographic and visual search and surveillance by military personnel were found not to violate the Posse Comitatus Act.

- Congress created a "drug exception" to the Posse Comitatus Act. Under recent legislation, the Congress authorized the Secretary of Defense to make available any military equipment and personnel necessary for operation of said equipment for law

---

[2]The language of the Posse Comitatus Act was further amended by congressional action reflected in P.L. 103-322 (1994).

[3]For further details, the reader is directed to: Lujan (1997); Department of the Army (undated); and to the notes of various court decisions refining the interpretation of the Posse Comitatus Act. For the latter, see United States Code, Title 18, Crimes and Criminal Procedures, Sections 1361 to 1950 2000 Cumulative Annual Pocket Part, St. Paul, Minn.: West Group, 2000, pp. 13–17.

[4]10 U.S. Code Sections 331 through 334 provide guidance. Section 332 states: "Whenever the President considers the unlawful obstructions, combinations, or assemblages, or rebellion against the United States, makes it impracticable to enforce the laws of the United States in any state or territory by the ordinary course of judicial proceedings, he may call into federal service such of the militia of any state, and use such of the armed forces to suppress the rebellion" (Lujan, 1997).

enforcement purposes. Thus, the Army can provide equipment, training, and expert military advice to civilian law enforcement agencies as part of the total effort in the "war on drugs."

- Use of a member of the Judge Advocate Corps as a special assistant prosecutor, while retaining his dual role in participating in the investigation, presentation to the grand jury, and prosecution, did not violate Posse Comitatus Act.

- The Coast Guard is exempt from Posse Comitatus Act during peacetime.

- Although brought under the Act through DoD regulation, described above, the Navy may assist the Coast Guard in pursuit, search, and seizure of vessels suspected of involvement in drug trafficking.

IMPLICATIONS FOR ARMY HOMELAND SECURITY ACTIVITIES

There is a rather diverse range of potential activities engendered in each of the homeland security task areas—domestic preparedness, COG, border and coastal defense, and continuity of operations—that may involve circumstances in which the Army is asked to assist domestic law enforcement. Accordingly, it is critical that the Army develop doctrine, leadership, and training programs that can provide clear and specific guidance on when and how the Posse Comitatus Act—as well as any other laws that proscribe Army activities in the domestic arena—applies and when it does not.

THREAT FINDINGS OF THE NUNN-LUGAR-DOMENICI ACT

Section 1402 of the Defense Against Weapons of Mass Destruction Act of 1996 (PL 104-201, September 23, 1996, also known as Nunn-Lugar-Domenici) provided the key congressional findings regarding threats, risks, and shortfalls in response capabilities that animated the Act. A total of 26 findings were provided in Section 1402:

(1)   WMD and related materials and technologies are increasingly available from worldwide sources. Technical information related to such weapons is readily available on the Internet, and raw materials for chemical, biological, and radiological weapons are widely available for legitimate commercial purposes.

(2)   The former Soviet Union produced and maintained a vast array of NBC WMD.

(3)   Many of the states of the former Soviet Union retain the facilities, materials, and technologies capable of producing additional quantities of WMD.

(4)   The disintegration of the former Soviet Union was accompanied by disruptions of command and control systems, deficiencies in accountability for weapons, weapons-related materials and technologies, economic hardships, and significant gaps in border control among the states of the former Soviet Union. The problems of organized crime and corruption in the states of the former Soviet Union increase the

potential for proliferation of nuclear, radiological, biological, and chemical weapons and related materials.

(5) The conditions described in paragraph (4) have substantially increased the ability of potentially hostile nations, terrorist groups, and individuals to acquire WMD and related materials and technologies from within the states of the former Soviet Union and from unemployed scientists who worked on those programs.

(6) As a result of such conditions, the capability of potentially hostile nations and terrorist groups to acquire nuclear, radiological, biological, and chemical weapons is greater than at any time in history.

(7) The President has identified North Korea, Iraq, Iran, and Libya as hostile states that already possess some WMD and are developing others.

(8) The acquisition or the development and use of WMD is well within the capability of many extremist and terrorist movements, acting independently from or as proxies for foreign states.

(9) Foreign states can transfer weapons to or otherwise aid extremist and terrorist movements indirectly and with plausible deniability.

(10) Terrorist groups have already conducted chemical attacks against civilian targets in the United States and Japan and a radiological attack in Russia.

(11) The potential for the national security of the United States to be threatened by nuclear, radiological, chemical, or biological terrorism must be taken seriously.

(12) There is a significant and growing threat of attack by WMD on targets not military in the usual sense of the term.

(13) Concomitantly, the threat posed to the citizens of the United States by nuclear, radiological, biological, and chemical weapons delivered by unconventional means is significant and growing.

(14)   Mass terror may result from terrorist incidents involving nuclear, radiological, biological, or chemical materials.

(15)   Facilities required for production of radiological, biological, and chemical weapons are much smaller and harder to detect than nuclear weapons facilities, and biological and chemical weapons can be deployed by delivery means other than long-range ballistic missiles.

(16)   Covert or unconventional means of delivery of nuclear, radiological, biological, and chemical weapons include cargo ships, passenger aircraft, commercial and private vehicles and vessels, and commercial cargo shipments routed through multiple destinations.

(17)   Traditional arms control efforts assume large state efforts with detectable manufacturing programs and weapons production programs but are ineffective in monitoring and controlling smaller, though potentially more dangerous, unconventional proliferation efforts.

(18)   Conventional counterproliferation efforts would do little to detect or prevent the rapid development of a capability to suddenly manufacture several hundred chemical or biological weapons with nothing but commercial supplies and equipment.

(19)   The United States lacks adequate planning and countermeasures to address the threat of nuclear, radiological, biological, and chemical terrorism.

(20)   The Department of Energy has established a Nuclear Emergency Response Team that is available in case of nuclear or radiological emergencies, but no comparable units exist to deal with emergencies involving biological or chemical weapons or related materials.

(21)   State and local emergency response personnel are not adequately prepared or trained for incidents involving nuclear, radiological, biological, or chemical materials.

(22)   Exercises of the federal, state, and local response to nuclear, radiological, biological, or chemical terrorism have revealed

serious deficiencies in preparedness and severe problems of coordination.

(23)   The development of, and allocation of responsibilities for, effective countermeasures to nuclear, radiological, biological, or chemical terrorism in the United States requires well-coordinated participation of many federal agencies and careful planning by the federal government and state and local governments.

(24)   Training and exercises can significantly improve the preparedness of state and local emergency response personnel for emergencies involving nuclear, radiological, biological, or chemical weapons or related materials.

(25)   Sharing of the expertise and capabilities of the Department of Defense, which traditionally has provided assistance to federal, state, and local officials in neutralizing, dismantling, and disposing of explosive ordnance, as well as radiological, biological, and chemical materials, can be a vital contribution to the development and deployment of countermeasures against NBC WMD.

(26)   The United States lacks effective policy coordination regarding the threat posed by the proliferation of WMD.

STATE AND LOCAL DOMESTIC PREPAREDNESS NEEDS

This appendix summarizes the results of three separate assessments of state and local preparedness: a 1995 survey of state and local preparedness by RAND; a 1997 National Institute of Justice survey of unmet technology needs; a 1997 study by FEMA; and a 1999 study by the Institute of Medicine and National Research Council.

RAND'S 1995 ASSESSMENT OF STATE AND LOCAL PREPAREDNESS

A 1995 RAND report revealed that, although there is concern about domestic preparedness issues, states and localities have limited resources for addressing the emerging threats:

> The case studies confirm in detail what the survey revealed in general terms. That is, communities perceived potential terrorism problems and have an interest in confronting terrorism before it erupts but in many cases are forced by budgetary, manpower, and other constraints to limit their terrorism preparedness. In such instances, cooperation with the FBI, through regular communication, training, and guidelines, is highly valued. Despite the resource and other constraints noted, the case studies reveal that a variety of successful terrorism preparedness formulas exist in communities both large and small. Large municipalities, such as New York City and Miami, have developed significant terrorism programs in close cooperation with the FBI and its regional joint terrorism task forces, whereas smaller communities, such as Kootenai County and Coeur d'Alene, Idaho, have worked to stay ahead of

nascent terrorism threats by forging close regional alliances and capitalizing on available FBI resources.

More generally, the case study findings suggest that a community's size, its resources, and the nature of the terrorism threats it confronts will influence both the strategic and tactical law enforcement response. Communities value the intelligence and support that the FBI provides, and municipalities highly value their communication with federal authorities. Localities are interested in adopting a strategic approach, in which intelligence, planning, and advance preparation are used to combat terrorism but lack the resources in many cases to maintain this more expensive approach. (Riley and Hoffman, 1995, p. x.)

The principal implications are as follows:

- The federal government is likely to be the principal source of resources for improving domestic preparedness.

- Localities see great value in assistance in planning, training, equipping, and exercising local capabilities.

- Localities see great value in access to federal law enforcement organizations, particularly the FBI, and are likely to value highly threat warning information, as well as access to relevant strategic, tactical, and operational intelligence.

NIJ'S 1997 SURVEY OF UNMET TECHNOLOGY NEEDS

The National Institute of Justice sponsored a study in 1997 that interviewed 195 individuals representing 138 agencies from 50 states and the District of Columbia about unmet technology needs for combating terrorism (National Institute of Justice, 1999). The top 15 identified technology needs are described in Table F.1. The list suggested a continuing need for

- technologies with improved performance characteristics (e.g., detection, assessment, communications, robots, personal protective equipment);

- technologies that, because they are currently very expensive or purchased in bulk quantities, need to be made more affordable

Table F.1

Top 15 Technology Needs of State and Local
Law Enforcement

National intergovernmental information system with current
   intelligence on terrorism
Improved means of detecting explosives
Improved and more readily available secure communications
Improved means of detecting and categorizing NBC threats
Improved interagency communications
Improved robots for disarming and disabling explosive devices
Improved affordable protective gear
Improved nonlethal weapons
Improved "see-through-the-wall" capability
Improved long-range video monitoring
Improved detection and tracing mechanisms for counter-
   measures for cyber attacks
Improved electronic listening devices
Improved training to combat terrorism
Improved containment vessels and vehicles for explosive
   devices
Improved night vision devices

SOURCE: National Institute of Justice, 1999, p. 4.

(e.g., detection and assessment equipment, personal protective
equipment); and

• improved communications and training.

THE 1997 FEMA STUDY

According to the 1997 Report to Congress on Response to Threats of
Terrorist Use of Weapons of Mass Destruction, FEMA was assigned
by the NSC to review the adequacy of the FRP to respond for WMD
events (DoD, 1997). As described by the report:

FEMA has been tasked by the NSC to review the adequacy of the
FRP to respond to nuclear, biological, or chemical (NBC) WMD
terrorism incidents and to identify and remedy any shortfalls in
stockpiles, capabilities, or training that would affect [the] ability to
respond. Scenarios describing NBC WMD incidents were used to
help Federal, State, and local responders focus on the capabilities
that would be required and to assess the adequacy of current capabilities to meet response requirements. The Federal effort included

a review of the coordination of consequence management activities with crisis management activities, an examination of the relationships among existing Federal interagency emergency plans, an assessment of the capabilities of the FRP to respond to an NBC WMD incident, the availability of medical capabilities for terrorism response, and procedures for military support of medical facilities and decontamination activities.

The assessment of the FRP and Federal capabilities focused on identifying shortfalls in stockpiles, capabilities, and training that would affect the Federal Government's ability to respond. In conducting the review and subsequent assessment, FEMA sought input from the 29 departments and agencies supporting the FRP. Comprehensive scenario-specific information was provided by key responding agencies including DoD, DOE, HHS, and EPA.

The DoD report then went on to summarize the findings of the FEMA report.

THE 1999 INSTITUTE OF MEDICINE/NATIONAL RESEARCH COUNCIL STUDY

In 1999, a study on chemical and biological terrorism was published by the Institute of Medicine and National Research Council. It provided an assessment of civilian capabilities for medical care in chemical and biological incidents. The capability areas in Table F.2 have been ranked in declining order of need at the local and state levels (i.e., the least capable areas are found in the top rows of the table).[1]

Although the table sheds little light on what performance improvements and costs might be associated with additional investments, the five areas given the lowest capability ratings for the localities and states were as follows:

*   Preincident intelligence and threat warning information.

---

[1] The rank-ordering was based on the number of times a capability was given a low rating in the first six columns (i.e., for local responders, initial treatment facilities, or state responders).

Table F.2

Relative Capabilities for Response to Civilian Chemical and Biological Incidents at Four Levels of Medical Care

Capability	Local Responders		Initial Treatment Facilities		State		Federal	
	Chem	Bio	Chem	Bio	Chem	Bio	Chem	Bio
Receipt of pre-incident intelligence	L	L	L	L	S	S	S	S
Detection and measurement of agent exposure in clinical samples	L	L	L	S	L	S	H	H
Methods/procedures for decontamination of those exposed	S	S	L	L	L	L	S	S
Availability, safety, and efficacy of drugs and other therapies	L	L	S	S	L	L	S	S
Detection, identification, and quantification of agents in the environment	S	L	L	L	S	S	H	S
Personal protective equipment	S	S	L	S	L	S	S	S
Safe and effective patient extraction	S	S	N/A	N/A	N/A	N/A	S	S
Methods for recognizing symptoms and signs in patients	S	S	S	S	L	L	S	S
Methods for recognizing covert exposure in populations	N/A	N/A	S	S	S	S	S	S
Mass-casualty triage techniques and procedures	S	S	S	S	L	L	S	S
Prevention, assessment, and treatment of psychological effects	S	S	S	S	S	S	S	S

NOTE: H = highly capable; S = some capability; L = little or no capability; and N/A = not applicable.

SOURCE: Institute of Medicine and National Research Council, 1999, p. 24.

- Detection and assessment equipment for environmental analysis and clinical samples.
- Mass decontamination capabilities.
- Vaccines and therapeutics.
- Personal protective equipment.

THE FEDERAL RESPONSE PLAN AND TERRORISM INCIDENT ANNEX

The Federal Response Plan—the mechanism by which FEMA coordinates federal disaster relief support to states and localities—and its Terrorism Incident Annex, provide the context and framework for DoD and Army roles in responses to WMD terrorism.[1] These documents establish the roles, responsibilities and relationships of various federal players in responding to a catastrophic terrorist incident.

The Terrorism Incident Annex envisions a possible flow from "crisis management" activities to "consequence management" activities in acts of WMD terrorism (see Figure G.1).

- Crisis management is defined by the FBI as "measures to identify, acquire, and plan the use of resources needed to anticipate, prevent, and/or resolve a threat or act of terrorism."

- Consequence Management is defined by FEMA as "measures to protect public health and safety, restore essential government services, and provide emergency relief to governments, businesses, and individuals affected by the consequences of terrorism."

As suggested by the figure, the annex also envisions the possibility that crisis and consequence management may operate concurrently.

---

[1]For radiological incidents, including radiological sabotage and terrorism, the Federal Radiological Emergency Response Plan (FRERP) Operational Plan (FEMA, 2000b) is also relevant.

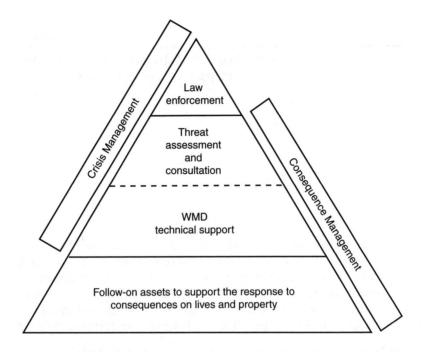

Figure G.1—Relationship Between Crisis and Consequence Management

Crisis Management

Another government document reaffirmed the FBI's federal lead responsibility for crisis management in responses to threats or acts of terrorism that take place within U.S. territory or in international waters and that do not involve the flag vessel of a foreign country.[2]

Consequence Management

The Robert T. Stafford Act "provide[s] an orderly and continuing means of assistance by the Federal Government to state and local

_____

[2]An unclassified FEMA abstract (1996) on a Presidential Decision Directive specifies the FBI's leadership role in crisis management activities. The FBI also has a WMD Incident Contingency Plan.

governments in carrying out their responsibilities to alleviate the suffering and damage which result" from emergencies and major disasters.[3] The Act does this by specifying mechanisms for the federal government to provide to states and localities assistance in planning, training and equipment, warning information, technical assistance, and other types of federal support prior to and during catastrophic incidents. The Act also defines the roles of the state and federal coordinating officers and other key elements of the response system.

These documents recognize the preeminent local and state role in disaster relief. For example, presidential declarations of major disasters and emergencies are premised on a governor's request for federal assistance, and federal responders are in a supporting role to local and state disaster officials. As a FEMA official put it:

> From its earliest beginnings, the United States has operated on two fundamental principles. The first is that State and local governments have the primary responsibility for disaster assistance. The second is that the Federal Government is responsible for the collective defense or national security of the respective states. (Goss, 1997.)

The Terrorism Incident Annex. The Terrorism Incident Annex was mandated by PDD 39, and aimed to provide additional guidance beyond the FRP that would improve the nation's "ability to respond rapidly and decisively to terrorism directed against Americans wherever it occurs, arrest or defeat the perpetrators using all appropriate instruments against the sponsoring organizations and governments, and provide recovery relief to victims, as permitted by law."

The Federal Response Plan (FRP). More broadly, the FRP provides the framework for federal responses to disasters and emergencies.[4]

---

[3]The existence of an emergency or major disaster is a presidential determination (Robert T. Stafford Act, 2000).

[4]According to FEMA (1999a):

> The FRP concepts apply to a major disaster or emergency as defined under the Stafford Act, which includes a natural catastrophe; fire, flood, or explosion regardless of cause; or any other occasion or instance for which the President determines that Federal assistance is needed to supplement State and local efforts and capabilities. Throughout the FRP, any reference to a disaster, major disaster, or

The FRP consists of 12 Emergency Support Functions (ESFs), and, as shown in Table G.1, the Army plays a prominent role in DoD's support to the FRP:

- For Public Works (ESF 3)—and the only ESF for which the DoD is responsible agency—the U.S. Army Corps of Engineers is the DoD point of contact (POC).

- The Army Corps of Engineers also is DoD POC for Energy (ESF 12), for which DOE is the responsible agency.

- The Director of Military Support (DOMS)—the Secretary of the Army's action agent for planning and executing DoD's Support Mission to civilian authorities in the United States—is DoD POC for two ESFs: Information and Planning (ESF 5), and Urban Search and Rescue (ESF 9).

Table G.1

The FRP and DoD POCs

ESFs	Responsible Agency	DoD POC
Transportation	DOT	CINCTRANS
Communications	NCS	OASD (C3I)
Public Works and Engineering	DoD	USACE
Fire-Fighting	USDA	FORSCOM
Information and Planning	FEMA	DOMS
Mass Care	Red Cross	DLA
Resource Support	GSA	DLA
Health/Medical Services	HHS	FORSCOM
Urban Search and Rescue	FEMA[a]	DOMS
Hazardous Materials	EPA	Navy, SUPV SALV
Food	USDA	DLA
Energy	DOE	USACE

SOURCE: FEMA, 1999b.

[a]We understand that DoD previously was responsible agency for Urban Search and Rescue.

---

emergency generally means a presidentially declared major disaster or emergency under the Stafford Act.

- By comparison, the only other service that is a DoD POC for an ESF is the Navy, for Hazardous Materials (ESF 10).

Although the foregoing covers the most obvious supporting Army roles, CINCTRANS, FORSCOM, and the Defense Logistics Agency (DLA), also can call on Army assets for DoD's support to other ESFs: transportation, fire-fighting, mass care, resource support, health/medical services, and food.

ARMY DOMESTIC PREPAREDNESS
TRAINING ACTIVITIES

Table H.1

Most DoD WMD Training Courses Are Army-Sponsored

Course Name	Agency/Sponsor
Chemical/Biological Countermeasures Training (CBCT)	U.S. Army Chemical School
Field Management of Chemical and Biological Casualties	USAMRICD
Medical Effects of Ionizing Radiation (MEIR)	(Armed Forces Radiobiology Research Institute (AFRRI)/ Uniformed Services University of the Health Sciences)
Medical Management of Biological Casualties	U.S. Army Office of the Surgeon General/USAMRIID
Medical Management of Chemical and Biological Casualties	USAMRICD/USAMRIID
NBC Domestic Preparedness Training Basic Awareness (Employee)	USA SBCCOM
NBC Domestic Preparedness Training Incident Command	USA SBCCOM
NBC Domestic Preparedness Training Responder–Awareness Courses	USA SBCCOM
NBC Domestic Preparedness Training Responder–Operations Courses	USA SBCCOM
NBC Domestic Preparedness Training Senior Officials Workshop	USA SBCCOM
NBC Domestic Preparedness Training Technician–Emergency Medical Services	USA SBCCOM
NBC Domestic Preparedness Training Technician Hazmat Courses	USA SBCCOM

Table H.1—continued

Course Name	Agency/Sponsor
NBC Domestic Preparedness Training Technician–Hospital Provider	USA SBCCOM
Nuclear Emergency Team (NET) Operations	(Defense Nuclear Weapons School)
Nuclear Hazards Training Course	(Defense Nuclear Weapons School)
Operational Radiation Safety	U.S. Army Chemical School
Radiological Accident Command, Control, and Coordination (RAC3)	(Defense Nuclear Weapons School)
Toxic Aid Automated Training	(DoD/ERDEC)
Toxic Chemical Training for Medical Support Personnel	U.S. Army CBDCOM
Preparing for and Managing the Consequences of Terrorism	(National Guard Bureau)

SOURCE: U.S. Army, SBCCOM, 1998.

NOTES: Non-Army agency/sponsors are in parentheses.

Table H.2

120 Cities to Be Trained by Army Domestic Preparedness Team

Akron, Ohio	Grand Rapids, Mich.	Oklahoma City, Okla.
Albuquerque, N.M.	Greensboro, N.C.	Omaha, Neb.
Amarillo, Tex.	Hialeah, Fla.	Orlando, Fla.
Anaheim, Calif.	Honolulu, Hawaii	Philadelphia, Pa.
Anchorage, Alaska	Houston, Tex.	Phoenix, Ariz.
Arlington, Tex.	Huntington Beach, Calif.	Pittsburgh, Pa.
Arlington, Va.	Huntsville, Ala.	Portland, Ore.
Atlanta, Ga.	Indianapolis, Ind.	Providence, R.I.
Aurora, Colo.	Irving, Tex.	Raleigh, N.C.
Austin, Tex.	Jackson, Miss.	Richmond, Va.
Bakersfield, Calif.	Jacksonville, Fla.	Riverside, Calif.
Baltimore, Md.	Jersey City, N.J.	Rochester, N.Y.
Baton Rouge, La.	Kansas City, Kan.	Sacramento, Calif.
Birmingham, Ala.	Kansas City, Mo.	Saint Louis, Mo.
Boston, Mass.	Knoxville, Tenn.	Saint Paul, Minn.
Buffalo, N.Y.	Las Vegas, Nev.	Saint Petersburg, Fla.
Charlotte, N.C.	Lexington-Fayette, Ky.	Salt Lake City, Utah
Chattanooga, Tenn.	Lincoln, Neb.	San Antonio, Tex.
Chesapeake, Va.	Little Rock, Ark.	San Bernardino, Calif.
Chicago, Ill.	Long Beach, Calif.	San Diego, Calif.
Cincinnati, Ohio	Los Angeles, Calif.	San Francisco, Calif.
Cleveland, Ohio	Louisville, Ky.	San Jose, Calif
Colorado Springs, Colo.	Lubbock, Tex.	Santa Ana, Calif.

Table H.2—continued

Columbus, Ga.	Madison, Wis.	Seattle, Wash.
Columbus, Ohio	Memphis, Tenn.	Shreveport, La.
Corpus Christi, Tex.	Mesa, Ariz.	Spokane, Wash.
Dallas, Tex.	Metairie, La.	Springfield, Mass.
Dayton, Ohio	Miami, Fla.	Stockton, Calif.
Denver, Colo.	Milwaukee, Wis.	Syracuse, N.Y.
Des Moines, Iowa	Minneapolis, Minn.	Tacoma, Wash.
Detroit, Mich.	Mobile, Ala.	Tampa, Fla.
El Paso, Tex.	Modesto, Calif.	Toledo, Ohio
Fort Wayne, Ind.	Montgomery, Ala.	Tucson, Ariz.
Fort Worth, Tex.	Nashville, Tenn.	Tulsa, Okla.
Fremont, Calif.	New Orleans, La.	Virginia Beach, Va.
Fresno, Calif.	New York, N.Y.	Warren, Mich.
Fort Lauderdale, Fla.	Newark, N.J.	Washington, D.C.
Garland, Tex.	Newport News, Va.	Wichita, Kan.
Glendale, Ariz.	Norfolk, Va.	Worcester, Mass.
Glendale, Calif.	Oakland, Calif.	Yonkers, N.Y.

NOTE: as of August 2, 1999.
Source: U.S. Army, SBCCOM, 1999b.

Table H.3

**Training by Army Domestic
Preparedness Team**

Quarter	Cities Trained
97Q3	5
97Q4	3
98Q1	13
98Q2	8
98Q3	5
98Q4	8
99Q1	8
99Q2	8

NOTE: As of August 2, 1999.
SOURCE: U.S. Army, SBCCOM, 1999c.

ARMY MISSION-CRITICAL FACILITIES AND SYSTEMS

This appendix illustrates the range of Army mission-critical facilities and systems.

MISSION-CRITICAL FACILITIES

In addition to the Headquarters, Department of the Army, and the CONUS Armies, Army mission-critical facilities include the Army's power-projection platforms, comprising installations, Air and Sea Ports of Embarkation (APOEs/SPOEs), and Depots and Ammunition Plants, identified in Tables I.1 through I.4.

Table I.1

Army Power Projection Platforms—Installations

Installation	Units	Deploying Soldiers
Fort Hood, Tex.	289	74,326
Fort Bragg, N.C.	253	48,236
Fort Drum, N.Y.	168	41,696
Fort Campbell, Ky.	176	37,269
Fort Stewart, Ga.	149	36,367
Fort Riley, Kan.	152	33,585
Fort Lewis, Wash.	152	26,524
Fort Carson, Colo.	93	21,178
Fort McCoy, Wis.	84	16,253
Fort Polk, La.	62	13,352

Table I.1—continued

Installation	Units	Deploying Soldiers
Fort Dix, N.J.	73	13,128
Fort Bliss, Tex.	45	11,138
Fort Sill, Okla.	45	11,106
Fort Benning, Ga.	59	11,061
Fort Eustis, Va.	59	6,390

Source: U.S. Army DCS (Logistics).

Table I.2

Army Power Projection Platforms—APOEs and Army Installations

APOE	Fort
Pope AFB, N.C.	Fort Bragg
Hunter AAF, Ga.	Fort Stewart
Lawson AAF, Ga.	Fort Benning
Alexandria, La.	Fort Polk
Gray AAF, Tex.	Fort Hood
Biggs AAF, Tex.	Fort Bliss
Altus AFB, Okla.	Fort Sill
Peterson AFB, Colo.	Fort Carson
McChord AFB, Wash.	Fort Lewis
Forbes Field, Kan.	Fort Riley
Volk Field, Wis.	Fort McCoy
Campbell AAF, Ky.	Fort Campbell
Fort Drum AAF, N.Y.	Fort Drum
McGuire AFB, N.J.	Fort Dix
Langley AFB, Va.	Fort Eustis

Source: U.S. Army DCS (Logistics).

Table I.3

Army Power Projection Platforms— SPOEs

SPOE	Fort
Wilmington, N.C.	Fort Bragg
	Fort Riley
Savannah, Ga.	Fort Stewart
	Fort Benning
	Fort Riley
Jacksonville, Fla.	Fort Campbell

Table I.3—continued

SPOE	Fort
Beaumont, Tex.	Fort Hood
	Fort Polk
	Fort Sill
	Fort Bliss
Galveston, Tex.	Fort Hood
Tacoma, Wash.	Fort Lewis
New York, N.Y.	Fort Drum
	Fort Dix
	Fort McCoy
Norfolk, Va.	Fort Carson
	Fort Eustis
Bayonne, N.J.	
Charleston, S.C.	
Long Beach, Calif.	
Morehead City, N.C.	
NWS Concord, Calif.	
Oakland, Calif.	
Port Hueneme, Calif.	
San Diego, Calif.	
Sunny Point, N.C.	

Source: U.S. Army DCS(Logistics).

Table I.4

Army Power Projection Platforms— Depots and Ammunition Plants

Milan Army Ammunition Plant, Tenn.
Anniston Army Depot, Ala.
Pine Bluff Arsenal, Ark.
Red River Army Depot, Tex.
McAlester Army Ammunition Plant, Okla.
Hawthorne Army Depot, Nev.
Tooele Army Depot, Utah
Iowa Army Ammunition Plant, Iowa
Crane Army Ammunition Activity, Ind.
Bluegrass Army Depot, Ky.
Letterkenny Army Depot, Pa.

Source: U.S. Army DCS (Logistics).

MISSION-CRITICAL SYSTEMS

"Mission-critical systems" are those systems critical to DoD's ability to meet its responsibilities and include command and control systems, satellite systems, inventory management systems, transportation management systems, medical systems and equipment, and pay and personnel systems (Curtis, 1998).

DoD-wide, approximately 2,300 systems are estimated to be mission-critical (Hamre, 1999), while the Army is estimated to have 376 such systems (GAO, 1998c, p. 10). Although an exhaustive list of Army mission-critical systems was unavailable, many mission-critical Army systems are included in the list of DoD mission-critical systems in Table I.5.

Table I.5

DoD Mission-Critical Systems

Army Sea-Lite Beam Detector
Standard Army Maintenance System–1
Standard Army Maintenance System–2
Army HELSTF Executive Controller
Army AN/TYQ-33, Tactical Combat Service Support Computer
  System–Enhanced
Army Standard Installation/Division Personnel System
Defense Communications and Army Switch Systems
Naval Space Command Mission Processing System
Integrated Satellite Control System
NESP EHF Low Data Rate Terminal
Integrated Verdin Transmit Terminal
Integrated Submarine Automated Broadcast Processing System
Nontactical Command Support System/Shipboard Nontactical
  Automated Data Processing Program I and II
Joint Maritime Command Information System Ashore
Joint Maritime Command Information System Afloat
Joint Maritime Command Information System Tac/Mobile
Joint Maritime Command Information System OBU/OED
Joint Maritime Command Information System Radiant Mercury
Inactive Manpower and Personnel Management Information
  System
Tomahawk Mission Planning
Tomahawk Afloat Planning System
Joint Services Imagery Processing System
Naval Communication Processing and Routing System
Common Source Routing File System

Table I.5—continued

Very Long Baseline Interferometry Mark III Correlator
Execution and Prioritization of Repairs Support System
AC-130U Gunship Avionics
Defense Attaché Worldwide Network
Defense Switched Network
Defense Fuels Automated Management System
NIMA Exploitation System
Automated Patient Evaluation System
Defense Medical Regulating Information System
Compliance Monitoring and Tracking System
Army National Guard's Standard Installation/Division
    Personnel System (SIDPERS)

SOURCES: Garamone, 1998; Stone, 1999.

Table I.6 identifies a number of future Army systems still in development that are potentially mission-critical.

Table I.6

Potential Future Army Mission-Critical Systems

Department of the Army Command and Control System
Army Global Command and Control System
Combat Service Support Automated Information Systems
    Interface
CONUS Freight Management System
Corps Theater ADP Service Center, Phase II
Defense Communications and Army Switched Systems
Defense Communications and Army Transmission Systems
Army segments of Defense Data Networks
Defense Message System–Army
Department Army Movements Management System–Redesign
Reserve Component Automation System
Standard Army Ammunition System
Standard Army Maintenance System
Standard Army Retail Supply System
Standard Installation/Division Personnel System
Sustaining Base Information Services
Tactical Management Information Systems
Transportation Coordinators' Automated Information for
    Movement System II
Unit Level Logistics System
Worldwide Port System

SOURCE: Assistant Secretary of the Army for Acquisition, Logistics and Technology.

RECOMMENDATIONS OF THE
DEFENSE SCIENCE BOARD

The Defense Science Board's 1996 report on defensive information warfare (IW) contained 50 recommended actions for DoD, summarized here (Defense Science Board, 1996).

1. Designate an accountable IW focal point.

2. Organize for IW defense (IW-D).

3. Increase awareness.

4. Assess infrastructure dependencies and vulnerabilities.

5. Define threat conditions and responses.

6. Assess IW-D readiness.

7. "Raise the Bar" with high-payoff, low-cost items.

8. Establish and maintain a minimum essential information infrastructure.

9. Focus the R&D.

10. Staff for success.

11. Resolve the legal issues.

12. Participate fully in critical infrastructure protection.

13. Provide the resources.

RECOMMENDATIONS OF THE PRESIDENT'S COMMISSION ON CRITICAL INFRASTRUCTURE PROTECTION

The President's Commission on Critical Infrastructure Protection (PCCIP) provided the outlines of a strategy for a layered defense that included activities in policy formulation; prevention and mitigation; information sharing and operational warning; counteraction (incident management); and response, restoration, and reconstitution (consequence management).

Policy formulation activities include

- assess national risk;
- integrate public and private sector perspectives;
- propose national objectives and develop strategies;
- propose and promote (new) legislation;
- assess and promote (new) regulations;
- influence private sector investments;
- prepare, recommend, and promote budget;
- manage and enforce implementation;
- shape the international environment; and
- issue the national policy.

Prevention and mitigation activities include

- provide effective education and awareness;
- set standards, certifications, and best practices;
- assess vulnerabilities and risks of system components;
- research advanced techniques and develop new technologies;
- negotiate funding;
- acquire the resources for protecting systems; and
- manage operations consistent with best practices.

Information sharing and operational warning activities include

- share information;
- analyze information and prepare threat advisories; and
- disseminate warnings.

Counteraction (incident management) activities include

- develop incident management policy and plan operations;
- deter, halt, or minimize an attack;
- implement defensive actions;
- punish perpetrators during or after an attack;
- control misinformation and manage perceptions; and
- coordinate incident and consequence management.

Response, restoration, and reconstitution (consequence management) activities include

- plan for the response to consequences;
- manage the response to consequences;
- plan for restoration and reconstitution; and
- manage restoration and reconstitution.

THE FEDERAL PROGRAM TO COMBAT
TERRORISM AND WMD

This appendix provides aggregate-level data on how the federal programs to combat terrorism and WMD are allocated.

FEDERAL SPENDING TO COMBAT TERRORISM AND WMD

Table L.1 describes governmentwide funding in terms of the five functional areas used to describe the overall federal program to combat terrorism and WMD.

As shown in the table, the shares allocated to each function are remarkably stable:

- Law enforcement and investigative activities (offensive activities) received 34.1 percent of the total funding for combating terrorism in the base budget for FY 1999 and 32.0 percent in the FY 2000 request, while funding for combating WMD was 7.1 and 6.3 percent of the WMD total, respectively.

- Preparing for and responding to terrorist acts (defensive activities) received 15.5 percent in FY 1999 and 15.1 percent in the FY 2000 request, while the WMD portion in the two years was 51.3 and 47.9 percent, respectively.

- The physical security of government facilities and employees (defensive activities) received 40.2 percent in FY 1999 and 40.7 percent in the FY 2000 request, while the WMD portion was 18.2 and 14.9 percent, respectively.

Table L.1

Funding for Combating Terrorism and WMD

	Terror FY 1999 Base	Terror FY 2000 Request	WMD FY 1999 Base	WMD FY 2000 Request
Law enforcement and investigative activities	$2,587 (34.1%)	$2,757 (32.0%)	$87 (7.1%)	$87 (6.3%)
Preparing for and responding to terrorist acts	1,175 (15.5)	1,302 (15.1)	629 (51.3)	664 (47.9)
Physical security of government facilities and employees	3,049 (40.2)	3,504 (40.7)	223 (18.2)	206 (14.9)
Physical protection of the national populace and national infrastructure	354 (4.7)	472 (5.5)	30 (2.4)	28 (2.0)
R&D	418 (5.5)	577 (6.7)	258 (21.0)	400 (28.9)

NOTE: Figures are expressed in dollar millions.

SOURCES: Office of Management and Budget (1999a, 1999b); Center for Nonproliferation Studies, Monterey Institute of International Studies, as of August 31, 1999.

- The physical protection of the national populace and national infrastructure (defensive activities) received 4.7 percent in FY 1999 and 5.5 percent in the FY 2000 request, with WMD funding at 2.4 and 2.0 percent, respectively.[1]

- R&D (supporting offense *and* defense) accounted for 5.5 percent of total spending in FY 1999 and 6.7 percent in FY 2000, while WMD-related funding was at 21.0 and 28.9 percent, respectively.

Federally, this spending was broken out as shown in Table L.2.

NATIONAL SECURITY COMMUNITY SPENDING TO COMBAT TERRORISM AND WMD

Table L.3 describes the FY 1999 and FY 2000 funding for National Security, including the DoD and the Intelligence agencies.

---

[1]This does not include funding for critical infrastructure protection, which amounted to $1.4 billion in the FY 2000 request.

Table L.2

Governmentwide Funding to Combat Terrorism

	FY 1999	FY 2000
Federal Government (total)	$9,647	$10,000
Combat WMD missions (total)	1,227	1,385
Law Enforcement and Investigative Activities	2,937	2,757
WMD figure for above function	87	87
Preparing for and Responding to Terrorist Acts	1,233	1,302
WMD figure for above function	629	664
Public health infrastructure/surveillance	44	65
Stockpile vaccines, antidotes, antibiotics	51	53
Planning/exercises	24	22
Training of first responders	90	87
Protective equipment for first responders	101	95
WMD detection equipment	105	128
State and local planning and assistance	113	123
Other	101	91
Physical Security of Government Facilities/Employees	4,600	3,504
WMD figure for above function	223	206
Physical Protection of National Population and Infrastructure	454	472
WMD figure for above function	30	28
R&D	423	577
WMD figure for above function	258	400
Pathogen genome sequencing	16	28
Vaccines/therapeutics	9	50
Detection/diagnostics	23	58
Personal and environmental decontamination	2	15
Modeling, simulation, systems analyses	4	8
Other	204	241

SOURCES: Office of Management and Budget (1999a, 1999b); Center for Nonproliferation Studies, Monterey Institute of International Studies, as of August 31, 1999.

NOTES: FY 1999 is amount enacted and does not include $50 million provided to DoD as part of the FY 1999 emergency supplemental bill. Funds are expressed in dollar millions.

Table L.3

National Security Funding to Combat Terrorism

	FY 1999	FY 2000
National Security Community (total)	$5,089	$5,052
Combat WMD missions (total)	140	196
Law Enforcement and Investigative Activities	2,385	2,191
WMD figure for above function	20	20
Preparing for and Responding to Terrorist Acts	592	600
WMD figure for above function	113	115
Public health infrastructure/surveillance	0	0
Stockpile vaccines, antidotes, antibiotics	0	0
Planning/exercises	1	1
Training of first responders	50	31
Protective equipment for first responders	0	0
WMD detection equipment	0	0
State and local planning and assistance	49	70
Other	13	12
Physical Security of Government Facilities/Employees	2,004	2,059
WMD figure for above function	0	0
Physical Protection of National Population and Infrastructure	16	18
WMD figure for above function	0	0
R&D	92	184
WMD figure for above function	7	62
Pathogen genome sequencing	0	4
Vaccines/therapeutics	0	0
Detection/diagnostics	0	34
Personal and environmental decontamination	0	12
Modeling, simulation, systems analyses	0	0
Other	7	12

SOURCES: Office of Management and Budget (1999a, 1999b); Center for Nonproliferation Studies, Monterey Institute of International Studies, as of August 31, 1999. Funds are expressed in dollar millions.

COUNTERPROLIFERATION PROGRAMS

Tables L.4, L.5, and L.6 detail the objectives, functional areas, and investments in the field of counterproliferation, including programs to counter paramilitary and terrorist threats.

Table L.4

Operational Objectives for Countering Proliferation/ Counterproliferation Functional Area Objectives

Proliferation Prevention	Effective and cooperative interagency support in export controls, treaty verification, and inspection support
	Detection, tracking, and protection of NBC weapons and means of delivery associated materials, components, and technologies
	Effective and timely data correlation and fusion
Strategic and Tactical Intelligence	Provide accurate, comprehensive, timely, and actionable foreign intelligence in support of national strategy for countering proliferation
	Effective and timely dissemination of operational intelligence to users
Battlefield Surveillance	Accurate NBC weapons and means of delivery target identification and characterization
	Time urgent response
	Prompt, reliable poststrike damage assessment and bomb-damage assessment
NBC Weapons and Means of Delivery Counterforce	High kill/neutralization probability against hardened, underground, and mobile NBC weapons and means of delivery targets
	Collateral effects characterization, minimization, and neutralization
Active Defense	Cost-effective, wide-area, low-leakage active air and missile defenses
	Collateral effects minimization/ neutralization
Passive Defense	Prompt, accurate NBC agent detection, identification, and early warning
	Individual and collective protection, decontamination, medical response, and postexposure therapies that minimize casualties, performance degradation, and operational and logistical impacts
	Availability of effective biological warfare vaccines
Countering Paramilitary, Covert Delivery, and Terrorist NBC Threats	Joint interagency readiness against NBC threats in the United States and overseas
	Prompt, effective worldwide response
	Timely and effective consequence management

SOURCE: CPRC, 1997, Table 1.1.

Table L.5

DoD and DOE Investments in Counterproliferation ACEs, FY 1998

Counterproliferation	DoD	DOE
Detection, identification, and characterization of biological warfare agents	$191.1	$19.0
Detection, characterization, and defeat of NBC weapons and means of delivery facilities with minimal collateral effects	83.9	
Detection, characterization, and defeat of underground facilities with minimal collateral effects		
Theater ballistic missile active defense	3,217.5	
Support for Special Operations Forces and defense against paramilitary, covert delivery, and terrorist NBC threats	151.1	41.1
Provide consequence management	21.5	
Cruise missile defense	18.1	
Collection, analysis, and dissemination of actionable intelligence to counter proliferation	0.8	
Robust passive defense to enable sustained operations on the NBC battlefield	364.9	
Biological Vaccine RDT&E and production to ensure stockpile availability	64.5	
Target planning for NBC weapons and their means of delivery targets	5.7	
Prompt mobile target detection and defeat	178.0	
Detection, tracking, and protection of NBC weapons and their means of delivery and related materials and components	3.0	297.2
Support export control activities of the U.S. government	16.2	16.5
Support inspection and monitoring activities of arms control agreements and regimes	569.9	115.6
Totals	4,886.1	489.4

NOTE: Figures are expressed in dollar millions.
SOURCE: CPRC, 1997, Table 2.1.

Table L.6

Key DoD Programs to Counter Paramilitary and Terrorist NBC Threats

Program/Project Title	Agency	FY 1998
New Initiatives in FY 1998		
Domestic Preparedness Initiative	ASD (SO/LIC)	$49.500
DoD's Force Protection Initiative	DSWA	4.500
Marine Corps CBIRF	USMC	20.200

Table L.6—continued

Program/Project Title	Agency	FY 1998
Consequence Management 911-BIO ACTD	ATSD (NCB)	a
CBD Program Antiterrorism Support	Joint	3.688
CP Support Programs		
First Responder Support	SOCOM	1.200
Specialized SOF Technologies and Prototype Devices	SOCOM	10.029
Joint EOD Readiness Sustainment	SOCOM Navy	0.656
Strongly Related CP Programs		
Counterterror Technical Support Program	ASD (SO/LIC)	29.087
Joint Physical Security Equipment	PDUSD (S&TS)	17.789
SO/LIC Analytical Support	ASD (SO/LIC)	1.611
EOD/LIC Program	ASD (SO/LIC)	4.165
Navy Joint Service EOD Systems Program	Navy ASD (SO/LIC)	4.720
Navy Joint Service EOD Procedures Program	Navy ASD (SO/LIC)	6.613
Joint Robotics Program	PDUSD (S&TS)	16.399

NOTE: Figures are expressed in dollar millions.

[a]ACTD demonstrations were completed in the first quarter of FY 1998 using FY 1997 dollars.

SOURCE: CPRC, 1997, Table 8.1.

NOTIONAL GPRA MEASURES OF PERFORMANCE

The Government Performance and Results Act of 1993 (GPRA) aims to improve governmental effectiveness by setting program goals, and measuring program performance against those goals.[1] While providing GPRA measures for most other defense activities, the current Report to the President and Congress (the Annual Defense Report, or ADR) includes no such measures for homeland security.

This appendix provides a consolidated listing of the measures of performance identified for each homeland security task area described in Chapters Four through Seven, measures that might be considered by the Army and DoD for use in their GPRA reporting for homeland security activities.[2]

DOMESTIC PREPAREDNESS AGAINST WMD

The measures of performance that should be considered for the domestic preparedness task area break out into three classes: those associated with prevention activities, those associated with pre-

---

[1]In the area of Domestic Preparedness, performance measures can be derived in part from the 1997 Counterproliferation Program Review Committee report, which provides potential measures for proliferation prevention; strategic and tactical intelligence; battlefield surveillance; NBC weapons and their means of delivery counterforce; active defense; passive defense; and countering paramilitary, covert delivery, and terrorist NBC threats. See CPRC, 1997, Table 1.1, reproduced as Table L.4 in Appendix L.

[2]Unlike most of the GPRA measures used by the Department of Defense, which are in terms of such inputs as the number of units of various kinds, we tried to design our measures to relate to performance outcomes or impacts.

paredness, and those associated with response.[3] Each is discussed separately.

Prevention Activities

Performance in terrorism and WMD prevention activities could be gauged by such quantifiable measures as

- terrorist incidents prevented;
- ratio of known preventions to known incidents;
- deaths possibly prevented;
- amount of damage possibly prevented;
- arrests/extraditions of terrorists; and
- proliferation incidents prevented.

These measures must be considered in the context of the base rate of terrorist and WMD-related activity, such as

- terrorist plans detected;
- domestic terrorist incidents;
- suspected incidents;
- deaths caused by domestic terrorism; and
- damage sustained in domestic terrorism.

They also would have to be considered in the context of hoaxes, idle threats, and other "noise."

---

[3]The Commission to Assess the Organization of the Federal Government to Combat the Proliferation of Weapons of Mass Destruction posited four national goals, for each of which required operational capabilities were identified. The national goals were proliferation prevention/denial, WMD deterrence (short of military action), WMD military action (including active defenses and/or retaliation), and WMD consequence management. See Commission (1999), Appendix H, pp. 155–167.

Preparedness Activities

Preparedness and response activities could be assessed by any number of measures.[4] To illustrate, consider the following:

- Estimated responsiveness, i.e., time until specific capabilities can be at the scene of an incident or increase in responsiveness since last employment or exercise.

- Estimated capacity of specific response units or overall response system to mitigate consequences (e.g., deaths and injuries) or increase in capacity.

- Assessed overall performance of response capabilities in training and field exercises.

- Number of hazmat (or other first responder teams) trained to a high level of capability for WMD.

- Number of U.S. cities trained to a level that provides highly responsive and capable WMD preparedness.

- Percentage of U.S. population that is covered by highly responsive and capable WMD preparedness.

Response Activities

Response activities could be assessed by such measures as the following:

- Percentage of mitigation attained, i.e., the number of deaths or injuries that otherwise would have occurred in an incident prevented as a result of response capabilities.

- Responsiveness, i.e., time until specific capabilities can be at the scene of an incident or increase in responsiveness since the last exercise or employment.

---

[4]As a practical matter, many preparedness and response activities blend together—the preparedness training and equipping that occurs well in advance of an actual incident favorably affects performance when employed.

- Actual capacity of specific response units or overall response system to mitigate consequences (e.g., deaths and injuries) or increase in capacity since the last exercise or employment.

COG

FEMA's most recent circular suggests a number of relevant performance measures in its discussion of the objectives and planning considerations for COG activities. Stated objectives for continuity of government include

- ensuring the continuous performance of an agency's functions/operations during an emergency;
- protecting essential facilities, equipment, records, and other assets;
- reducing or mitigating disruptions to operations;
- reducing loss of life, minimizing damage and losses; and
- achieving a timely and orderly recovery from an emergency and resumption of full service to customers.

Planning considerations suggest that a viable COG capability

- must be maintained at a high level of readiness;
- must be capable of implementation both with and without warning;
- must be operational no later than 12 hours after activation;
- must maintain sustained operations for up to 30 days; and
- should take maximum advantage of existing agency field infrastructures.

Generally speaking, then, the key performance measures for COG are the degree to which the consequences of emergencies can be mitigated, and the speed with which government functions and services can be restored. Our recommendation is that planning should aim to reestablish a sort of nominal or basic level of civil authority within 12 hours, as suggested by FEMA.[5]

CONTINUITY OF OPERATIONS

Performance measures for continuity of operations and COG activities appear to be somewhat similar, although the specific activities depend on which aspect of this problem set is considered.

Prevention Activities

Because the threats are assumed to overlap with those in the domestic preparedness task area—state and nonstate sponsors of terrorism and disaffected domestic groups—the same sorts of prevention-based performance measures apply, e.g., the number of actual attacks, the number of known, credible attack plans discovered, and the number of preventions.

Preparedness Activities

Threat and risk analyses would lead to a prioritization of potential mission-critical targets, whether focused on the continuity of headquarters operations, critical facilities, or critical systems and networks. A wide range of preparedness activities could then be undertaken, including improving defenses (e.g., hardening for facilities, improved network security for systems) and contingency planning for relocation.

Measures for preparedness activities would aim to reduce the level of damage and the time that any set of mission-critical assets was unavailable. These measures could include

- percentage of mission-critical facilities that have a high capability to withstand attack (e.g., blast effects or introduction of chemical or biological attack);

---

[5]As in the discussion of performance levels for domestic preparedness activities, policymakers might set lower or higher performance criteria.

- expected maximum time that normal operations of mission-critical organizations or facilities are likely to be disrupted;
- expected maximum time mission-critical facilities are unavailable; and
- expected maximum time until mitigation or reconstitution capabilities are deployed.

Response and Reconstitution Activities

Some of the operational measures associated with responses in the domestic preparedness area also would apply to response activities. Added to these, however, would be the speed at which headquarters could be relocated to alternative sites where they would be at lower risk.

In addition to response performance, one also needs to consider performance in terms of the speed with which basic functions and services can be restored. Perhaps the best measure would be time, i.e., the time until operations can resume at their normal tempo.

Threat Campaigns

An additional measure of performance would be the ability to sustain the full range of continuity operations over a sustained threat campaign that involved multiple attacks in dispersed locations.

BORDER AND COASTAL DEFENSE

Measures of performance are analogous to the measures described in our earlier discussion of domestic preparedness. As in that case, activities should be measured in terms of their responsiveness, i.e., the time until core capabilities can be on-scene and, once on-scene, their capacity to capture, neutralize, destroy, or otherwise eliminate the threat of WMD and other potentially mass casualty-producing weapons:

- The probability of detecting WMD before it enters the United States, whether on land, sea, or in the air.

- The time until smugglers can be located and targeted.

- The time until WMD can be secured, rendered safe, and safely transported to a secure location.

- Both measures of actual preventions (e.g., preventions or arrests for smuggling such weapons, planned attempts that were disrupted), and measures of the apparent base level of threat activity (e.g., suspected smuggling attempts).

Preparedness activities for border and coastal defense thus need to be measured by the national capability to detect weapons and agents of interest before they can be introduced into the United States, and the ability to secure them, render them safe, and transport them to a secure location.

Refugee Resettlement Operations

The key measures of performance for refugee management operations are capacity measures, both in terms of the total number of refugees that can be processed and in terms of the rate at which they can be processed. See Table 7.2, which provides several different measures of processing capacity for six past Army resettlement operations.

BIBLIOGRAPHY

Agence France-Presse, "Russian Hackers Reportedly Accessed U.S. Military Secrets," September 12, 1999, at http://www.nandotimes. com.

Allison, Graham, Matthew Bunn, Ashton Carter, John Deutch, Richard Falkenrath, John Holdren, Robert Newman, and Joe Nye, "Defending the United States Against Weapons of Mass Destruction," unpublished memorandum to the U.S. Senate, June 2, 1997, at http://ksgnotes1.harvard.edu/BCSIA/Library.nsf/wwwdocsname/defend_US.

American Civil Liberties Union, "ACLU Says Broad New Anti-Terrorism Measure Could Encroach on Americans' Rights," ACLU news release, January 25, 1999, at http://www.aclu.org/news/1999/n012599a.html.

"Anthrax Advisory from WMD Operations Unit of the Federal Bureau of Investigation," December 1998, at http://www.emergency.com/fbiantrx.htm.

Assistant Secretary of the Army for Acquisition, Logistics and Technology, U.S. Department of the Army, Washington, D.C., at http://sarda.army.mil/acat/ais.htm.

Assistant Secretary of the Army for Financial Management and Comptroller, *The Army Budget: FY 00/01 President's Budget*, Washington, D.C., February 1999a.

_____, *FY 00/01 President's Budget Highlights*, Washington, D.C., February 1999b.

Associated Press, "CIA Employing Stealth Tactics to Preempt Terrorist Attacks," March 1, 1999.

Association of the U.S. Army, 1999–2000 Army Greenbook.

Avalon Project, at http://www.yale.edu/lawweb/avalon/avalon.htm.

Bacon, Kenneth, DoD News Briefing, January 13, 2000.

Bender, Bryan, "US DoD Clamps Down on Threats over the Internet," *Jane's Defence Weekly*, Vol. 32, No. 9, September 1, 1999.

Berkowsky, Pamela B., and Charles Cragin, Joint Statement of Pamela B. Berkowsky, Assistant to the Secretary of Defense for Civil Support, and Charles Cragin, Principal Deputy Assistant Secretary of Defense for Reserve Affairs, to the Senate, Committee on Armed Services, March 24, 2000.

Betts, Richard K., "Analysis, War, and Decision: Why Intelligence Failures Are Inevitable," *World Politics*, Vol. 31, No. 1, October 1978, pp. 61–89.

_____, "The New Threat of Mass Destruction," *Foreign Affairs*, January/February 1998, pp. 26–41.

Byrne, Sean J., "Defending Sovereignty: Domestic Operations and Legal Precedents," *Military Review*, March/April 1999.

Cable News Network, "Pentagon Says Computers Invaded by Hackers," CNN.com, February 25, 1998, http://www.cnn.com.

_____, "Hackers Target Pentagon Computers: Cyber 'War' Over Access Under Way," CNN.com, March 5, 1999a, http://www.cnn.com.

_____, "Pentagon 'At War' With Computer Hackers," CNN.com, March 5, 1999b, at http://cnn.com/TECH/computing/9903/05/pentagon.hackers.

_____, "FBI on Offensive in 'Cyber War,' Raiding Hackers' Homes," CNN.com, June 20, 1999c, http://www.cnn.com.

Campbell, Matthew, "Russian Hackers Steal US Weapons Secrets," *London Sunday Times*, July 25, 1999.

Carter, Ashton B., John M. Deutch, and Philip D. Zelikow, "Catastrophic Terrorism: Tackling the New Danger," *Foreign Affairs*, November/December 1998a, pp. 81–94.

_____, *Catastrophic Terrorism: Elements of a National Policy*, Cambridge, Mass.: Harvard University Press, 1998b.

Carus, Seth, "The Threat of Bioterrorism," *Strategic Forum*, Institute for National Strategic Studies, National Defense University, No. 127, September 1997.

Close Up Foundation, "U.S. Policy Toward Cuba," at http://www.closeup.org/cuba.htm, 1999.

Commission to Assess the Organization of the Federal Government to Combat the Proliferation of Weapons of Mass Destruction, *Combating Proliferation of Weapons of Mass Destruction*, Washington, D.C., July 1999, p. 1.

Committee on R&D Needs for Improving Civilian Medical Response to Chemical and Biological Terrorism Incidents, Health Science Policy Program, Institute of Medicine, and Board on Environmental Studies and Toxicology, Commission on Life Sciences, National Research Council, *Chemical and Biological Terrorism: Research and Development to Improve Civilian Medical Response*, Washington, D.C.: National Academy Press, 1999.

Computer Emergency Response Team Coordination Center (CERT/CC), CERT Coordination Center Annual Reports, 1994–1998.

_____, "CERT®/CC Statistics, 1988–1998," at http://www.cert.org/stats/cert_stats.html, 1999.

Computer Security Institute and Federal Bureau of Investigation, 1999 CSI/FBI Computer Crime and Security Survey, 1999, at http://www.gocsi.com.

Congressional Quarterly, "Clinton Signs Defense Bill Despite Budget Increase," *1996 CQ Almanac*, Washington, D.C.: *Congressional Quarterly*, 1997, p. 8–8.

Counterproliferation Program Review Committee, *CPRC Report to Congress on Activities and Programs for Countering Proliferation and NBC Terrorism*, Washington, D.C., May 1997.

Curtis, William A., prepared statement by William A. Curtis, Special Assistant for Year 2000, Office of the Assistant Secretary of Defense (Command, Control, Communications, and Intelligence) to the House Committee on Government Reform and Oversight, Subcommittee on Government Management, Information, and Technology, June 10, 1998, at http://www.defenselink.mil:80/speeches/1998/t19980610-curtis.html.

DAMO-SSW, "Integrating Reserve Component (RC) into the Army's Information Operations (IO) Mission," information paper, January 25, 1999.

Defense Science Board, *Report of the Defense Science Board Task Force Task Force on Information Warfare—Defense (IW–D)*, Washington, D.C., November 1996.

_____, *DOD Responses to Transnational Threats*, 1997 Summer Study Task Force report, sponsored by the Office of the Under Secretary of Defense for Acquisition and Technology, Washington, D.C.: USGPO, October 1997.

Department of the Army, *Justification of Estimates for Fiscal Year 2000*, Washington, D.C., 1999.

_____, *Domestic Disaster Assistance: A Primer for Attorneys*, The Judge Advocate General's School, Center for Law and Military Operations, Charlottesville, Va., undated.

Department of Defense, *Proliferation Threat and Response*, Washington, D.C., 1996.

_____, *Domestic Preparedness Program in the Defense Against Weapons of Mass Destruction*, Washington, D.C., May 1, 1997, at http://www.defenselink.mil/pubs/domestic/index.html.

_____, Office of the Assistant Secretary of Defense (Public Affairs), "Reserve Integration Moves Forward with Establishment of Consequence Management Program Integration Office," OSD (PA)

News Release, March 17, 1998a, http://www.defenselink.mil/news/Mar1998.

_____, "Joint Task Force on Computer Network Defense Now Operational," DoD Press Release No. 658-98, December 30, 1998b, http://www.defenselink.mil/news/Dec1998/b12301998_bt658-98.html.

_____, *Nuclear/Biological/Chemical (NBC) Defense: Annual Report to Congress*, Washington, D.C., March 1999a.

_____, *Reserve Component Employment Study 2005 Study Report*, Washington, D.C., June 1999b.

_____, *DoD Insider Threat Mitigation Plan*, Final Report of the Insider Threat Integrated Process Team, June 1999c, For Official Use Only.

_____, DoD News Briefing by Secretary of Defense Cohen, September 16, 1999d, at http://www.defenselink.mil:80/news/Jul1999/t07221999_t0722y2k.html.

Department of Defense Tiger Team, *Department of Defense Plan for Integrating National Guard and Reserve Component Support for Response to Attacks Using Weapons of Mass Destruction*, Washington, D.C., January 1998, at http://www.defenselink.mil/pubs/wmdresponse/.

Department of Energy, *Historical Records Declassification Guide*, Chapter Six, "Nuclear Emergency Search Team (NEST)," CG-HR-1, 1999, at http://www.etde.org/html/osti/opennet/document/cghr1/cghr1c.html.

Deutch, John, "Press Briefing by Deputy Secretary of Defense John Deutch," The White House, December 1, 1994.

_____, "Foreign Information Warfare Programs and Capabilities," DCI Testimony, June 25, 1996, at http://www.cia.gov.

Dertouzos, James N., Eric V. Larson, and Patricia A. Ebener, *The Economic Costs and Implications of High-Technology Hardware Theft*, Santa Monica, Calif.: RAND, MR-1070-AEA, 1999.

Director of Military Support (DOMS), "Director of Military Support Brief," undated, at http://www.dtic.mil/doms/infobrief.

"DoD: Infrastructure Protection Program Badly Underfunded," *Defense Information and Electronics Report,* August 6, 1999, p. 1.

Dower, John, "Hiroshima, Nagasaki, and the Politics of Memory," *Technology Review,* August 1995, at http://www.techreview.com/articles/aug95/AtomicDower.html.

Ellis, James, David Fisher, Thomas Longstaff, Linda Pesante, and Richard Pethia, *Report to the President's Commission on Critical Infrastructure Protection,* CERT® Coordination Center, Software Engineering Institute, Carnegie Mellon University, Pittsburgh, Pa., January 1997.

Emerson, Steven, "America's Doomsday Project," *U.S. News and World Report,* August 7, 1989, pp. 26–31.

Executive Order 10222, "Providing for Certain Transfers to the Federal Civil Defense Administration," March 8, 1951.

Executive Order 11179, "Providing for the National Defense Executive Reserve," September 22, 1964.

Executive Order 11795, "Delegating Disaster Relief Functions Pursuant to the Disaster Relief Act of 1974," July 11, 1974.

Executive Order 12127, "Federal Emergency Management Agency," March 31, 1979a.

Executive Order 12148, "Federal Emergency Management," July 20, 1979b.

Executive Order 12241, "National Contingency Plan," September 29, 1980.

Executive Order 12472, "Assignment of National Security and Emergency Preparedness Telecommunications Functions," April 3, 1984.

Executive Order 12656, "Assignment of Emergency Preparedness Responsibilities," November 18, 1988.

Executive Order 12657, "Federal Emergency Management Agency Assistance in Emergency Preparedness Planning at Commercial Nuclear Power Plants," November 18, 1988.

Executive Order 13010, "Critical Infrastructure Protection," July 15, 1996.

Falkenrath, Richard A., "Confronting Nuclear, Biological, and Chemical Terrorism," *Survival*, Vol. 40, No. 3, Autumn 1998, pp. 43–65.

Federal Bureau of Investigation, *Terrorism in the United States*, various years.

Federal Emergency Management Agency, "Continuity of the Executive Branch of the Federal Government at the Headquarters Level During National Security Emergencies," Federal Preparedness Circular 60, November 20, 1990.

_____, Unclassified FEMA Abstract on PDD-39, March 8, 1996, at http://www.fas.org/irp/congress/1996_hr/a950603.htm.

_____, *An Assessment of Federal Consequence Management Capabilities for Response to Nuclear, Biological, or Chemical (NBC) Terrorism*, Washington, D.C., February 1997a, For Official Use Only.

_____, *Federal Response Plan Notice of Change Number FEMA 229*, Chg 11, February 7, 1997b, at http://www.fas.org/irp/offdocs/pdd_39_frp0.htm.

_____, *Introduction to the Basic Plan of the Federal Response Plan*, April 1999a.

_____, *Federal Response Plan*, Washington, D.C., April 1999b, at http://www.fema.gov/r-n-r/frp/frpfull.pdf.

_____, *Terrorism Incident Annex*, Washington, D.C., April 1999c, at http://www.fema.gov/r-n-r/frp/frpterr.pdf.

_____, "Federal Executive Branch Continuity of Operations (COOP)," Federal Preparedness Circular 60, July 26, 1999d.

_____, "Mt. Weather Emergency Assistance Center," 2000a, at http://www.fema.gov/pte/weather.htm.

_____, *Federal Radiological Emergency Response Plan (FRERP) Operational Plan*, 2000b, at http://www.nrc.gov/NRC/AEOD/ER/FRERP/frerp.html.

Federation of American Scientists, "Continuity of Government," 1999a, at http://www.fas.org/nuke/guide/usa/c3/cog.htm.

_____, "Operation Safe Harbor/Operation Able Manner," 1999b, at http://www.fas.org/man/dod-101/ops/safe_harbor.htm.

_____, "Operation Sea Signal/Joint Task Force 160," 1999c, at http://www.fas.org/man/dod-101/ops/sea_signal.htm.

Frank, Diane, "Agencies Lay Groundwork for Intrusion-Detection Network," *Federal Computer Week*, May 11, 1999, at http://www.fcw.com.

Freeh, Louis J., statement of Louis J. Freeh, Director, Federal Bureau of Investigation, to the Senate Committee on Intelligence, *Threats to U.S. National Security: Hearing Before the Senate Select Committee on Intelligence*, 105th Congress, January 28, 1998.

_____, *Ensuring Public Safety and National Security Under the Rule of Law: A Report to the American People on the Work of the FBI, 1993–1998*, Washington, D.C., undated, at http://www.fbi.gov/library/5-year/5YR_report_.PDF.

Garamone, Jim, "Pay Up 3%, Contingencies Funded in DoD Budget," American Forces Information Service, March 6, 1996.

_____, "Some Critical DoD Systems Won't Make Y2K Deadlines," American Forces Press Service, June 30, 1998, at http://www.defenselink.mil:80/news/Jun1998.

_____, "DoD Examines Joint Task Force Concept for Civil Support," American Forces Information Service, August 17, 1999, at http://www.defenselink.mil/news/Aug1999/n0081799_9908175.html.

General Accounting Office, "Information Security: Computer Attacks at Department of Defense Pose Increasing Risks," statement of Jack L. Brock, Jr., Director, Defense Information and Financial Management Systems Accounting and Information Management Division, Washington, D.C.: GAO/T-AIMD-96-92, May 22, 1996a.

_____, *Information Security: Computer Attacks at Department of Defense Pose Increasing Risks*, Washington, D.C.: GAO/AIMD-96-84, May 1996b.

_____, *Defense Computers: Year 2000 Computer Problems Threaten DOD Operations*, Washington, D.C.: GAO/AIMD-98-72, April 1998a.

_____, *Combating Terrorism: Threat and Risk Assessments Can Help Prioritize and Target Program Investments*, Washington, D.C.: GAO/NSIAD-98-74, April 1998b.

_____, *Defense Computers: Army Needs to Greatly Strengthen Its Year 2000 Program*, Washington, D.C.: GAO/AIMD-98-53, May 1998c.

_____, *Combating Terrorism: Opportunities to Improve Domestic Preparedness Program Focus and Efficiency*, Washington, D.C.: GAO/NSIAD-99-3, November 1998d.

_____, *Combating Terrorism: Observations on Federal Spending to Combat Terrorism*, Washington, D.C.: GAO/T-NSIAD/GGD-99-107, March 11, 1999a.

_____, *Combating Terrorism: Observations on Biological Terrorism and Public Health Initiatives*, Washington, D.C.: GAO/NSIAD-99-112, March 16, 1999b.

_____, *Combating Terrorism: Use of National Guard Response Teams Is Unclear*, Washington, D.C.: GAO/NSIAD-99-110, May 1999c.

_____, *Combating Terrorism: Issues to Be Resolved to Improve Counterterrorism Operations*, Washington, D.C.: GAO/NSIAD-99-135, May 1999d.

_____, *Combating Terrorism: Use of National Guard Response Teams in Unclear*, Washington, D.C.: GAO/T-NSIAD-99-184, May 1999e.

_____, *Combating Terrorism: Analysis of Potential Emergency Response Equipment and Sustainment Costs*, Washington, D.C.: GAO/NSIAD-99-151, June 1999f.

_____, *Combating Terrorism: Use of National Guard Response Teams Is Unclear*, Washington, D.C.: GAO/T-NSIAD-99-184, June 23, 1999g.

_____, *Combating Terrorism: Analysis of Federal Counterterrorist Exercises*, Washington, D.C.: GAO/NSIAD-99-157BR, June 1999h.

_____, *Chemical and Biological Defense: Program Planning and Evaluation Should Follow Results Act Framework*, Washington, D.C.: GAO/NSIAD-99-159, August 1999i.

_____, *Chemical and Biological Defense: Coordination of Nonmedical Chemical and Biological R&D Programs*, Washington, D.C.: GAO/NSIAD-99-160, August 1999j.

Gordon-Hagerty, Lisa E., statement of Lisa E. Gordon-Hagerty, Director, Office of Emergency Response, Acting Director, Office of Weapons Surety Defense Programs, Department of Energy, October 1, 1997.

Goss, Kay C., "America Preparing for the Consequences of Terrorism," presentation before the NATO Civil Emergency Preparedness Symposium, Moscow, Russia, April 22, 1997, http://www.fema.gov/pte/gosspch11.htm.

Graham, Bradley, "U.S. Studies New Threat: Cyber Attack," *Washington Post*, May 24, 1998, p. A1.

_____, "Pentagon Plans Domestic Terror Team; Critics Fear Too Much Military Interference in Civilian Emergency Response," *Washington Post*, February 1, 1999, p. A2.

Grange, David L., and Rodney L. Johnson, "Forgotten Mission: Military Support to the Nation," *Joint Forces Quarterly*, No. 15, Spring 1997, pp. 108–115.

Gup, Ted, "Doomsday Hideaway," *Time*, December 9, 1991, pp. 26–29.

_____, "The Doomsday Blueprints," *Time*, August 10, 1992, pp. 32–39.

Hamre, John J., "Information Vulnerability and the World Wide Web," Deputy Secretary of Defense memorandum, 1998a.

_____, "Web Site Administration," Deputy Secretary of Defense memorandum, December 7, 1998b.

_____, briefing on year 2000 issues, DoD News Briefing, January 15, 1999, at http://www.defenselink.mil.

Hoffman, Bruce, "Terrorism, Homeland Defense, and the U.S. Army," briefing, March 1999.

Howard, John D., *An Analysis of Security Incidents on the Internet*, Ph.D. dissertation, April 7, 1997, at http://www.cert.org/research/JHThesis/Start.html.

Iklé, Fred C., *Defending the U.S. Homeland: Strategic and Legal Issues for DOD and the Armed Services*, Washington, D.C.: Center for Strategic and International Studies, January 1999.

Institute of Medicine and National Research Council, *Chemical and Biological Terrorism: Research and Development to Improve Civilian Medical Response*, Washington, D.C.: National Academy Press, 1999.

"In the President's Words: Assessing the Risk of Germ Warfare," *New York Times*, January 22, 1999.

Joint Chiefs of Staff, *Shape, Respond, and Prepare Now: A Military Strategy for a New Era*, Washington, D.C., 1997a.

_____, *Joint Doctrine Encyclopedia*, Washington, D.C., 1997b.

_____, Joint Strategic Review 1999, Washington, D.C., 1999.

"Joint Department of State, Department of Energy, and DoD Memorandum of Understanding for Responding to Malevolent Nuclear Threats Outside U.S. Territory and Possessions," January 28, 1982.

"Joint Federal Bureau of Investigation, Department of Energy, and Department of Defense Agreement for Response to Improvised Nuclear Device Incidents," February 27, 1980.

Kaufmann, Arnold F., Martin I. Meltzer, and George P. Schmid, "The Economic Impact of a Bioterrorist Attack: Are Prevention and Postattack Intervention Programs Justifiable?" *Emerging Infectious Diseases*, Vol. 3, No. 2, April–June 1997, pp. 83–94.

Keeter, Hunter, "DISA Stands Up Computer Network Defense Center," *Defense Daily*, August 12, 1999, p. 7.

Kelley, Jack, "Bin Laden Was Stopped Seven Times," *USA Today*, February 24, 1999, p. 1A.

Larson, Eric V., and Glenn A. Kent, *A New Methodology for Assessing Multilayer Missile Defense Options*, Santa Monica, Calif.: RAND, MR-390-AF, 1994.

Lauder, John, Unclassified Statement for the Record by Special Assistant to the DCI for Nonproliferation John A. Lauder on the Worldwide WMD Threat to the Commission to Assess the Organization of the Federal Government to Combat the Proliferation of Weapons of Mass Destruction, as prepared for delivery on 29 April 1999.

Lawrence Livermore National Laboratory, "WATS," 1999, at http://www.llnl.gov/nai/technologies/technet2.htm.

Lujan, Thomas R., "Legal Aspects of Domestic Employment of the Army," *Parameters*, Autumn 1997, pp. 82–97.

Macko, Steven, "FBI Says There Is a Marked Increase in Number of Domestic WMD Terrorist Threats," ERRI Daily Intelligence Report, ERRI Risk Assessment Services, Vol. 4, No. 276, October 3, 1998, at http://www.emergency.com/doma-wmd.htm.

Messmer, Ellen, "Kosovo Cyber-War Intensifies: Chinese Hackers Targeting U.S. Sites, Government Says," CNN.com, 1999, at http://www.cnn.com.

Miller, Judith, and William J. Broad, "Clinton Describes Terrorism Threat for 21st Century," *New York Times*, January 22, 1999.

Mitchell, Russ, "Why Melissa Is So Scary," *U.S. News & World Report*, March 12, 1999, http://www.usnews.com/usnews/issue/990412/12viru.htm.

Monterey Institute for International Studies, Center for Nonproliferation Studies, 1999, at http://cns.miis.edu/.

MSNBC, "Does U.S. Need Anti-Terror Troops? Pentagon, FEMA at Odds over Plans for Homeland Command," February 1, 1999, at http://www.msnbc.com/news/236665.asp.

National Defense Panel, *Transforming Defense: National Security in the 21st Century*, Washington, D.C., December 1997.

National Institute of Justice, Office of Justice Programs, U.S. Department of Justice, "Inventory of State and Local Law Enforcement Technology Needs to Combat Terrorism," NIJ Research in Brief, Washington, D.C., NCJ 173384, January 1999, at http://www.ojp. usdoj.gov/nij.

National Research Council, *Realizing the Potential of C4I: Fundamental Challenges*, Washington, D.C.: National Academy Press, 1999.

Nuclear Regulatory Commission, *Federal Radiological Emergency Response Plan (FRERP)—Operational Plan*, Washington, D.C., 1996, at http://www.nrc.gov/NRC/AEOD/ER/FRERP/frerp.htm.

Office of the Assistant Secretary of Defense (Public Affairs), "DoD Announces Plans for 17 New WMD Civil Support Teams, News Release No. 017-00, January 13, 2000.

Office of Management and Budget, unclassified report on governmentwide spending to combat terrorism, March 3, 1999a.

_____, annex on domestic preparedness to report on government-wide spending to combat terrorism, March 30, 1999b.

Ogata, Sadako, United Nations High Commissioner for Refugees at the International Seminar on "The Indochinese Exodus and the International Response," Tokyo, October 27, 1995, at http://www. unhcr.ch/refworld/unhcr/hcspeech/27oc1995.htm.

O'Harrow, Robert, Jr., "Computer Security Proposal Is Revised: Critics Had Raised Online Privacy Fears," *Washington Post*, September 22, 1999, p. A31.

Parachini, John, "U.S. Governmental Spending to Combat Terrorism: Chart and Analysis," Center for Nonproliferation Studies, Monterey Institute for International Studies, 1999, at http://www.cns. miis.edu/research/cbw/ternarr.htm.

Peterson, Gordon L., "An Advocate for Jointness," *Sea Power*, Vol. 43, No. 2, February 2000, p. 9.

President's Commission on Critical Infrastructure Protection, *Critical Foundations: Protecting America's Infrastructures*, Washington, D.C., October 1997a.

_____, *Fact Sheet: President's Commission on Critical Infrastructure Protection*, Washington, D.C., October 1997b.

Public Broadcasting Service, "AWOL Arsenal," The News Hour with Jim Lehrer, March 19, 1998, at http://www.pbs.org/newshour/bb/military/jan-june98/nukes_3-19.html.

_____, "Meltdown at Three Mile Island," The American Experience, 1999a, at http://www.pbs.org/wgbh/amex/three/index.html.

_____, "Russian Roulette," Frontline, 1999b, at http://www.pbs.org/wgbh/pages/frontline/shows/russia/.

Public Law 105-261, *The Strom Thurmond National Defense Authorization Act for Fiscal Year 1999*, October 17, 1998.

Reserve Forces Policy Board, "Reserve Component Programs," FY 1998, report, 1999.

Riley, Kevin Jack, and Bruce Hoffman, *Domestic Terrorism: A National Assessment of State and Local Law Enforcement Preparedness*, Santa Monica, Calif.: RAND, MR-505-NIJ, 1995.

Robert T. Stafford Disaster Assistance and Emergency Relief Act, 42 U.S.C. 5121, et seq., 2000, at http://www.fema.gov/library/Stafact.htm.

Rubin, Barnett R., "Afghanistan: The Forgotten Crisis," Writenet (UK), February 1996, at http://www.unhcr.ch/refworld/country/writenet/wriafg.htm.

Saldarini, Katy, "Pentagon Slack May Lead to Cyber-Attack, Report Says," GovExec.com, at http://www.govexec.com.

Schwartau, Winn, "Cyber-vigilantes Hunt Down Hackers," CNN.com, January 12, 1999, at http://www.cnn.com.

Seipel, Chris, "Consequence Management: Domestic Response to Weapons of Mass Destruction," *Parameters*, Autumn 1997, pp. 119–134.

Stone, Paul, "Reserve Components on Guard for Y2K," American Forces Press Service, May 19, 1999, at http://www.defenselink.mil:80/news/May1999.

"Tired of Hacks, U.S. Army Switches to Macs," *TechWeb News*, September 10, 1999, at http://www.techweb.com.

U.S. Army, *Army Strategic Planning Guidance*, Washington, D.C., April 16, 1999.

U.S. Army Concepts Analysis Agency, *Force Employment Study (FES)*, Bethesda, Md.: U.S. Army Concepts Analysis Agency, CAA-SR-91-4, February 1991.

U.S. Army, Soldier Biological Chemical Command (SBCCOM), "Compendium of Weapons of Mass Destruction Courses Sponsored by the Federal Government," July 1998, at http://www.sbccom.apgea.army.mil/ops/dp/fr/compendiumfinal.pdf.

_____, "Domestic Preparedness Fact Sheet," 1999a, at http://dp.sbccom.army.mil/fs/dp_overview.html.

_____, "120 Cities Fact Sheet," 1999b, at http://dp.sbccom.army.mil/fs/fs_120c.html.

_____, "Domestic Preparedness Training Report," 1999c, at http://dp.sbccom.army.mil/tr/index.html.

U.S. Army Special Operations Command (USASOC), 1999, at http://users.aol.com/armysof1/Missions.html.

U.S. Congress, Fiscal Year 1997 Defense Authorization Bill, Public Law 104-201 (Defense Against Weapons of Mass Destruction Act of 1996, or the Nunn-Lugar-Domenici legislation), September 23, 1996.

U.S. House of Representatives, Committee on National Security, Report of the Committee on National Security, House of Representatives, on H.R. 3616, Report 105-532, May 12, 1998a.

_____, Section 1402 of Public Law 105-261, "The Strom Thurmond National Defense Authorization Act for Fiscal Year 1999," October 17, 1998b.

_____, Armed Services Committee Military Research and Development Subcommittee Hearings on Domestic Preparedness, March 11, 1999a.

_____, H.R. 106-162, Report of the Committee on Armed Services, on H.R. 1401, National Defense Authorization Act for Fiscal Year 2000, Report 106-50, May 24, 1999b.

U.S. Senate, Committee on the Judiciary, Subcommittee on Technology, Terrorism, and Government Information, *Crime, Terror, & War: National Security & Public Safety in the Information Age,* November 1998.

_____, Committee on Armed Services, National Defense Authorization Act for Fiscal Year 2000, report to accompany S. 1059, May 17, 1999.

U.S. State Department, "Haiti: Haitian Migrants," January 23, 1997, at http://www.state.gov/www/global/prm/Haiti.html.

_____, *Patterns of Global Terrorism 1998,* Washington, D.C., May 1999.

Unzueta, Silvia M., "The Mariel Exodus: A Year in Retrospect," Metropolitan Dade County Government, Office of the County Manager, April 1981, at http://home.earthlink.net/~gwinslow/doc033.htm.

Uranium Information Centre Ltd., "Hiroshima, Nagasaki, and Subsequent Weapons Testing," Nuclear Issues Briefing Paper #29, June 1999, at http://www.uic.com/au.nip29.htm.

Varma, D. J., "Subcontinent in Web War," Fairfax I.T., 1999, at http://newslinx.internet.com/newstopics/hacking.html.

Ware, Willis H., *The Cyber-Posture of the National Information Infrastructure,* Santa Monica, Calif.: RAND, MR-976-OSTP, 1998.

Warner, Edward L., testimony to the Senate Armed Services Subcommittee on Emerging Threats and Capabilities, March 23, 1999.

Weiner, Tim, "Blowback," *New York Times Magazine,* March 13, 1994a.

_____, "Pentagon Book for Doomsday Is to be Closed," *New York Times*, April 18, 1994b, p. A1.

The White House, "Remarks by the President in Television Address to the Nation," September 15, 1994a.

_____, "Proliferation of Weapons of Mass Destruction," press release, November 14, 1994b.

_____, PDD-62, "Protection Against Unconventional Threats to the Homeland and Americans Overseas, May 22, 1998a.

_____, PDD-63, "Critical Infrastructure Protection (CIP)," May 22, 1998b.

_____, "Fact Sheet: Summary of Presidential Decision Directives 62 and 63," May 22, 1998c.

_____, *A National Security Strategy for a New Century*, Washington, D.C., October 1998d.

_____, PDD-67, "Ensuring Constitutional Government and Continuity of Government Operations," October 21, 1998e.

_____, "Text of a Letter from the President to the Speaker of the House of Representatives and the President of the Senate," November 12, 1998f.

_____, "Funding for Domestic Preparedness and Critical Infrastructure Protection," fact sheet, January 22, 1999a.

_____, "Press Briefing by Attorney General Janet Reno, Secretary of HHS Donna Shalala, and Richard Clarke, President's National Coordinator for Security, Infrastructure, and Counterterrorism," January 22, 1999b.

_____, "Preserving America's Privacy and Security in the Next Century: A Strategy for America in Cyberspace," press release, September 16, 1999c.

Windrem, Robert, "Pentagon-FEMA Battle over Plans for Homeland Military Command," NBC News, January 31, 1999.

Wohlstetter, Albert, "The Delicate Balance of Terror," Santa Monica, Calif.: RAND, P-1472, 1958, at http://www.rand.org/publications/classics/wohlstetter/P1472/P1472.html.

Wolfe, Frank, "Task Force Monitoring Cyber Intrusions Around the Clock," *Defense Daily*, July 27, 1999, p. 1.

Zoellick, Robert B., National Security Strategy and the Defense Budget Statement of Robert B. Zoellick, President and CEO, Center for Strategic and International Studies, to the Committee on the Budget of the U.S. Senate, February 24, 1999, at http://www.csis.org/hill/ts990224.html.